VIETNAM TASK

THE 5TH BATTALION
THE ROYAL AUSTRALIAN REGIMENT, 1966-67

VIETNAM TASK

THE 5TH BATTALION
THE ROYAL AUSTRALIAN REGIMENT, 1966–67

ROBERT J. O'NEILL

ANU PRESS

ANU PRESS

Published by ANU Press
The Australian National University
Canberra ACT 2600, Australia
Email: anupress@anu.edu.au

Available to download for free at press.anu.edu.au

ISBN (print): 9781760465377
ISBN (online): 9781760465384

WorldCat (print): 1344217245
WorldCat (online): 1344217262

DOI: 10.22459/VT.2022

This title is published under a Creative Commons Attribution-NonCommercial-NoDerivatives 4.0 International (CC BY-NC-ND 4.0) licence.

The full licence terms are available at
creativecommons.org/licenses/by-nc-nd/4.0/legalcode

Cover design and layout by ANU Press. Cover photograph: Two Fifth Battalion soldiers on patrol, Ptes. G. Cassidy and B. Everard (*Army Public Relations*).

First edition © 1968 Robert J. O'Neill
Second Edition © 1995 5 RAR Association
This Edition © 2022 5 RAR Association

Contents

Plates	vii
Diagrams	xi
Symbols Used in Diagrams	xiii
Foreword	xvii
Introduction	1
1. The Problem	5
2. Holsworthy to Vietnam	19
3. The Clearance of Nui Dat	29
4. An Experiment in Night Movement	53
5. The Reclamation of Binh Ba	69
6. A Frustrated Effort	89
7. Assistance for Duc Thanh	103
8. Clearing a Mountain	117
9. Securing Route 15	139
10. Return to Nui Thi Vai	145
11. The Western Approaches	167
12. An Isolated Outpost	179
13. A Re-evaluation of Strategy	191
14. Against the Village Cadres	205
15. In the Long Hai Hills	223
16. Interdiction in the East — the Horseshoe and the Fence	239
17. The Final Balance	253
Appendix A	261
Fifth Battalion Roll of Honour Vietnam 1966–67	

Appendix B · 263
    Citation accompanying the award of the Distinguished Service Order to Lieutenant Colonel J. A. Warr
    Citation accompanying the award of the Military Cross to Second Lieutenant M. G. J. Deak
    Citation accompanying the award of the Military Cross to Second Lieutenant J. D. McAloney
    Citation accompanying the award of the Military Cross to Second Lieutenant D. C. Rainer
    Citation accompanying the award of the Military Medal to Private C. J. Cogswell
    Citation accompanying the award of the Military Medal to Private P. Fraser
    Citation accompanying the award of a Mention-in-Despatches (Posthumously) to Corporal N. J. Womal

Appendix C · 271
    5 RAR Nominal Roll, 1966–67

About the Author · 287
    Other Publications by the Author

Index · 291

Plates

The Prime Minister, Mr Harold Holt, and Second Lieutenant Roe, a member of our advance party, at Bien Hoa, 25 April 1966 (see Chapter 2). 33

A bridge on Route 15 between Ba Ria and Vung Tau destroyed before our arrival by the Viet Cong. 34

Brigadier Jackson and General Westmoreland on board HMAS *Sydney* to welcome C Company to Vung Tau, 2 May 1966 (see Chapter 2). 34

Colonel Warr (centre) planning helicopter requirements with Lieutenant Brinnon of the 68th US Army Aviation Company (left) and Major Hannigan, operations officer, First Australian Task Force (right) at Vung Tau, May 1966 (see Chapter 2). 49

Major Carroll (right) and Corporal Western, his radio operator, at the battalion helicopter rehearsal before Operation Hardihood, May 1966 (see Chapter 2). 49

During the first hours of Operation Hardihood on 24 May 1966 (see Chapter 3): Lieutenant Hartley (centre) with his radio operator and the ubiquitous Le Van Yen, a fluent French speaking herbalist. 50

Private Allen (left) and Corporal Cleary with Viet Cong panji spikes encountered on Operation Hardihood (see Chapter 3). 50

Staff Sergeant Mick Seats, assistant to Captain White, giving treatment to a sick baby. Medical aid was given to the villagers several times each week. 83

Unloading the guns of 105 Field Battery at Tennis on Operation Sydney, 6 July 1966. They were carried inside APCs (shown in the rear) so that the Viet Cong would not know our strength (see Chapter 4). 84

Pte. Jerry Bruin of B Company distributing captured Viet Cong rice to the villagers from whom the Viet Cong had taken it in the first place. 84

Operation Sydney at Duc My, 20 July 1966. In the foreground is the
Viet Cong prisoner whose capture is described in Chapter 4. He had
just been resuscitated by Captain White (kneeling) and his capture
had been controlled by Second Lieutenant Rainer MC, shown
standing, centre. 101

A service in the village church at Binh Ba conducted by Father Joseph,
village priest, and Father Williams, battalion padre; attended by
members of C Company under Second Lieutenant Neesham (left). 102

The five Ngai Giao villagers of military age who had no identity cards
being guarded by members of D Company under Sergeant Witheridge
(standing right), Operation Crowsnest, 3 October 1966
(see Chapter 7). 102

Pte Shoebridge and L/Cpl Bryan supporting Pte Riik after a booby trap
explosion had wounded several members of C Company on Nui Thi
Vai on 8 October 1966, during Operation Canberra (see Chapter 8). 133

Members of C Company after clearing a helicopter pad on the slopes of Nui
Thi Vai to evacuate the men wounded by booby traps on 8 October.
Major Miller is standing bottom centre without hat. 133

Second Lieutenant Deak MC, Reconnaissance Platoon commander,
at Phuoc Hoa during Operation Hayman in November 1966
(see Chapter 11). The platoon soon established friendly relations
with the people. 134

B Company after dismounting from APCs in the Binh Ba rubber plantation
before patrolling an area crossed by tracks used by the Viet Cong. Pte.
Barney Gee is the forward scout. 134

The officers of the Fifth Battalion in January 1967. 153

Four members of the Intelligence Section by the model of An Nhut which
they prepared in early February 1967 before Operation Beaumaris
(see Chapter 14). From left: Pte. Colin Ross, Pte. Noel Clare, L/Cpl.
Colin Bruce, Cpl. Bob Williams. 154

Second Lieutenant Bob Askew, a helicopter pilot of 161 Recce Flight, who
performed outstanding feats of flying in support of our operations. 154

Major Maizey—a historic photograph of the second-in-command. 154

One of the eight inch guns of the 1st/83rd US Artillery Regiment
stationed at Nui Dat. These guns possess extraordinary precision
over long ranges (see Chapter 15). 183

PLATES

An APC of A Squadron, 3rd Cavalry Regiment, controlling ox cart traffic along Route 2 near Nui Dat. The APCs supported most of our operations.   183

Commencing the planning after the An Nhut reconnaissance, 12 February 1967 (see Chapter 14): from left, Colonel Warr, Major Carroll and the author.   184

The battalion lifting off from Luscombe Field, Nui Dat, late in the afternoon of 18 February 1967 to launch Operation Renmark (see Chapter 15). This was the only operation for which we carried steel helmets. The risk of Viet Cong mortar bombardment of Battalion Headquarters was appreciable.   184

Members of D Company beginning the defences at the Horseshoe, March 1967 (see Chapter 16). A Sioux helicopter of 161 Recce Flight is hovering below the rim of the crater.   201

Pte. Wales of D Company looking south from the crest of the Horseshoe over Dat Do towards the Long Hai hills on the horizon.   201

Building the fence around Dat Do, March 1967 (see Chapter 16).   202

Sergeant Chinh, our senior Vietnamese interpreter, at Binh Ba (see Chapter 14).   202

The handover. Colonel Warr presenting Colonel Smith, CO 7 RAR, with the 'tiger pig', 26 April 1967 (see Chapter 17).   202

Intelligence officer Captain Bob O'Neill briefing soldiers in 5 RAR's open-air theatre, 'The Mayfair'.   288

Diagrams

Fig. 1. Phuoc Tuy province, May 1966. 4

Fig. 2. The corps areas and major towns, South Vietnam. 7

Fig. 3. The provinces, major towns and Viet Cong bases, 3 Corps area. 8

Fig. 4. Major roads, 3 Corps area. 12

Fig. 5. The movements of A and D Companies to clear the Viet Cong away from Nui Dat, Operation Hardihood, 24–31 May 1966. 37

Fig. 6. The movements of B and C Companies, Operation Hardihood, 24–31 May 1966. 39

Fig. 7. An example of the many ambushes planned by Major McQualter. This ambush was set on the Suoi Da Bang by B Company on the night of 29–30 May 1966. 46

Fig. 8. The rifle companies move in towards Nui Dat before commencing to build the defences of the base, Operation Hardihood, 1–4 June 1966. 48

Fig. 9. The company movements during the search around Nui Nghe, Operation Sydney One, 6–17 July 1966. 56

Fig. 10. Placing the cordon around Duc My on the night of 19–20 July 1966, Operation Sydney Two. 65

Fig. 11. The cordoning of Binh Ba, 7–8 August 1966, Operation Holsworthy. 74

Fig. 12. The search for the Viet Cong who survived the battle of Long Tan on 18 August 1966, Operation Darlinghurst. 94

Fig. 13. The blocking operation west of Binh Ba, Operation Toledo, 2–8 September 1966. 99

Fig. 14. The company movements during the preliminary clearance of Nui Thi Vai to secure Route 15, Operation Canberra, 6–10 October 1966. 123

Fig. 15. The company dispositions while the American convoys were using Route 15, Operation Robin, 11–16 October 1966.   140

Fig. 16. The company movements to dislodge the Viet Cong encountered on Operation Canberra from Nui Thi Vai, Operation Queanbeyan, 17–26 October 1966.   147

Fig. 17. The cordoning of Phuoc Hoa on the night 6–7 November 1966, Operation Yass.   174

Fig. 18. The clearing of Viet Cong from Long Son island, Operation Hayman, 8–12 November 1966.   176

Fig. 19. The second cordoning of Binh Ba, Operation Caloundra, 9–10 January 1967.   209

Fig. 20. The cordoning of An Nhut, Operation Beaumaris, 13–14 February 1967.   217

Fig. 21. The search of the Viet Cong base areas in the Long Hai hills, Operation Renmark, 18–22 February 1967.   230

Fig. 22. Phuoc Tuy province, May 1967.   259

Symbols Used in Diagrams

SIZE SYMBOLS

Infantry

⊠ Brigade or Task Force (3000 men)

⊠ Battalion (800 men)

⊠ Company (80-110 men on operations)

⊠ Platoon (25-30 " ")

⊠ Half Platoon (12-15 " ")

⊠ Section (6-9 " ")

Cavalry (APC's)

⌘ Squadron (36 APC's)

⌘ Troop (10 ")

⌘ Section (3 ")

Artillery

⌶ Battery (6 guns)

⌶ Platoon (2 guns - Vietnamese)

HEADQUARTERS

⌐ Basic symbol to which is added the size symbol e.g.

⌐⊠ HQ of a battalion

UNIT IDENTIFICATION

⊠5 5 RAR

B⊠5 B Company 5 RAR

HELICOPTER LANDING ZONES

(LZ) or ⊤

DATE-TIME GROUP

e.g. 020908 — 0908hrs on 2nd day of month.

WEAPONS

↕ 81 mm. mortar

ABBREVIATIONS

MOR	Mortar	RECCE	Reconnaissance	PF	Popular Forces (Vietnamese)
PNR	Pioneer	OP	Observation Post	RF	Regional Forces (")
ATK	Anti Tank	MFC	Mortar Fire Controller	INT	Intelligence

xiii

TO THOSE MEMBERS OF THE
FIFTH BATTALION WHO DIED
IN VIETNAM

Foreword

by Lieutenant General Sir Reginald Pollard,
KBE, CB, DSO,
Honorary Colonel,
The Royal Australian Regiment

Fifth Battalion, The Royal Australian Regiment, was the first of our battalions composed of regulars and national servicemen to be committed to operations in Vietnam and to establish themselves at Nui Dat. They, 'the Tiger Battalion', were the leading element of the First Australian Task Force assigned the role of clearing and keeping the Viet Cong out of Phuoc Tuy province, an area which the Communists had used at will since 1945.

During 1967, as their Honorary Colonel, I visited them in Vietnam. Again, as so often in the past, I was impressed by the professional skill and confidence with which a young battalion was meeting the challenge of war under new and demanding conditions. Despite the difficulties of being first on the ground, their morale was high and they were doing their duty well.

The spirit of the battalion is admirably captured in this account of its operations in Vietnam, written by one who took part in them, and it graphically portrays the qualities of stoical endurance, compassion and bluff good humour characteristic of Australian soldiers in the field, be it on the beaches of Gallipoli, the trenches of Flanders, the sands of the desert or the paddy fields and jungles of South Vietnam.

The operations in Vietnam were fought under difficult and hostile conditions in an environment alien to most Australians. Those who took part can be proud of their achievements and their contribution to the maintenance of democratic freedom in South East Asia.

The author, Major Bob O'Neill, former Rhodes Scholar and a graduate of the Royal Military College, Duntroon, has a ready pen and a flair for recapturing the atmosphere of the events he describes. I commend this book for its obvious sincerity and moving portrayal of the anatomy of the Vietnam conflict at close range. I believe the book will live as a powerful reminder to those who took part in the operations described, as a memorial to those who failed to return and as an inspiration in courage and self-sacrifice to all who may read it.

Introduction

Every man sees a war in which he fights from two points of view. The one is his own, his view of his personal life in relation to the harsh environment of battle; the other is the outlook of his unit which makes him share closely the corporate experience of this unit and gives that unit an individual entity and character with its own peculiar difficulties and joys, its own failures and successes. The extent to which either of these two viewpoints dominates a man's thinking depends on his closeness to the direction of his unit. A forward scout carrying a rifle on a jungle track knowing little more than his activities for that day has little to divert his attention from his immediate personal environment, while a commander is so deeply involved with the fate of his unit that he tends to identify almost completely with it.

Somewhere in between are most soldiers. As a member of the Battalion Headquarters, I saw the war largely in terms of the battalion as a whole and I was able to experience our first operation from the point of view of a rifle company as its second-in-command. At the same time I have tried to give an impression of what it was like from an individual standpoint to participate in this war.

The war of this book is not the war of the teach-ins and the abstract debates nor is it the war of many journalists. It is the story of eight hundred men who landed from helicopters at Nui Dat on May 24, 1966, and who for the following year took part in the restoration of South Vietnamese Government control to the people of Phuoc Tuy.

I began writing this account on May 24, 1966, the first day of our first operation, and most of the descriptions of actions and places are unchanged from what I wrote in a small, green, loose leaf note book at the time of their occurrence. These pages were mailed to my wife every few days for her information, editing and typing, and to preserve them from the monsoon rains. During my leave after returning from Vietnam these accounts were woven together to make the book.

There are many people whom I must thank for their assistance. Most of them are the members of the Fifth Battalion who provided me with information and encouragement to keep writing at times when I felt more like forgetting the whole project. I am grateful to those who have helped with the preparation of the diagrams, to the Director of Army Public Relations, to Captain H. A. D. White and to Colin Bruce for permission to publish their photographs. Finally I must thank my wife, Sally, for her perseverance and for the quality of her criticism of the draft, often in the face of stubborn defence by a husband who tended to hold each postern as if it were his keep.

VIETNAM TASK

Fig. 1. Phuoc Tuy province, May 1966.

1
The Problem

South Vietnam is a country of remarkable geographic differences. Within a few hundred miles one passes through the ruggedness of the Annamite Chain, the rich tangle of growth on the plain around Saigon and the flat watery expanse of the Mekong Delta in the south, one of the richest rice-producing areas of the world. These geographic differences have partitioned the country into four fairly natural subdivisions which have been used by the Vietnamese Government as the basis for the four military regions comprising the country and through which the war against the Viet Cong is controlled. Each of these regions contains a corps of two or three Vietnamese divisions and they are numbered in order from north to south.

The First Corps area, adjoining North Vietnam, includes the mountains of central Annam and the coastal plain from which the vital cities of Hue, the old imperial capital of Annam, and Da Nang, the greatest military base in the north, have risen. The Second Corps area is dominated strategically by the central mountain plateau which stretches around Kontum and Pleiku. Sparsely populated, this area is the largest of the four, covering nearly three hundred miles out of South Vietnam's length of seven hundred. The coastal plain is narrower than in the First Corps area but it is nonetheless important because of the multitude of sea infiltration routes which its length offers to craft from North Vietnam. The Third Corps area borders on the southern extremity of the Annamite mountains. Essentially a broad plain of some hundred miles in diameter, the area includes the approaches to Saigon and the rice fields, gardens and rubber plantations which are so vital to the sustenance of daily life and commerce in the capital. The Mekong Delta begins within twenty miles to the south of Saigon at a line linking the sea with the long tongue of Cambodia which juts south-eastwards, pointing directly at Saigon and coming within fifty miles of it. The Fourth Corps boundary runs from the tip of this Cambodian peninsula south-eastwards to the sea. The plains of reed and paddy stretch southwards for nearly two hundred miles to the tip of Cape Ca Mau, Vietnam's southernmost extremity. The Fourth Corps area is peculiarly vital because of its enormous food production potential for whichever side controls it. Formerly a complement to the more industrialised Tonkin, its significance has been well appreciated by the contenders.

The effects of geography go further than to divide South Vietnam into a number of regions, for they have greatly determined the nature of the fighting which has occurred in each area. Proximity to North Vietnam is one key factor. In general the more northwards one goes the more one encounters North Vietnamese regular troops rather than the southern Viet Cong, so that the war in the First Corps area consists of fairly conventional large scale operations against divisional sized formations of North Vietnamese. The mountainous expanses and sparseness of the population of the Second Corps area offer more scope to the small bands of Viet Cong guerillas and, since it is further down the Ho Chi Minh Trail from North Vietnam, it is much more difficult for the North Vietnamese to maintain large numbers of troops there than in the First Corps area. The peculiar strategic importance of the Second Corps area is its potential for splitting South Vietnam into two pieces which may then be consumed separately. The Viet Cong were nearly successful in carrying out this manoeuvre before the weight of the American build-up had come into effect. The presence of the First Air Cavalry Division at An Khe in the central mountains and of the two Korean divisions near the central coast has blocked the way for further Viet Cong moves of this sort. The Fourth Corps area, made up of countless tiny villages and hamlets and inhabited by great numbers of extremely poor peasants, lent itself ideally to the warfare of local insurgency from which Asian Communism has sprung. The village guerilla squad is the essential element of the Viet Cong forces in this area. The overcrowding and poverty of the settlements have provided good conditions for Viet Cong recruiting and the Fourth Corps area has been an important source of manpower for Viet Cong forces in other parts of Vietnam.

1. THE PROBLEM

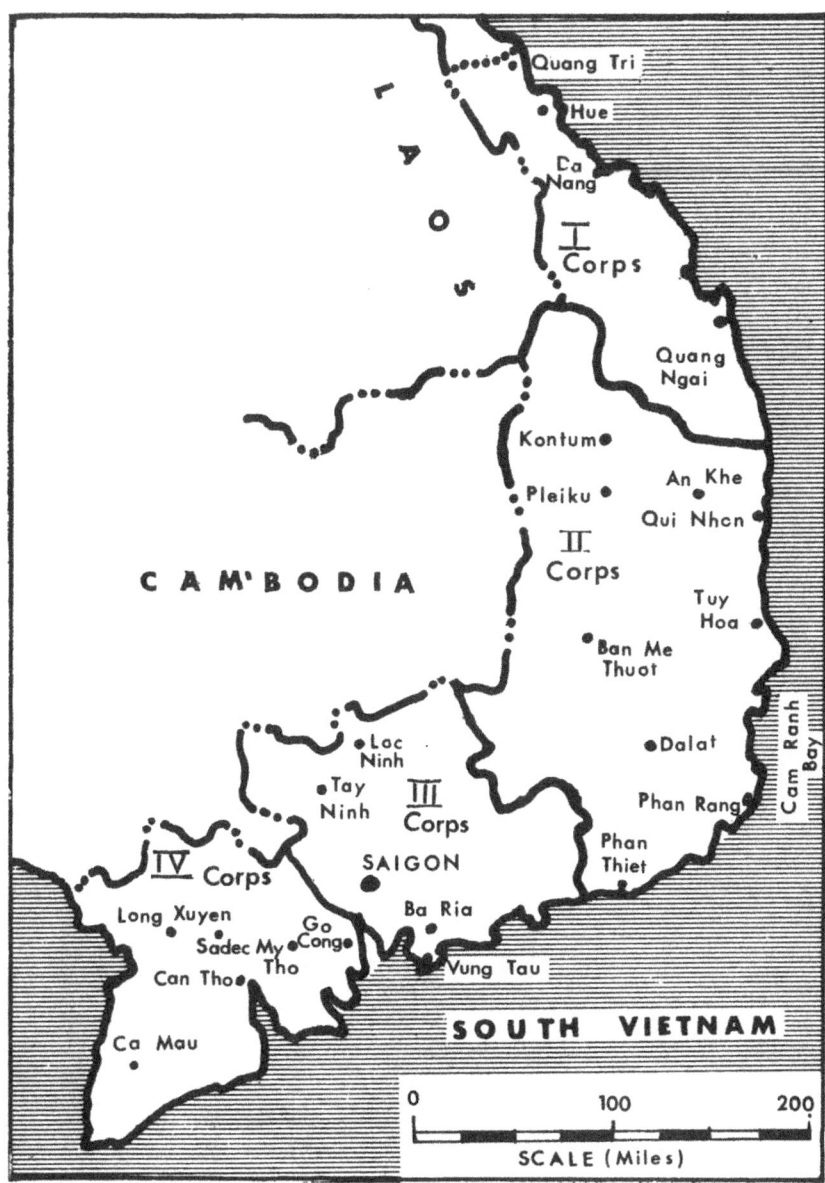

Fig. 2. The corps areas and major towns, South Vietnam.

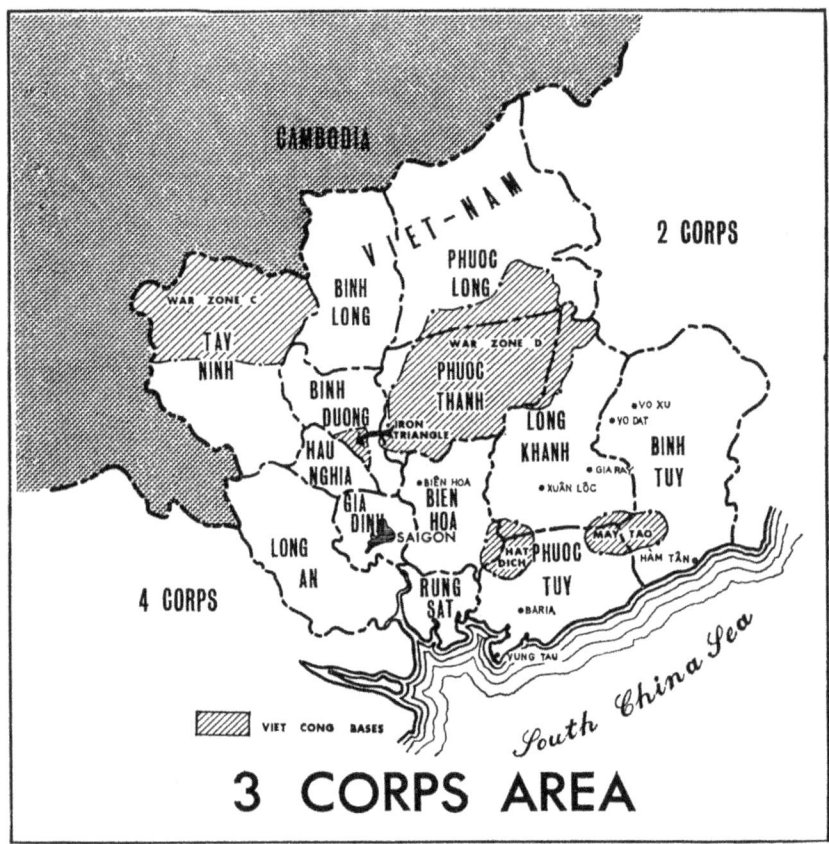

Fig. 3. The provinces, major towns and Viet Cong bases, 3 Corps area.

The most important recipient of men from the delta has been the Third Corps area. The country around Saigon could have provided the key to a swift end to the war and victory for the Viet Cong when they went over into their final stage of fighting battles in large formations of divisional size. The Third Corps area has not been a particularly good supplier of men for the Communist ranks and the journey by foot from North Vietnam through Laos and Cambodia is over four hundred miles. Consequently, many of the Viet Cong main force or regular units in the Third Corps area have been drawn from the Mekong Delta.

The Third Corps area may be considered in terms of four subdivisions. The south-western corner contains Saigon and the rice-producing province of Long An. Both of these are relatively easy for the Government to control since they are close to the main troop concentrations and they do not contain any tracts of wild country from which large numbers of Viet Cong can operate. However in the north-western sector, embracing the provinces of Tay Ninh, Hau Nghia, Binh Long and Binh Duong, lies the great belt of jungle known to the Viet Cong as War Zone C. From this area they have directed the whole of the war in South Vietnam and they have built up their forces in the area to several regiments. Many of their bases both in War Zone C and in other areas were established in the nineteen-forties for use against the French and thus they are extremely well developed and protected. The north-eastern sector contains the province of Phuoc Long and the northern half of Long Khanh province. Stretching into both provinces is the vast, sparsely populated expanse of War Zone D. Although this area has not been as crucial to the Viet Cong as War Zone C, it has been a major area of support for the Communists and usually contains some regiments of main force Viet Cong. The south-eastern sector consists of Bien Hoa, southern Long Khanh, Phuoc Tuy and Binh Tuy provinces. This area has also supported several regiments of Viet Cong based on two areas in the north-western and north-eastern corners of Phuoc Tuy. The Hat Dich area in north-western Phuoc Tuy overlaps Bien Hoa province to the west and Long Khanh to the north. The May Tao mountains link north-eastern Phuoc Tuy with Binh Tuy to the east and Long Khanh to the north and provide the second Viet Cong base. Phuoc Tuy and Binh Tuy provinces are important because they are on the sea coast. The port of Vung Tau, situated at the end of a long peninsula jutting out from Phuoc Tuy, is of major importance for, in conjunction with the road link to Saigon, Route 15, it can take much of the pressure off the crowded port facilities of Saigon and obviate the need for some vessels to negotiate the miles of tortuous narrow channels which thread the mangroves which lie all around the southern side of the capital. Long Khanh and Binh Tuy provinces are traversed by National Route 1, the main road link with the north, and both contain important rubber plantations.

The security of Saigon itself was threatened directly from two areas, the one to the north, the other to the south. The great area of mangroves which shrouds the mouth of the Nha Be river to the south is known as the Rung Sat. Its mangroves provide a direct labyrinthine link of tiny channels for Viet Cong sampans to bring men and supplies from the Fourth Corps area into the Third Corps area via Phuoc Tuy and the Hat Dich region. The thousands of small islands amongst the swamps provide many hides for Viet Cong guerillas, supply and transport sections and for their sappers who attempt to blow up shipping in the confines of the Long Tau river, the channel through to Saigon. One ship disabled for a day could delay another thirty for the same time. To the north of Saigon in the sharp angle formed by the junction of the Saigon river and Route 13 lies another patch of dense jungle known as the Iron Triangle. From this triangle the Viet Cong controlled, supplied and supported all Communist activity in the capital only twenty miles away.

The insertion and growth of Communist forces in the Third Corps area had been long and carefully planned. In the mid nineteen-forties they established War Zones C and D and a major base in the south-eastern part of Phuoc Tuy along the coast. The Viet Minh then took control of the major axes of communication leading from Saigon, thus tying the French down to a number of isolated garrisons. None of these posts could easily support the others, while the Viet Minh were able to concentrate locally superior forces when they chose because they enjoyed relative freedom of movement. After 1954 the major Viet Minh units in the south were either disbanded or went for temporary refuge and training to North Vietnam. However, cadres of Communists were left behind in the less controlled areas and in the bases such as War Zones C and D. In 1957 these began expanding and re-emerged as the Viet Cong. By 1959 local companies were being formed, by 1961 battalions, by 1964 regiments and in 1965 divisional staffs were formed to co-ordinate and command the regiments.

The strategy appeared to be similar to that of the Viet Minh, i.e. to concentrate and train enough men to form a strong fighting force capable of inflicting defeat on the Government troops, then to cut Saigon off from the main provincial centres and finally administer the *coup de grâce* to a dying regime. Unfortunately for this plan the commitment of American ground troops to the war began before the design could be executed. Just at the stage when the Viet Cong were established with several regiments in the Third Corps area and were cutting the major roads, forcing the Government out of many of the smaller villages, the First US Infantry Division, the 25th US Infantry Division and the 173rd US Airborne Brigade arrived to re-establish control over the provinces immediately to the north-west and north-east of Saigon and to provide an airborne mobile reserve capable of hitting the Viet Cong anywhere within the Third Corps area.

1. THE PROBLEM

However Route 15, the road between Saigon and Vung Tau, was still in Viet Cong hands and the security of Vung Tau itself was menaced directly to the point of mortar bombardment. From the Hat Dich and May Tao bases the Viet Cong were taking hold of most of Phuoc Tuy and parts of Long Khanh, Bien Hoa and Binh Tuy provinces. Over one hundred miles of Route 1 and the whole of Route 2, the north-south road linking Ba Ria, the capital of Phuoc Tuy with Xuan Loc, the capital of Long Khanh, were both under Viet Cong control. It was to this area that the First Australian Task Force was committed with the aim of restoring Government control to Phuoc Tuy and of clearing the Viet Cong off the southern sections of Routes 2 and 15.

Phuoc Tuy occupies a fairly level stretch of the central plain, approximately rectangular in shape, forty miles from east to west and thirty from north to south. Three large groups of hills or mountains thrust their way up through the thick green carpet of rich vegetation which covers the province. In the north-east the May Tao mountains rise to between two and three thousand feet. Centrally on the southern coast the Long Hai hills raise a spine of over one thousand feet in height, which juts into the South China Sea opposite the Vung Tau peninsula. Parallel to the south-western coast and the edge of the Rung Sat run the Dinh hills in a line eight miles long to the north-west and over sixteen hundred feet high. Various small hills are dotted about the broad plain such as Nui Nghe and Nui Dat in the central part of the province but these hills are too low and isolated to allow their use as a fortified defensive position which could become a major obstacle. The eastern third of the province, Xuyen Moc district, is divided off by the Song (river) Rai which drains the western slopes of the Annamite mountains away to the north-east. The Song Rai, fifty feet wide in some places, is an appreciable obstacle to mechanised vehicles, while it offers a navigation route for small craft to pass from the coast into the central eastern part of Phuoc Tuy within easy access of the Viet Cong bases. The island of Long Son off the south-west coast of the province is the final major geographic feature. Four miles long and over a mile in width, the island is crowned by the heights of Nui Nua from which a single Viet Cong machine gun post continually dominated the whole of the populated eastern half.

VIETNAM TASK

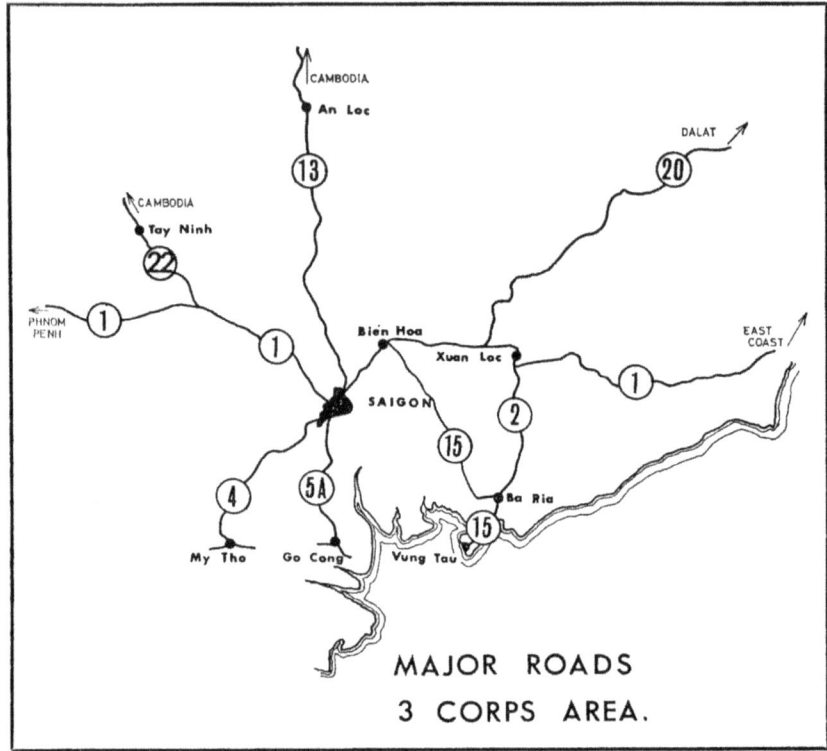

Fig. 4. Major roads, 3 Corps area.

The heart of the province is the south central region. This area provides good paddy fields and gardens and it contains over three-quarters of the population of Phuoc Tuy. Several fishing villages have grown up along the coast and they reap an ample harvest from the sea, sufficient to establish a flourishing trade with the Saigon fish market. However, this heart area occupies less than one quarter of the province. The remainder is covered for the most part by thick jungles inhabited by isolated communities of hunters, peasants, charcoal burners and, of course, by the Viet Cong. The town of Ba Ria, officially called Phuoc Le, situated at the crossing point of the Song Dinh and at the junction of the Saigon–Vung Tau road with the main roads to the east and north, has grown to a population of some twenty thousand people and become the seat of the provincial administration. This position, well to the south of the province and directly linked to the major base of Vung Tau, saved the provincial administration from falling into the hands of the Viet Cong in 1965. As one travels eastwards from Ba Ria one passes through the towns of Long Dien and Dat Do, a few

1. THE PROBLEM

miles apart. Twelve miles east of Dat Do lies the village of Xuyen Moc, the only appreciable settlement in the whole of the eastern third of the province. The three are joined to Ba Ria by Route 23 and each has given its name to an administrative district of the province. Several villages skirt the northern edge of the central cultivated area, chief of which is Hoa Long, three miles north-east of Ba Ria, while several other small villages lie to the north of Hoa Long, several miles apart, surrounded by small cleared areas and then by the all-embracing jungle.

The road network of the province has grown up around this framework. Route 15 runs northwards from Vung Tau to Ba Ria, and connects with the fishing and wood cutting villages along the western coast on its way north-west towards Bien Hoa and Saigon. This road was reconstructed by the French after the Second World War and traces of the old sunken cart road are still visible adjacent to the broad double strip of the new road. The maintenance of the security of Route 15 was complicated by two factors. First, the road is overlooked by the Dinh hills for most of its course in Phuoc Tuy. Viet Cong observation posts could see any traffic approaching from miles off and could launch ambushes from the steep hillsides or set up taxation points to take badly needed money from the Vietnamese civilians who used the road. Second, as with any coast road, Route 15 crosses a large number of small streams and thus there are many bridges and small culverts for the Viet Cong to blow up, cutting the road. Route 23 links Ba Ria with the towns and villages to the east, passing through open flat country covered with low scrub or through paddy fields until it reaches the outpost of Xuyen Moc. From there it runs to Ham Tan, twenty-five miles to the east in Binh Tuy province. Route 23 also crosses a great number of streams, including the broad Song Rai which had been spanned by a steel bridge nearly one hundred yards long. Thus, this road was also very vulnerable and could be controlled by taxation points along the twelve empty miles between Dat Do and Xuyen Moc.

Ba Ria is connected to the north by Route 2, a French road which runs with many straight stretches for over thirty miles to Xuan Loc. The biggest bend in its length is at Hoa Long where the road swings from the north-east to the north. The advent of Route 2 was of great economic importance to Phuoc Tuy because it opened up the unused central northern part of the province. This country was well suited to the growing of rubber trees and plantations were established by the major French firms after the First World War. The rubber trees begin at Hoa Long, where they stretch in an arc around the north-western side of the village and then run eastwards for a few miles to the villages of Long Phuoc and Long Tan. The next plantation is centred around the hamlet of An Phu, which lies on Route 2, four miles north of Hoa Long. From An Phu onwards to Xuan Loc the road runs through an almost continuous belt of plantations—the most important of which are those at Binh Ba, Ngai Giao and Xa Bang, the Courtenay Plantation on the border with Long Khanh province and the Ong Que Plantation in southern Long Khanh.

The population distribution within Phuoc Tuy may be seen from the above to be concentrated around the central hub with three arms of villages radiating out to the north-west, the north and the east along each of the major roads. 103,000 persons live in Phuoc Tuy. Of these, nearly 70,000 live around the central southern rice-growing area, 15,000 are strung out along each of the north-western and northern arms and 2,000 live at Xuyen Moc and along the eastern axis. These people are administered by six districts, three of which are the heavily populated areas around Ba Ria, Long Dien and Dat Do. The fourth is the territory east of the Song Rai, Xuyen Moc district; the fifth, Long Le district, is commanded from Hoa Long and stretches westwards across the Dinh hills to include the villages along Route 15 and Long Son island; and the sixth, Duc Thanh district, is commanded from near Ngai Giao, and covers the north-western third of the province.

The province is administered by a military government possessing a certain degree of autonomy in local affairs but coming under the command of the Third Vietnamese Corps via the Eighteenth Vietnamese Infantry Division whose headquarters are located at Xuan Loc. The Province Chief was Lieutenant Colonel Le Duc Dat, a cavalry man who began his service with the French. Dat's lithe figure was often to be seen darting around the district headquarters or in any village which our operations affected. By any standards Dat was energetic. Compared with the peasantry of Phuoc Tuy he was a dynamo. His conversation was sharp and incisive. He was very easy for us to work with, not least because he spoke moderate English as well as excellent French. Phuoc Tuy was a good province for an allied nation to work in because there were no major scandals or disloyalty. Dat was a hard man and although his political activities led to his re-posting in October, 1967, he was a very capable administrator. He was not particularly happy in his job. Once when I asked him why he had given some captured Viet Cong saboteurs a heavy sentence he wheeled around and said: 'For sixteen years I have been fighting these people—for sixteen years they have ruined my life and killed my friends. I will be lenient to a Viet Cong regular who is fighting because he is forced to, but to saboteurs and spies who are all volunteers I will not be lenient!'

The District Chiefs were mostly captains in the South Vietnamese Army. They were completely responsible for all the affairs of their districts, from food, health and housing to justice and military security. To ask one officer, unaided by any save a few clerks and policemen, to cater for all these needs of up to 30,000 people and to administer the writ over one hundred square miles of territory does not make for good government. Yet with the shortage of administrators and soldiers in South Vietnam any permanent enlargement of the district staffs was not feasible. Fortunately the American adviser system worked down to the level of districts and each Vietnamese captain had an American captain or major alongside him. However, the American was there to advise and while he could be of some moral support to his District Chief he could not remove much of the weight of decision making.

The Viet Cong first appeared in the villages of Phuoc Tuy in 1959. For the next year or so they confined their activities to the political front, holding meetings, recruiting members for the Party, propagandising against the Diem regime and organising their own administrative system for the province. In 1961 the first armed bands of Viet Cong challenged the Government's authority. One of the first targets for the marauding companies of regulars who came down into Phuoc Tuy from War Zone D was Route 15, which was attacked, ambushed, blown up and used for tax gathering with increasing frequency until by 1965 it had passed into Viet Cong control to the degree that even a battalion of Government troops with an armoured escort could not guarantee passage for themselves.

The armed forces of the Viet Cong fall into three categories. Their hard core is the regular soldier who serves for a period of several years and who can be moved to wherever he is needed. These soldiers are usually organised into regiments or divisions and are referred to as main force units. The main force have become augmented increasingly by North Vietnamese regulars so the term must be taken to include both the southern Viet Cong regulars and the northerners. The main force are augmented and assisted by local forces of two kinds, the provincial mobile and the village guerilla units. The provincial mobile units are recruited usually from the guerillas in the province in which they serve. They are full time soldiers and receive a small wage to keep their families alive. They have the advantages of intimate knowledge of the area in which they are fighting and of close contact with some of the people. They can act as guides and suppliers for the main force units and can provide them with detailed information of local Government activities, fortifications and strengths. The mobile force units are also equipped heavily enough to mount their own offensive actions and constitute a continuous threat to Allied troops within their particular province. The village guerilas are only part time soldiers, lightly equipped, usually with only an old French or American rifle, and are not well trained. The guerilas assist the mobile forces in much the same way as the latter assist the main force units. They can also carry out small raids and assassinations, collect taxes and carry messages.

Parallel to this structure of the Viet Cong Armed Forces is the Communist Party organisation which controls and co-ordinates all activity at each level, including military action. Hence, regional main force divisions are controlled by the regional Party committee, provincial mobile units are controlled by the provincial Party committees and the guerilas are directed by their village Party committees.

The Phuoc Tuy Party committee began to build up its own mobile force in 1961 when one company of infantry was raised. This was augmented by another in the following year and so the D445 Provincial Mobile Battalion was formed. In succeeding years several village committees were established and they in turn produced their crop of guerilas which went to make up squads and platoons so that by 1966 there were four district companies of guerilas within Phuoc Tuy.

The obvious areas for the Viet Cong to use for their bases were the uninhabited fastnesses of jungle which cover the northern half of the province. In the north-western corner lay the abandoned village of Hat Dich. This was taken over by the Viet Cong and used as a base for operations against the villages in central, northern and western Phuoc Tuy. In the north-east they took over the village of Thua Tich and organised it into a model Communist settlement as a commune even to the extent of using Viet Cong money. From these two centres the influence of the Viet Cong spread, beginning with the northern villages who, under the Diem regime, scarcely knew that there was a government in Saigon. Gradually, between 1961 and 1964 the villages of Xa Bang, Ngai Giao and Binh Ba came under Viet Cong control, leaving only the North Vietnamese Catholic refugee village of Binh Gia outstanding as a centre of resistance to the Viet Cong.

1. THE PROBLEM

While the north was being infiltrated another thrust was being pressed into the northern edge of the central region. Long Tan and Long Phuoc were taken over as Viet Cong villages and from these influence was exerted over Hoa Long. However the presence of the Long Le District Headquarters probably saved Hoa Long from complete takeover. Pressure was also applied from the east. Route 23 was cut in nine places by blowing up bridges and culverts, including the main bridge across the Song Rai. The district headquarters at Xuyen Moc was isolated and was to remain in a state bordering on siege for several years. A base area was established in the Long Hai hills and from here a significant degree of control was exerted over all the villages of the south central region. In particular, the Viet Cong achieved access to the rice harvest and so were able to establish the basis for the support of much larger forces within Phuoc Tuy. They also took control of the eastern coastline and so were able to receive direct shipments of specialised equipment over the miles of beaches, making Phuoc Tuy even more suitable for use as a main Viet Cong base.

Several of the villages along the western coast were infiltrated. Again two North Vietnamese Catholic refugee villages, Long Cat and Ong Trinh South, held out and preserved their independence. However the establishment of bases in the Dinh hills and the presence of guerillas in the villages along Route 15 gave the Viet Cong firm control over the area. Long Son island was taken over as a rest and training centre and as a terminal point for some of the supplies which came from the Mekong Delta across the Rung Sat. Several landing points were established from which the supplies were moved northwards to Hat Dich.

Much of this expansion had been due to the efforts of the D445 Battalion but on several occasions main force units were made available for operations in Phuoc Tuy and from 1964 onwards 274 Regiment was frequently on the scene. The forces of the Government were at full stretch everywhere in Vietnam as a result of the decline of the Army since 1954 and all Colonel Dat had at his command were a battalion of regulars and a few companies of regional force soldiers, most of whom were poorly trained and equipped and lacked leadership at the lower levels. With the tide of Viet Cong success rising throughout Vietnam in the early nineteen-sixties there were no forces spare to help Dat and he had to make do as best he could. He decided to hold on to the district headquarters as vital ground from which some vestige of control and communication could be maintained. There seemed no point in wasting troops trying to defend villages which would stretch his forces too thinly on the ground.

By early 1966 the headquarters of Xuyen Moc and Duc Thanh districts were isolated and all districts except Ba Ria itself were heavily infiltrated. Even Ba Ria was attacked and Colonel Dat's house mortared as retaliation for one assault which he had led against what had become the fortified Viet Cong village of Long Phuoc. The Viet Cong had established very large scale bases in the northern half of the province and had moved two main force regiments, 274 and 275, in to make up the teeth of the Fifth Viet Cong Division with headquarters in the May Tao mountains. Thus there were by this time seven battalions of Viet Cong with heavy fire support units active within the province and the outlook for the Government was black. Consequently it was with rejoicing that Dat received the news that the Australian Task Force of two battalions of infantry and one regiment of artillery was to be stationed in Phuoc Tuy. The Task Force was to arrive in May 1966 to begin clearing the Viet Cong forces out of the central area of the province and to help restore the authority of the Government over the people of Phuoc Tuy.

2
Holsworthy to Vietnam

The Fifth Battalion, The Royal Australian Regiment, was born on March 1st, 1965, at Holsworthy in the military wilderness on the outskirts of Sydney. Since the Fifth and the Sixth were the first battalions of The Royal Australian Regiment to be composed of a mixture of regulars and national servicemen, their formation and development was a particularly vital experiment for this was to be the model for the infantry battalions of the Army from then onwards. The core of the Fifth Battalion was made up of members of the First Battalion. Major J. A. Warr, the senior administrative staff officer of the First Battalion, was given the task of organising the split of the First Battalion and of administering command over the Fifth Battalion for the first month of its existence.

In April, the command of the battalion passed to Lieutenant Colonel P. H. Oxley. It was announced then that in September both Colonel Oxley and Major Warr were to be promoted. The former was to take command of the Third Training Battalion, the latter was to become the commanding officer of the Fifth Battalion. The two officers agreed that Major Warr would accept responsibility for all decisions which would affect the battalion after September 1st.

The First Battalion was in the final stages of its preparations for departure to Vietnam and so the Fifth came in for more than its usual share of routine chores and administrative duties. In order to foster a high spirit in the new battalion, the idea of becoming known as the 'Tiger Battalion' was introduced and this spread rapidly and spontaneously amongst its members. From that time on Fifth Battalion were the Tiger Battalion, from the gold of their lanyards to the tiger tails tied onto the kitbags leaving for Vietnam in April 1966.

Command of the battalion passed to Lt. Col. Warr in September 1965. He was faced with the responsibilities of preparing the battalion for war in the last six months of its training and of leading the battalion while it was stationed in Vietnam. Colonel Warr had been a soldier since 1944 when he had joined up as a private. After a year of experience in the ranks he gained selection for Duntroon. He graduated in December 1947 and went to Japan as a platoon commander with the 67th Battalion and the Third Battalion, The Royal Australian Regiment. He served in Korea with the Third Battalion, and was severely wounded, full recovery taking several years. During this time he occupied a number of staff positions in Victoria, studying part time at Melbourne University. In 1957, he attended the Australian Staff College at Queenscliff and in 1959 he went to Canada for two years on exchange duties with the Canadian Army. On returning to Australia he served as a company commander and staff officer with the First Battalion, RAR, until the formation of the Fifth.

During late 1965 the battalion went through an upheaval. A great number of officers' repostings fell due, there were many vacancies on establishment which became filled and some three hundred troops, both regular and national servicemen, came to the battalion in January 1966 so that the composition of the battalion was fifty per cent new. Although the newcomers were all trained soldiers they had not worked together as a team and so they had to be exercised first as sections, then as platoons, and then as companies before the battalion could operate as a whole.

The new second-in-command was Major Stan Maizey. A Duntroon graduate, Major Maizey had served in Korea and Malaya and was a graduate of the Australian Staff College. A Company was commanded by Major Bert Cassidy, one of the few members of the battalion who had fought in the Pacific theatre in the Second World War. He had also served in Malaya. B Company's commander was Major Bruce McQualter who at 29 was the youngest of a young group of company commanders. Bruce was a Duntroon graduate and he had also served in Malaya as a platoon commander during the emergency. C Company was commanded by Major Noel Granter who as one of the first group of post war national servicemen had gone on to graduate from the Officer Cadet School at Portsea, just in time to serve in the closing stages of the Korean commitment. He came to the Fifth Battalion directly from a staff posting in Malaysia. Major Paul Greenhalgh came to D Company with a background similar to that of Bruce McQualter. They had both graduated from Duntroon at the same time and Paul had also served in Malaya during the emergency. However, Paul had also spent a few years with the Special Air Service. Administration Company was commanded by Major John Miller, a Portsea graduate who had also served in Malaya. Major Max Carroll, another Portsea graduate, commanded Support Company. Max was also well acquainted with jungle warfare and had been mentioned in despatches for his leadership of the tracking team in Malaya. He had just graduated from Staff College.

The important common denominator of all the company commanders was service in Malaysia. While all of these officers were young and had not worked together as a team they were dedicated and hardworking, and they had the capacity to get along with each other. Thus the foundations of a happy battalion were laid.

For variety our adjutant was an Englishman, Captain Peter Isaacs, who had been commissioned into the British Army and served in Germany before coming to Australia. The intelligence officer at that time was Captain Don Willcox, a Duntroon graduate with Malayan experience, who had come to the battalion from the Intelligence Corps. Captain Ron Shambrook was the quartermaster and Captain Tony White was the medical officer. Tony's experience had included many notable battles at Cambridge and Sydney Universities and he almost knew which way to put his gaiters on when he came to the battalion. Captain Brian Ledan came to us as signals officer.

Compared with the earlier battalions of The Royal Australian Regiment this was a young group of officers to lead the Fifth into battle. But although most of them were not substantive in the ranks which they held, there was a good leaven of experience of the sort of conditions under which the battalion would have to fight. In particular this was provided by the Malayan emergency and this knowledge and experience supported the battalion in Vietnam until it had learned all the local lessons which were to give it complete confidence in being able to cope with the Viet Cong.

The time schedule gave the battalion three more months from January to be ready for operational commitment. This was not to say that we were to be fighting the Viet Cong in April, but we thought that any time we had after that would have to be regarded as a bonus. In January, Colonel Warr sent each of the rifle companies off in turn into the Gospers mountains for a shakedown while Battalion Headquarters roamed over the Holsworthy Range learning how to move itself and to establish itself in a defensive harbour. The training was undertaken with a spirit of urgency and the long hours and weekends which the work entailed were given cheerfully by all members. Range practices began in the dawn hours and went on until 10 pm. Training in night movement, lectures on Vietnamese history, culture and customs and language classes for the whole battalion often went on until 11 pm. The days themselves were given to specialised work such as booby trap training at the School of Military Engineering and tactical field firing exercises.

In February, each company went in turn to the Jungle Training Centre at Canungra. There in the rain forests of South Queensland many of us met jungle for the first time and became accustomed to the strange feeling of not being cold after a drenching by a tropical rain storm. The first week was worse than the whole of our year in Vietnam put together, for we had to propel our reluctant bodies over rope courses, across rivers dangling from flying foxes, over an assault course and finally over a thing called a confidence course which speedily removed any confidence I had left in my capacity for negotiating obstacles. We then brushed up our ability to creep about the jungle without getting lost in a maze of valleys which all looked the same, clad with so much growth that the furthest one could see to take a compass bearing was twenty yards or so. In the third week we exercised as companies in the depths of the Wiangaree State Forest. Here it was easy to move silently on the rotting leaves lying around the trunks of giant trees which shut out the sky with a translucent green canopy. We met some rather interesting practical problems of the Vietnamese war, for besides 'enemy' troops in the forest were groups dressed as civilian woodcutters. Sometimes these civilians were not what they appeared to be but guerillas carrying messages. What to do with a man who appeared to be a genuine civilian was a real problem. If he had seen some of our troops he could easily slip off and inform some armed Viet Cong. Therefore we had the mutual displeasure of their apprehension for the course of the operation. We learned that it was far better to hide and avoid discovery unless it was imperative for the safety of the civilian to hold him with us.

2. HOLSWORTHY TO VIETNAM

The training at Canungra was of the greatest value. Once we had learned to cope with its jungle and torrential rains, Vietnam held little that was totally new, except of course, the Viet Cong. The three weeks at Canungra rounded off our training in tactics at company level.

In March, the battalion began its first integral exercise. We flew up to Richmond from the rough aero-paddock behind Holsworthy and set off into the Gospers country on exercise Ben Tiger. We learned how to carry out a co-ordinated advance into rough, enemy-held territory, some of the rudiments of how to live on helicopter resupply and some of the problems of assembling the battalion at night for a dawn attack. The next phase was to build a defensive position which could be held against the mortar and artillery bombardments for which the Viet Cong are famous. This was an experience we were to be very glad of two months later. The battalion then came under command of the First Task Force for exercise Iron Lady which aimed at practising the co-operation of the essential elements of the Task Force. We set off for a week to learn the ruses for trapping Viet Cong when searching a wide stretch of difficult country; to camp on windy ridges and to get splendidly fit climbing in and out of gorges in quest of enemy and water. The battalion then reassembled for an attack on an enemy redoubt.

After a long hike out of the mountains we came together to hear the verdict of the Task Force Commander, Brigadier Douglas Vincent. We assembled in lines in the cold dawn mist after making camp, dog tired, at ten o'clock the previous night. Of course it had poured with rain to add to the confusion of the darkness and the rocks on the razor backed ridges, so we were a collection of very sober-minded individuals as we waited for the commander's arrival.

In a way it was like the minutes before the announcement of examination results. One's mind flew back over all the happenings of the past three months—months which had been crowded with activity and effort from one end to the other with the exercises, with studies of Vietnam, with the evening language classes, and with the weeks when we had begun firing on the range at dawn and had finished at ten o'clock at night. It had been hectic and everyone had tried hard, but had we reached a standard high enough to fit us for action against the Viet Cong? We knew that Brigadier Vincent would be honest with us for he always had been. Certainly we knew when we had not been up to standard! So when he told us that he thought we were fit to go to Vietnam and that he would look forward to commanding a Task Force of which the Fifth Battalion was a component we felt that we had reached a goal. The battalion had got through its adolescence and was about to start active life.

Orders for movement to Vietnam came very soon after this exercise. Most of the battalion were to fly, but one company was to go by sea with the heavy baggage and equipment on board the converted aircraft carrier HMAS *Sydney*. Noel Granter drew the unlucky number out of Stan Maizey's hat and so C Company left Australia on the *Sydney* on April 19th and spent twelve slow days wallowing and rolling its way to Vung Tau. Here the *Sydney* stood off the coast for a day while sailors threw lumps of explosive at random over the side to discourage any Viet Cong who might try to fix limpet mines to the hull.

C Company was met by the advance party of the battalion which had flown to Vung Tau in early April under the command of John Miller. On arrival, the advance party had spent a few days with the First Battalion, RAR, who were completing their tour of duty in Vietnam at the great base of Bien Hoa city, fifteen miles north-east of Saigon. The Australian forces had been allotted an area of sand dunes facing on to the eastern coast of the Vung Tau peninsula for a base camp and ultimately for use as a logistic support base for the Task Force when it had moved up into Phuoc Tuy. Beginning from nothing and working in a heat of 110 degrees, Major Miller began to lay the area out and started work on tent lines, defences, and with some ingenuity talked a passing American bulldozer driver into digging the latrines. The Viet Cong threat to the Vung Tau camp was not great for they had no forces on the Vung Tau peninsula. However, two months previously 275 Regiment had come across from the Long Hai peninsula on rafts to mortar the Vung Tau air field. Our part of the coast faced towards the Long Hai peninsula, so we had to take into account the possibility of harassing fire from mortars.

While this activity was going on at the Vung Tau base, two members of the battalion, Max Carroll and his batman, were out on operations. Major Carroll's main function within the battalion organisation was not the direct command of Support Company, for it functioned as a number of separate specialist teams such as the signallers, the mortars and the pioneers, but to be the commanding officer's chief staff officer and the battle second-in-command. This system was adapted from American practice in which this officer was referred to as the S3. The First Battalion had pioneered its use and we had taken it on after Colonel Warr's visit to the First Battalion in Vietnam in January 1966. Its great merit was that it left the commanding officer more freedom to think about what his next moves in a battle should be, or to plan the battalion's next operation, or to think about the long-term effectiveness of the various types of operation which we could undertake.

Of course the system was very dependent on the man who was the S3 for he had to work very closely with the commanding officer. It was essential that he had graduated from Staff College for he had to write the battalion operation orders which were the guide lines for all our efforts. Often the amount of detail required by the type of war which we were fighting involved an order of over thirty pages in length, so the job was a very burdensome one. The Fifth Battalion was very lucky to have had Max Carroll for this appointment. A recent graduate of Staff College, he was a very volatile combination of energy and human warmth. With his intenseness he was able to perceive the implications of any move suggested by the company commanders in a flash. His judgement regarding when to take a decision himself and when to refer a problem to the colonel was sound.

A wartime radio net, conducted with the security precautions appropriate to denying information to a listening enemy intercept service, is a dreadfully impersonal thing, yet Max had the facility for making one feel that the essence of one's problem was fully grasped and sympathised with, so that the answer he gave was a genuine weighing up of all the relevant factors rather than the automatic 'press on regardless' type. Max stayed as S3 until the end of the year, when reluctantly, Colonel Warr granted Max his often expressed desire to command a rifle company. It was not at all surprising that Max was awarded another mention in despatches for his work in Vietnam.

It was vital that Max should find out as much as possible at first hand about operations in Vietnam before the battalion was committed to action so he had gone with the advance party in early April in order to accompany the 173rd US Airborne Brigade, the formation with which the First Battalion had operated, on a fast moving, hard hitting action. While the rest of the battalion was getting itself to Vietnam, Max and his batman were upholding Australian discretion by digging foxholes over the Vietnamese countryside.

As the second-in-command of B Company at that time, I had to bring the second plane load of the company across to Vietnam. At Holsworthy, I made a final round of clearing my office forever, aware that at least I had a sea of activity into which to plunge while our families faced all the anxieties of waiting for twelve months to pass. The company paraded at 5 pm on Thursday, May 12th, in the stillness of the early evening. Everything around the camp seemed unusually precious—the quiet huts which we had got to know so well, the green grass and the tall gum trees. We called the names one by one and I was snapped out of my pensiveness to find that eighteen out of the ninety-one men were absent. However they all arrived during the next half hour, most having slipped into Liverpool for a few too many final beers on their native soil.

We drove out to Richmond air base by bus, feeling frightfully cold against the night air coming off the mountains, clad in our jungle greens ready for business in Vietnam on the following morning. After weighing in, we were free for an hour or so. There was a large crowd of relatives and friends—wives, children, fathers, mothers, and fiancées—some of whom were making their private distress public, and the atmosphere was rather emotionally charged.

As we emerged from our final briefing to board the waiting Boeing 707, the crowd became excited and then cheered, at first self-consciously and then with full assertion of their spirits. We climbed the gangway and saw the small distant faces and waving arms recede quickly into the distance as we taxied down the runway.

The flight to Manila was uneventful. We arrived at 8.30 am local time on a hot humid morning, sat in yet another characterless international lounge for half an hour and sampled some excellent San Miguel beer. One hour and fifty minutes away lay Saigon. The aircraft stewards, all male, said with some pride that they had volunteered to take us. We refrained from remarking that we had volunteered to get out of the aircraft at the other end and that no one was insuring our lives for £75,000. They were very willing and energetic assistants when the time came for me to brief the passengers with their landing instructions and to hand out the weapons to everybody.

We became excited to see the Vietnamese coast—a wide belt of yellow sand separating the blue sea from the green jungle. We descended into Saigon very steeply from 37,000 feet, because the pilot did not want to spend more time close to the ground than he could help. It was very turbulent and, coupled with the sight of the expanses of green jungle which abound close to Saigon, the effect was a little unnerving.

Than Son Nhut air base was a mass of parked aircraft, row upon row, thousands of yards long—bombers, tactical fighters, supersonic fighter-bombers, transports of all descriptions and a myriad tiny reconnaissance aircraft and helicopters. We filed out of the aircraft and moved into buses with wire grids over the open windows to prevent Viet Cong cyclists from dropping in hand grenades as they rode past. A few hundred yards away was a large, fat bellied C 123 transport aircraft into which we loaded our equipment and ourselves and in which we were sealed to await take off. We waited for nearly an hour in a temperature of 85 degrees and in ninety per cent humidity so we were fairly tired by the time we reached Vung Tau, some twenty minutes away by air. Bruce McQualter was waiting to give us a cheery welcome and to whisk us off in a convoy of Land Rovers and trucks to see some of the local sights en route to the battalion camp.

The camp was sited on an uneven stretch of dunes, some rising to fifty feet above the valleys which thrust blindly amongst them. The tents were laid out in company areas within a four hundred yard square. Tents were pitched fairly closely together, rather like a Citizen Military Forces camp in Australia, but surrounded by the protection of sandbag walls, thrown up by those of the battalion who had arrived earlier. We guessed that we would have a short period for acclimatisation and preparation before we attempted to establish ourselves in Phuoc Tuy; but until Colonel Warr had received his orders from the commander of the 173rd Airborne Brigade, who was in charge of the operation to establish the Task Force base securely in Phuoc Tuy, we could only estimate that we had about two weeks to become acquainted with the terrain and with American methods of operation in so far as they would affect the battalion.

Part of our acclimatisation was to clamber about in the Ganh Rai mountains which capped the broad end of the Vung Tau peninsula in a steeply sloping bulbous mass of green jungle and smooth brown rock. Occasional reports of small Viet Cong groups hiding in the mountains had been received, so there was some element of realism in carrying out a search of the area. However, we discovered nothing more than a few magnificent views over the peninsula and the Ganh Rai Bay which stretched away to the dark green fuzz of the Rung Sat. Crowning the summit were the ruins of a massive French fortress and gun emplacement sited to protect the seaward approaches to Saigon. Given over to the tenancy of rats and snakes, their whitewashed interior walls covered with the graffiti of Vietnamese lovers, and their exteriors disappearing beneath an envelopment of softly coiling creepers, they seemed to hang a large provocative question mark before our eyes. This feeling recurred to me on every occasion that we came across the deserted or ruined forts of the French which were strewn about the country in profusion. They asked 'What do you newcomers think you can achieve?' and they admonished 'Find methods which are more successful than the ones which we found!'

The most enjoyable experience of those first days in Vietnam was a close friendship which sprang up between our battalion and the 68th US Aviation Company. The 68th flew Iroquois helicopters, the normal means of transport for troops on operations. Since they were stationed at Vung Tau air base it seemed likely that they would be supporting us in the future. Perhaps one of the factors which precipitated the friendship was that they were also 'tigers', with the distinction that they were the 'Top Tigers', and their motto 'Every man a tiger'. But they needed to be, for helicopter pilots, always in short supply, flying several assault missions per day and spending minutes hovering defencelessly within range of Viet Cong machine guns, had one of the least enviable jobs in Vietnam. Furthermore, most of them were on their second tour of duty. Consequently we knew we could learn a lot from the 68th and were all the more glad when they laid aside several days of their own timetable to brush up our helicopter techniques and to introduce us to newer types of helicopter than those we had seen before. It brought a great feeling of confidence to have a close friendship with the men who would be bringing us the food and ammunition on which we relied and who would depend to a certain extent for their safety on our judgement in choosing and protecting landing zones.

The time at Vung Tau passed quickly in the succession of activities, all fascinating because of the newness of the environment and their relevance to our immediate future. As the days went by it became possible to place increasing emphasis on direct preparations for the battalion's first operation—Operation Hardihood.

3

The Clearance of Nui Dat

The location of the Task Force base depended upon several factors, none of which could be ignored without seriously prejudicing the operational prospects of the Australian commitment. As a base containing some three thousand troops it had to be supplied with a great tonnage of food, ammunition, equipment and building materials every day. Consequently, there had to be a good road capable of taking heavy traffic, even at the height of the monsoon, between the base and Vung Tau. This road had to be capable of being kept secure without a great deal of continuous effort such as had worn out the best mobile forces of the French at Hoa Binh or An Khe. Water was not a serious problem in the wet season but many of the streams of Phuoc Tuy dry up in the long rainless period which lasts from November to May, so the base had to be near a major watercourse.

Because the aim of the Task Force was to break the hold of the Viet Cong over the central region of the province it was logical that the base should both command the main approach to this area and be fairly centrally located within the province so that forces might be deployed quickly with lines of communication kept as short as possible. The base had to be capable of resisting strong Viet Cong attacks by forces of up to divisional size, so it had to occupy a location which suited the construction of a tactically sound defensive position. In particular it had to avoid the dominating effect of the Dinh and the Long Hai hills. The base had to be well away from the inhabitants of the province so that its weapons could fire at an attack from any direction without endangering the civilian population.

It was also important for the security of the base that a large zone be established around the perimeter into which entry was restricted, so that spies, reconnaissance teams and mortar crews were denied the protected access which the Viet Cong could obtain through mingling with the local people. The space requirements for the accommodation of the Task Force within its perimeter were quite appreciable, for not only were three thousand men to be fitted in, but provision had to be made for a medium length airstrip, indispensable for the rapid transport of men and urgent materials. The airstrip also imposed a requirement for level ground and safe approaches. Finally, the base had to be fitted into Phuoc Tuy in a manner which would cause the least possible economic disruption to the Vietnamese who used the land and the roads.

These considerations reduced the choice of site to two alternatives. The base had to be close to Route 2 in order to command central Phuoc Tuy with good communications. North of Hoa Long, surrounding the knoll of Nui Dat, was a large disused rubber plantation with a flat piece of fairly open ground in the centre. Further north of Nui Dat was the well established French plantation of Binh Ba, with an airstrip capable of taking the heaviest transport aircraft we were likely to need. Binh Ba offered the advantages of immediate air communications and of a well developed area equipped with large buildings, a hospital and a good water supply. However, the airstrip was in the centre of a working plantation on which three thousand people depended for their livelihood. Since security requirements for a base in this plantation would have caused the closure of many sections of the plantation, Binh Ba was clearly unsuitable for our location.

The Nui Dat area contained some dozen houses grouped together in the hamlet of An Phu but the area between An Phu and Hoa Long, nearly two miles away, was uninhabited and was not used for gardens. Hence, although it would be necessary to resettle the inhabitants of An Phu, use of the Nui Dat area would cause very little disruption to the lives of the local people. Nui Dat also had the advantage of shorter road communications and thus of more security for our traffic. Water supply appeared to be a problem for the engineers since there were only two perennial creeks skirting the area and none flowed through it. Some careful adjusting of perimeters was necessary to take in suitable water points on these two creeks. Nui Dat itself, a steep-sided, tree-clad hillock, rising some

3. THE CLEARANCE OF NUI DAT

two hundred feet above the plain, provided convenient observation of the surrounding country for several miles. Fire from its slopes could sweep a large area and it was a useful point for siting radio aerials.

Once the decision for Nui Dat had been taken, some long range preparations were begun. In February, 1966, the 173rd US Airborne Brigade, with the First Battalion, RAR, flew into Binh Ba and carried out a sweeping operation around the area of the plantation to disrupt the Viet Cong and learn a little more of the enemy's activities in central northern Phuoc Tuy. The Viet Cong villages of Long Phuoc and Long Tan were entered by joint Vietnamese-American operations in April 1966 after heavy fighting. The population of both of these villages were resettled in surrounding villages such as Dat Do, Long Dien and Hoa Long. While this movement of people crushed the two villages as centres of Viet Cong activity, it spread a thinner layer of Viet Cong across the other villages which the Task Force would have to deal with later—particularly in Hoa Long at its back door.

The Task Force was fortunate in having the assistance of the 173rd Airborne Brigade for mounting the operation to establish the base at Nui Dat. Because the Fifth Battalion was the only Australian unit available for the operation, command of the operation was given to the Americans. The Fifth Battalion was to function as an integral part of the Brigade, exactly as the First Battalion had done, until the Task Force Headquarters was installed at Nui Dat. We were very glad to be with the 173rd because of their familiarity with the area of operations and their previous experience of working with an Australian battalion. If the Viet Cong had decided to respond to our arrival at Nui Dat with either of their main force regiments we would have needed the additional strength given by the American brigade.

While the battalion was training with the 68th Aviation Company at Vung Tau, four of us were sent off on a helicopter reconnaissance of central Phuoc Tuy. The party consisted of Stan Maizey, Peter Isaacs, Captain Bob Milligan, the second-in-command of C Company, and myself. The helicopters were heavily armed for they had to carry out another mission as well. Each of the four aircraft carried fourteen rockets and six machine guns and two of them were armed with a two-inch grenade launcher in the nose. These four aircraft were what are known as gun ships and they normally escorted the passenger ships of the aviation company.

We climbed up out of the Vung Tau air base rapidly and set off at 2,000 feet and 100 miles an hour, moving up the long peninsula. The countryside beneath was dead flat, making the view like a page from an atlas. The Dinh hills rose on our right, flanking our path. The bright green plain of central Phuoc Tuy stretched away to the north and along the littoral were miles of mangroves divided by serpentine stretches of rivers and oxbows. The smoothness of these curves could have been inscribed with a compass or a French curve. We sped on to Ba Ria, landing to be briefed by Colonel Thurman, senior adviser to Colonel Dat. Armed with the latest information regarding the activities of the Viet Cong to the north, we set off again from the short air strip whose margin was littered with the carcasses of destroyed helicopters.

The pilots flew in tight formation at tree top height, so that we could have a good look at the ground around Nui Dat. We did not linger in any one area in case the suspicions of the Viet Cong were aroused and our eventual landing at Nui Dat strongly opposed. After a few swings over the area, the aircraft set off to the north-west. A few hundred yards further on bullets began whizzing past our helicopter. Immediately the laughing, boyish humour of the crew was discarded. The left door gunner had seen where the fire was coming from and had marked the position by hurling down a white smoke grenade. The whole team went into action as a single body. The four helicopters abruptly wheeled into line ahead and swooped down on the Viet Cong. The leading aircraft fired its machine guns and then two rockets. As it passed over the target the second helicopter took over and the leader wheeled around to the rear of the line to follow through again if necessary. It took two passes to silence the fire of the small group of black-clad figures. Probably the men on the ground had not realised that this patrol was made up of gun ships.

We then circled Binh Ba. It was fascinating to know that there was a large group of Viet Cong directly beneath us, for there were several hundred main force soldiers in the plantation. They had been digging up the airstrip by making rows of short shallow pits across it from one side to the other. Evidently this move was to prevent a similar operation to the one in February. The helicopters led off towards their goal, Thua Tich. The long regular lines of Binh Gia passed beneath us as we admired the defences of the village which had kept the Viet Cong at bay for two years. Thua Tich was still being used as a base by the Viet Cong so the gun ships were visiting it on a harassing raid. Their rockets swiftly reduced a couple of recently built storage huts to ashes and we flew back across miles of green jungle and then rubber trees, gardens, rice paddies and yellow sand to Vung Tau.

The Prime Minister, Mr Harold Holt, and Second Lieutenant Roe, a member of our advance party, at Bien Hoa, 25 April 1966 (see Chapter 2).

A bridge on Route 15 between Ba Ria and Vung Tau destroyed before our arrival by the Viet Cong.

Brigadier Jackson and General Westmoreland on board HMAS *Sydney* to welcome C Company to Vung Tau, 2 May 1966 (see Chapter 2).

3. THE CLEARANCE OF NUI DAT

On May 17th the two battalions of the 173rd Brigade, the 1st/503rd and the 2nd/503rd, flew in to the Nui Dat area to commence a sweep of the surrounding countryside. The 1st/503rd Battalion was accompanied by Peter Isaacs and Brian Ledan. A few days later they reported back to Vung Tau with news of the operation. The Americans had encountered several groups of Viet Cong of company size and it was apparent that there was at least one enemy battalion in the area of Nui Dat, assisted by some companies of guerillas. One of the American companies had been badly mauled on the first day of the operation. At 3.30 pm on May 17th, B Company of the 1st/503rd was moving up the western slope of Hill 72, one and a half miles north of Nui Dat. They knew that they were being followed by a Viet Cong rifleman carrying a radio, but they did not know that in their path were a Viet Cong company who were being guided by the man with the radio. The Americans were caught in the deadly cross fire of a box ambush to which were quickly added 60 mm. mortar bombs. By the time that they had extricated themselves they had lost eight killed and twenty-three wounded—a heavy blow for an infantry company to sustain.

While the American sweep was continuing, Colonel Warr was finalising his plans.

The tasks of the Fifth Battalion in Operation Hardihood were first to clear the area to the north and east of Nui Dat to a distance of five thousand metres so that enemy mortar fire could not reach the future base area, and second, to establish a defensive position to give security to the Nui Dat area while the other units of the Task Force concentrated in the new base. Therefore, the first part of the operation entailed a sweep over a quadrant-shaped piece of country with a radius of about three miles. It was possible that Viet Cong forces of up to regimental size were in the area and therefore the battalion had to be sufficiently concentrated to allow the companies to reinforce each other within an hour or two. The area of operation was divided into several sections so that all four companies could search simultaneously. Their routes were planned to be at least several hundred yards apart to avoid the risk of two companies clashing unwittingly. The thickness of the vegetation limited visibility to twenty yards in many places and to make half a mile an hour was fair progress. Each of the company areas was given natural boundaries, such as tracks or streams, rather than arbitrary lines drawn on a map so that the searching patrols could see clearly when they had reached the limit of their areas and the commencement of the territory in which the next company would be operating. The area to be searched was divided so that D Company moved to the southern area around Nui Dat, C Company went to the central area a mile north of Nui Dat, and A and B Companies covered the northern edge of the area. As the second-in-command of B Company, I shall be describing this operation from that company's point of view.

On May 23rd, the day before we were to begin the operation a battalion parade was held on the beach. Colonel Warr addressed us on the importance of the first operation from the point of view of both the nation and the battalion and exhorted us to remember what we had learned during our training. As we made our final preparations there was a slight growth of tension. Men became more serious-minded as they concentrated on packing their equipment, cleaning their weapons and pondering the operation which was to introduce them to the activity in which they would be immersed for the following twelve months. We were all very conscious of the importance of doing well during the coming days, not least for the reason that if the Viet Cong came to regard us as a weak battalion they would harry us all the more, whereas if they respected our proficiency they would probably stay out of our way and leave us to concentrate on the re-establishment of government control in the villages.

The morning of May 24th was dull and misty. Reveille was very early as the companies began taking off in helicopters shortly after dawn, in approximately half company groups. My lift took off at 0936 hours, punctual to a few seconds. The helicopters seemed to be amazingly close together in the air. From a distance they looked like a long line of cherry stones hanging and bobbing on strings. From close up it was like driving on a motorway with a third dimension added to the movements of the vehicles around one. The country looked quiet and sleepy, clad in small wraps of white mist which clung around the tall trees. The landing area was a broad flat hilltop in front of a rubber plantation which formed the north-western extremity of the An Phu sector. Rubber trees ran along two sides and low scrub began on the other two. This landing zone was code named Hudson. The name stuck after the operation and whenever we referred to that ground it was simply called Hudson. When we landed we saw a few members of the 2nd/503rd Battalion standing around, washing and smoking and looking very wet for it had rained hard earlier that morning. The wet season was well under way. As we waited in the rubber for the companies in front to shake out and move off, we were deafened by the American artillery and mortars which were firing in support of an engagement which was taking place a mile and a half away.

3. THE CLEARANCE OF NUI DAT

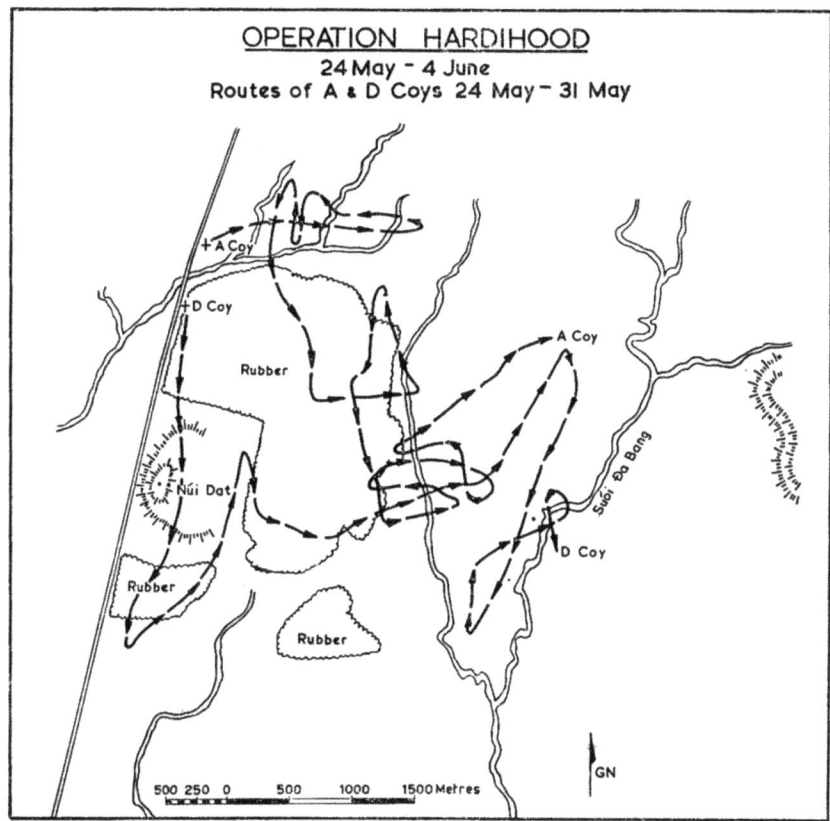

Fig. 5. The movements of A and D Companies to clear the Viet Cong away from Nui Dat, Operation Hardihood, 24–31 May 1966.

We moved off about 1 pm just as a group of eleven Vietnamese were being escorted into Battalion Headquarters by members of A Company, who had been searching the houses of An Phu. We passed through bananas, around the hamlet and crossed Route 2. The narrow strip of French bitumen looked a little forlorn in these wild surroundings. On the eastern side of the road we moved into scrub. The heat in the open was punishing for no air stirred in the tall grass and one had a feeling of being stifled. We were saturated by perspiration in ten minutes so that our jungle green shirts looked black. After clearing nearly a mile of country we made camp near the crest of Hill 72 at 5 pm. An hour later Bruce sent out a water party to fill up our depleted bottles from a creek some two hundred yards to the south-east.

A Company had encountered a number of Viet Cong further away to our south-east during the afternoon and were following them up, so the water party, members of Five Platoon under Sergeant Hassall, were treading warily. Shortly after reaching the stream and posting scouts around the water point the party was fired on. Everyone went to ground and the fire was returned. During a pause Private Noack, one of the water party, stood up to move to another position. As soon as he rose up he was hit by a burst of sub machine gun fire. Just then, A Company reached the stream from the other side and drove the Viet Cong off to the north. A stretcher was quickly assembled by Five Platoon, while Corporal Ron Nichols, the company medic, had dashed forward and dressed Noack's wound. It was my task to call Battalion Headquarters on the radio and request a medical evacuation helicopter. For some peculiar reason these helicopters were known as Dust Off helicopters —probably a code name which stuck because of its convenient length and unambiguous sound when spoken over a poor radio net.

The next forty minutes were crowded with activity as we awaited the Dust Off. The defences of the company had to be sited properly and checked to see that each of the three platoons was linked in with each of the other two on its flanks. The siting of each of the ten machine guns had to be individually checked to see that the main approaches to the company position were covered by fire and that each gun was capable of giving mutual support to its neighbours by firing across their front in the event of the latter receiving a frontal assault. While I was doing this, Bruce was arranging for A Company to pass through our position so that they could make camp to our north-west. A landing zone fifty yards across was cut for the Dust Off and Noack was carried to the edge of the clearing. He had been hit in the side and the back and the wound looked serious. Nichols had given him some morphine but he was still in pain and complained of lack of feeling in his legs. Bruce spent several minutes talking with Noack and giving what comfort he could. We were very thankful to see the helicopter appear overhead just as darkness was gathering. The pilot saw our coloured smoke marker and confirmed the colour so that he knew he was not being lured to a killing ground by the Viet Cong. A huge Negro medic jumped out of the aircraft when it landed. He looked jet black in the gathering gloom. His direct brusqueness seemed professional and reassuring. We returned to digging the defences before darkness became complete, keenly aware that we were close to the point at which the American company had been attacked and feeling rather uneasy, wondering what Viet Cong force might be gathering to pounce on our position whose location had been betrayed by the Dust Off helicopter.

3. THE CLEARANCE OF NUI DAT

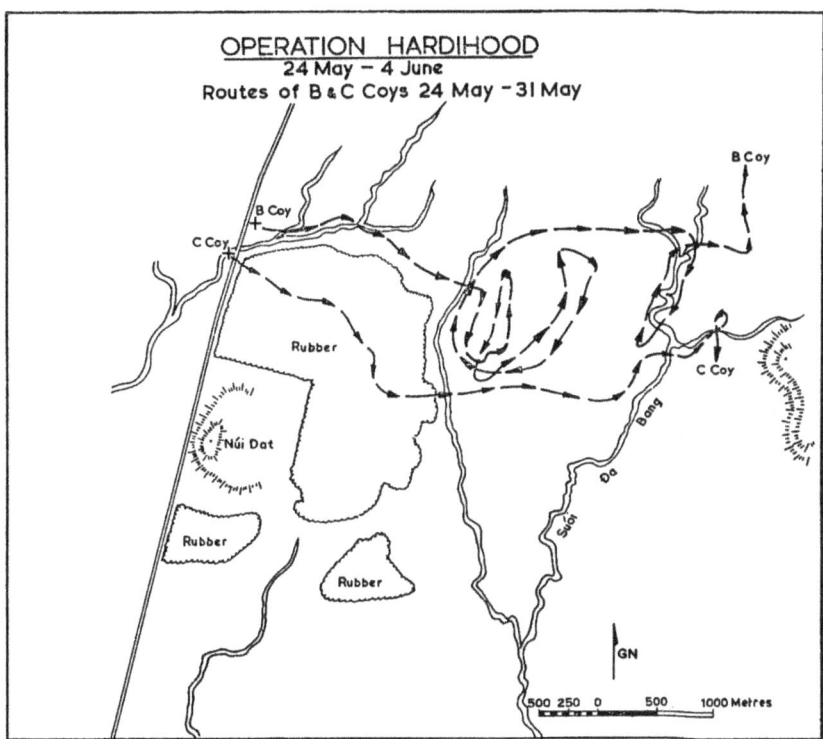

Fig. 6. The movements of B and C Companies, Operation Hardihood, 24–31 May 1966.

As events turned out we need have had no worries, but we were shaken by the realisation that death could come in this war without warning and without knowledge of the assailant's intentions or numbers. At 10 pm we received a call on the radio from Battalion Headquarters. Noack had died in the helicopter on the way to Vung Tau. The worst had happened and its acceptance was very difficult.

On the following morning we pressed on through country which was a mixture of low scrub, overgrown banana plantation and tangled secondary jungle. There were several open areas in our path which had to be negotiated carefully lest an ambush lay lurking on the edges waiting to catch us in the centre. The country was carefully searched as we went, so progress was slow. Near midday we came to some low forest, through which two well used ox cart tracks ran, one of which had been used by a rubber tyred vehicle in the past few days. These tracks were obviously part of the Viet Cong road network which ran from the coast to the inland bases. We laid an ambush on one track but then received orders to move half a mile to the south-east to clear some huts.

Soon after starting off, Five Platoon saw two Viet Cong in black pyjamas and carrying rifles running through the bushes a few hundred yards away. As we were moving down a long gentle hill we heard a rushing scuffle coming through the bush and were startled by three wild pigs who dashed through our formation. Shortly afterwards, the forward elements of Five Platoon, who were leading, crossed over a small ridge in front of us. Suddenly they went to ground, firing vigorously at a hut some fifty yards ahead in which were four Viet Cong with rifles. The enemy fled into the thick scrub at the back of the hut, deserting their tools and equipment. We burned the hut so that it could shelter no more Viet Cong.

As we moved carefully through the dense bush in the wake of the fleeing Viet Cong two more huts were discovered. This area was a small Viet Cong base. Each hut contained a bed and beneath each bed was a bunker. On the roof of one hut were two hand grenades without their strikers. They were triggered to explode at the least disturbance. We set fire to the huts and moved well away from the sharp explosions which sent showers of metallic fragments through the air near the huts. We camped for the night in a large banana plantation. It was quiet and peaceful under the weird sail-like shapes of the huge banana leaves, silhouetted against the soft moonlight of the tropical sky.

Early the following morning three helicopters arrived bringing food. After their departure, a fourth helicopter, bearing Colonel Warr, appeared. It landed and suddenly a burst of firing broke out from the southern edge of the landing area. The Viet Cong had been lurking close by awaiting an opportunity to strike us a sharp blow. A clearing patrol forced the Viet Cong away. The helicopter had three holes in it—one in an oil line. The pilot said he would chance getting it off the ground again if Colonel Warr agreed. Colonel Warr had finished conferring with Bruce about the coming phase of the operation. He climbed into the helicopter with a light remark about the pleasures of the unknown. The machine took off successfully, climbed to fifteen hundred feet and disappeared over the western horizon to Battalion Headquarters.

Bruce then moved the company to a hilltop in the banana plantation, some five hundred yards away. We arrived without incident and I proceeded to lay out the company defences. Bursts of machine gun fire rattled out on

3. THE CLEARANCE OF NUI DAT

our northern flank. Two Viet Cong had walked straight into our position from the north, directly onto one of Four Platoon's machine guns. Bullets also came into our position from the south-east, so we temporarily had the impression that the Viet Cong were all around us and the next few minutes were rather exciting. Four Platoon set off in pursuit of the two who had walked into them. They found a lot of blood and brought back one sandal, blood covered, made from an old rubber tyre. Known as Ho Chi Minh sandals they were the normal footwear of the Viet Cong. The amount of blood on the trail indicated that one had been killed. The other must have hidden the body before making off.

During the afternoon several of our patrols went out, locating some Viet Cong huts and a bunker which they destroyed. One patrol saw a group of Viet Cong crossing a piece of open ground which was over a thousand yards away from them. Lieutenant Pott, commander of Six Platoon, ordered one of his machine guns to open fire, more to give the Viet Cong a fright than to hit them, for at that distance accuracy is almost impossible. However, a patrol from A Company found a body riddled by our machine gun bullets near that open ground on the following day.

During the night we set an ambush on the track which the two Viet Cong had used in the morning. The night passed uneventfully if a little tensely, for once again we had given away our position in the afternoon by taking a helicopter resupply.

On the morning of May 27th we moved off to clear another area which lay fifteen hundred yards away to the north-east. The country which we passed through was extremely beautiful. The jungles were a little thorny and tangled in places, but much of the country was lush and green, rather like an overgrown English park. Great festoons of greenery hung down from the high trees on long vines and lianas like an absurdly overdone Baroque ornament. Short green grass carpeted the ground. Even the mosquitoes seemed elegant. They had black bodies, very slender, and their legs were banded with black and white.

Patrolling through that sort of country had its own peculiar atmosphere of tension. The hot sun beat down and was reflected from the ground in a slow moving stream of heated air which enveloped the body. All around the air was filled with the clicking and whirring of insects and jungle birds. Heat dripped from everything around and poured in torrents from our brows. The scenery shimmered. Even the metallic sounds of the birds seemed to glint and shimmer with the heat.

We moved in two groups. Five Platoon was separated from the remainder of the company and investigated the area to the south of our line of march. The northerly route was quiet, but Five Platoon had a more successful morning. They encountered a Viet Cong defensive position, which was occupied by five men. The platoon commander, Lieutenant O'Hanlon, ordered an attack which drove out the Viet Cong, who left a considerable trail of blood. On following this blood trail, voices were heard. One wounded Viet Cong attracted attention to himself and surrendered. Our chaps bandaged his wounded leg and splinted it in case it had been broken. He accepted a cigarette and a drink of water. Within twenty minutes of receiving his wound he was flying to the same hospital which we used at Vung Tau. Near the huts of the base Five Platoon discovered a cache containing 1,300 pounds of rice. Disposal of captured rice is always a problem when it is found in such large quantities as it is seldom possible to lift it out by helicopter or by road. Often the only expedient which can be used for denying the rice to the Viet Cong is to blow it up. Five Platoon were forced to do this because the helicopters supporting us were too fully committed to carry out the rice and no more helicopters were available.

The company formed a harbour around a wide clearing in the forest. Bruce positioned men in ambushes along a track which ran through the clearing. Around mid-afternoon we jumped into our weapon pits at the sound of firing just outside our perimeter. Two Viet Cong had walked into our western ambush. They had come up the track quite casually with their weapons, American M1 rifles, slung on their shoulders. One of the men was killed by a burst of machine gun fire. The other, wounded, dropped his rifle and equipment and ran into the trees.

It was my task to take out the small patrol to bring in the body and the equipment. We went down to the ambush position from where we could see two thin bare legs protruding from behind a bush. We cautiously approached the clearing where he lay, for his companion or others could have been lurking nearby. The body was a pitiful sight; the ageless features of the oriental may have been deceptive but he looked only eighteen and pathetically thin. However, his weapon and equipment laden with grenades and ammunition swiftly dissolved much of my remorse, for he was armed and trained to kill us. I searched him, finding only some unimportant papers in a plastic document case and a cigarette lighter in his pockets. We carried him back to camp and buried him.

3. THE CLEARANCE OF NUI DAT

As we finished blowing up the captured grenades and ammunition a flurry of shots broke out on the northern side of our harbour. The companion who had escaped had evidently come back to take a good look at us in order to carry a full report to his commander. We attempted to capture him but the thickness of the bush gave him too much cover. Since our position and numbers had been observed we prepared our defences for the night with great care, laying ambushes on all likely approaches. Around midnight, peals of thunder broke the silence like artillery and rain crashed down in sheets. I soon found myself lying in a stream of water three inches deep. Fortunately the heat of the night made it a small matter if one was wet. However I became rather anxious for our security, because the rain made it impossible to detect any movement outside our perimeter: we would not have known that the enemy was upon us until he had entered our defences. Fortunately, as so often, these fears were groundless and no one bothered us. Also, determination to get some sleep was a good antidote to anxiety. As time went by we found that we were frightened only if we had enough energy left over to feel fear.

On the 28th of May we set off to move further to the east where some more Viet Cong tracks lay. At 10 am we had a welcome stop and our first wash since the beginning of the operation. We changed our clothes and took our feet out of our boots for the first time in four days. However, the dry socks stayed dry for five minutes only as we then waded through a deep, swiftly flowing creek, the Suoi Da Bang, swollen by the recent heavy rains. After slithering and clawing our way up the far bank, which was ten feet high, we headed into thick bamboo.

Bruce halted the company at 2 pm on top of a steep ridge overlooking a well used track which followed the line of the Suoi Da Bang. Then we received a radio warning from Max Carroll to stay off the high ground in case we struck a Viet Cong force which was too big for us to handle. An enemy battalion had been located further south down the valley, and A Company had almost collided with it. The enemy intentions were uncertain. The battalion may have been coming up the valley to attack us or it may have been preparing to withdraw. We repacked our equipment and commenced to move back into the valley. Six Platoon descended from the ridge first in order to secure our northern flank against any Viet Cong who might have been coming down the track. Two minutes later several bursts of machine gun fire sent everyone to the ground. Six Platoon had encountered several Viet Cong coming south on the track. The confidence displayed by the Viet Cong was remarkable, right through this phase of the operation. Possibly this was the result of many years of undisputed possession of the area, but on many occasions, such as this one, the Viet Cong ignored all precautions and walked down the centre of the track talking loudly and with their weapons slung on their shoulders where they could not be used on the instant if they were ambushed.

The Viet Cong had arrived on the scene just as Six Platoon were crossing the track, so there was no opportunity for surrounding them and cutting off their escape. One of our forward scouts opened fire and was quickly supported by his section's machine gun. One Viet Cong was killed and at least two others wounded. Bruce called in artillery onto the line of withdrawal taken by the survivors. The dead man was searched and then buried. The whole action had taken up some thirty minutes, so Bruce decided to return to the security of the ridge line for the night and to continue the search in the morning.

At this stage the whole of the Fifth Battalion was being redeployed to form a line of ambushes along the Suoi Da Bang. Many Viet Cong had been encountered along this valley by the other companies and there was the possibility of the whole battalion of Viet Cong in the south attempting to move up the valley and link up with the main force regiment which was to the north of us.

We had gone only two hundred yards in the morning when five shots cleaved the air. The forward scout of the leading platoon had seen one Viet Cong moving towards him and had quickly called up the second scout. Unseen by the enemy, the two scouts had split up so that the one could cover the Viet Cong with his rifle, while the other worked around to try to get close enough to capture him. When the latter scout was close enough to the Viet Cong to challenge him he called on him in Vietnamese to surrender. The Viet Cong dropped behind a log and made no reply. When he was told to surrender a second time he darted off into the scrub. However he was not quick enough to escape the fire which had been covering him in case he attempted flight and he was cut down.

After the burial the company moved southwards again. The route lay through a maze of bamboo clumps whose low arching branches forced us to duck and stoop while thousands of sharp little thorns snared our clothing and equipment. We rested on a small sandy spit at the junction of a stream with the Suoi Da Bang, and felt, very sharply, the huge distinction between the moments when one was being shot at and those when one was not. The war seemed rather like a tramp through the bush for 95 per cent of the time: it was that vital 5 per cent which made the difference—the time when danger threatened, or when one imagined that it threatened. At times it was very easy to put the thought of danger right out of mind. This may have been merely a human defence mechanism, but perhaps it was also a rationalisation for only seldom was one bothered enough by the dangers to feel fear.

After this rest we went on to the next creek junction where we laid an ambush for the night. Several tracks cut the creeks at this point and Bruce arranged a brilliant series of ambushes so that all the approaches were covered, and if enemy caught in one ambush tried to break and run away they would run into another. However, the Viet Cong made no movement that night and we lost our sleep for no gain.

On the morning of May 30th we found an extensive Viet Cong camp. It was several years old and the defences were in poor condition, but some of the huts had been used recently. The amount of work which had been put into a tunnel system connecting two strong points was surprising. What was the purpose of this defensive installation in the heart of territory which had been securely in the hands of the Viet Cong for years? I could only suppose that it had been built as a training exercise.

It became apparent that the Viet Cong battalion had moved eastwards to avoid contact, for D Company had found their camp which had been hurriedly vacated by an enemy who left many tracks leading to the east.

The battalion plan was to concentrate the companies closer together in another series of ambushes in case the Viet Cong attempted to re-use the Suoi Da Bang track. We moved some five hundred yards to the north and found ourselves in the ironical situation of ambushing the Viet Cong from the security of one of their old camps. I made myself very comfortable behind the piled rocks of a Viet Cong sangar for the next two days. This pause afforded us a very welcome rest and a chance to dry out our saturated equipment and bedding. This was confined to our packs when we were on the move and so never had an opportunity to dry out from one day's deluge to the next.

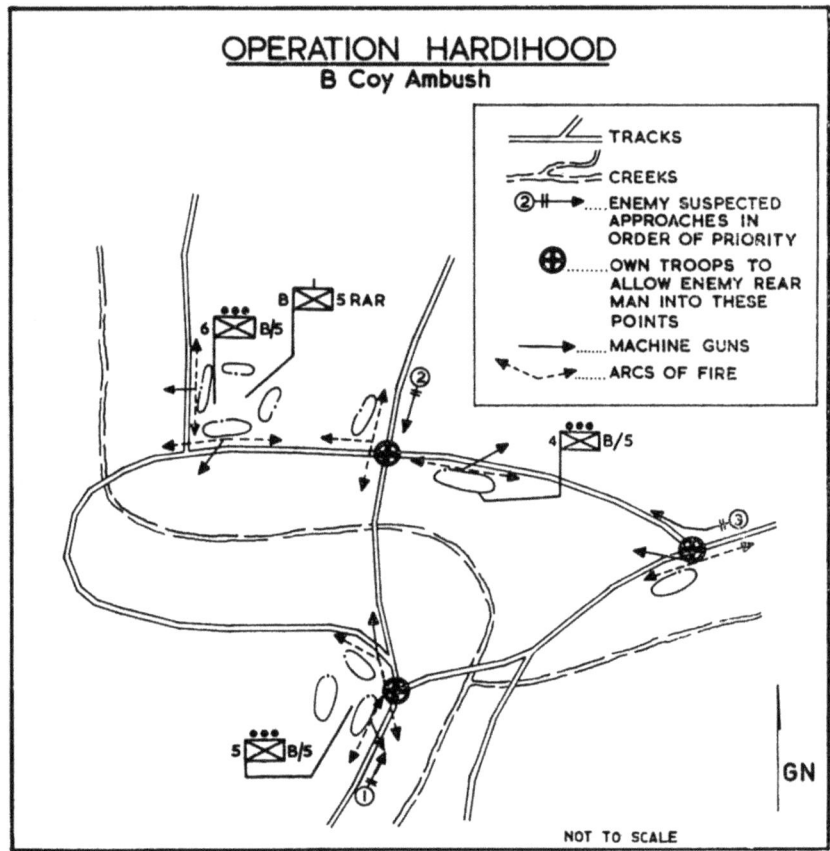

Fig. 7. An example of the many ambushes planned by Major McQualter. This ambush was set on the Suoi Da Bang by B Company on the night of 29–30 May 1966.

Evidently the Viet Cong were vacating the whole area for no contacts with them were made by any of the companies—the first day of the operation on which this had happened. After a peaceful and dry night we continued to man our ambushes on a ridge line. The position abounded with fascinating insects and other wild life: big butterflies with black wings splashed with turquoise which glittered and shone, fat friendly brown lizards, bloated by the richness of the local provender, and black ants with large mandibles which we called chomper ants. These had eaten a hole in my groundsheet six inches square during the night. During the day we aired our feet. A couple of hours in the fresh air restored those whitish lumps of wrinkled flesh to something nearer their normal appearance.

We made no contact with the Viet Cong in this ambush. The other companies encountered a few however, and C Company took two prisoners, a man and a woman who had bumped into the company position without knowing that it was there. Another group of Viet Cong who probed C Company were heard by an interpreter to remark 'Australians! Be careful!'

After a few more days of sweeping the area it was apparent that the Viet Cong had departed and that we could now prepare to develop the battalion's permanent base at Nui Dat. On June 2nd the companies moved back into the immediate vicinity of Nui Dat and occupied a wide arc around the north-eastern side, about one thousand yards out from the hill. When I was back in the base area I went across to the camp of the 173rd Airborne Brigade on the opposite side of Route 2 to see what I could scrounge. Several others must have beaten me to that idea for when I asked for a few items which I said were still on their way to us on board the HMAS *Sydney*, the American Supply Sergeant replied, 'Well goddam, that *Sydney* must be the biggest ship in the world—the *Queen Elizabeth*, the *Enterprise* and the *United States* all rolled into one. There's so much gear on board it!'

During the following days Colonel Warr laid out the battalion defences and the companies began to dig themselves in. Once everyone had a weapon pit with thick overhead cover for protection from shelling, work was commenced on the perimeter wire. The companies were still widely dispersed with only A and B Companies near their final positions. This was because the whole Task Force area had to be patrolled every day and it was necessary to have one company, D Company, at the southern extremity, some thousand yards south of Nui Dat, while another company, C Company, had to be on the eastern flank a similar distance out from Nui Dat.

During this week the other units of the Task Force began concentrating at Nui Dat. The headquarters flew in on June 5th and began to take over control of the Fifth Battalion from the American brigade which departed from Nui Dat on June 8th, having rendered us most vital assistance. In helping the Australian Task Force to become established, the Americans had suffered 23 killed and 160 wounded.

VIETNAM TASK

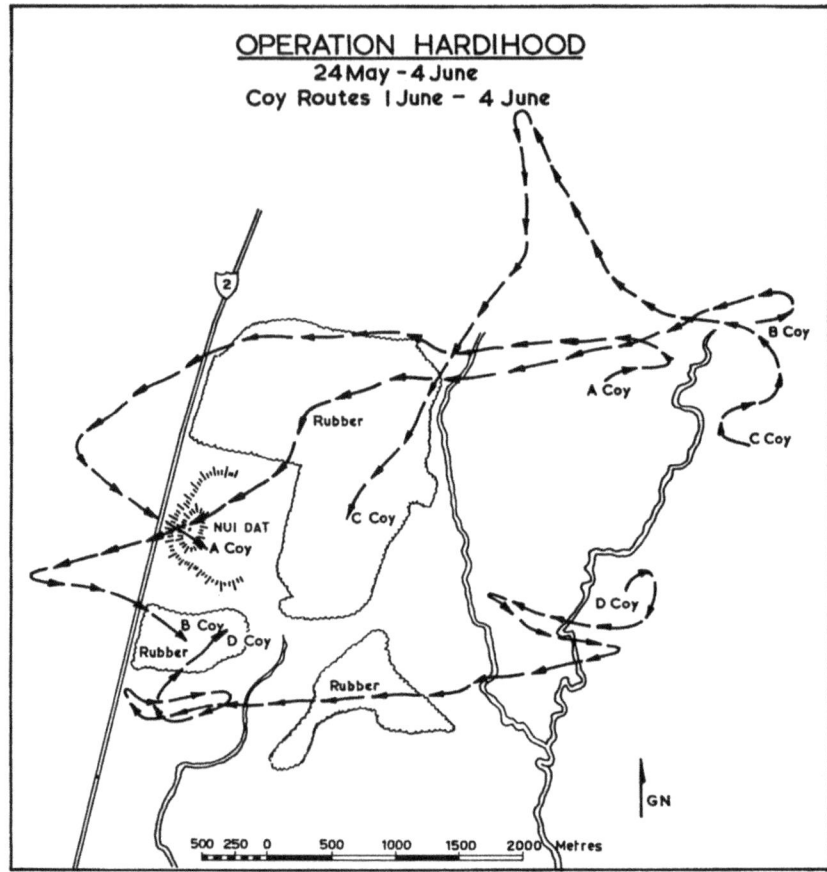

Fig. 8. The rifle companies move in towards Nui Dat before commencing to build the defences of the base, Operation Hardihood, 1–4 June 1966.

As we dug ourselves in around Nui Dat the Viet Cong were not sitting idly by. Each night they began to creep up to our positions to see where we were, where the wire was sited and how effective it was. They waved lights about on poles in attempts to locate our machine guns by drawing their fire. However, no one fired unless they had a man within very close range and the machine guns were under orders not to fire at all unless a heavy attack came in. This probing was normal procedure for the Viet Cong in preparing a large scale attack and it tended to confirm an intelligence report which we had received that 274 Regiment was planning to attack our position on a night around June 12th in order to throw us out of Phuoc Tuy and restore their loss of face amongst the local people.

3. THE CLEARANCE OF NUI DAT

Colonel Warr (centre) planning helicopter requirements with Lieutenant Brinnon of the 68th US Army Aviation Company (left) and Major Hannigan, operations officer, First Australian Task Force (right) at Vung Tau, May 1966 (see Chapter 2).

Major Carroll (right) and Corporal Western, his radio operator, at the battalion helicopter rehearsal before Operation Hardihood, May 1966 (see Chapter 2).

VIETNAM TASK

During the first hours of Operation Hardihood on 24 May 1966 (see Chapter 3): Lieutenant Hartley (centre) with his radio operator and the ubiquitous Le Van Yen, a fluent French speaking herbalist.

Private Allen (left) and Corporal Cleary with Viet Cong panji spikes encountered on Operation Hardihood (see Chapter 3).

3. THE CLEARANCE OF NUI DAT

In October 1966 we captured the diary of Nguyen Nam Hung, deputy commander of 274 Regiment, who had commanded the group of reconnaissance teams which probed us in early June, so I can relate both sides of the events which occurred at that time. Hung had set off from his base in the Hat Dich area on June 4th in order to examine our position. He formed a small base to the north of us on June 6th, from which his men made their patrols. They saw the Americans depart on June 8th and he recorded that several of his men were wounded by our sentries as they probed our defences. The Regiment moved down from its base and concentrated near Nui Nghe, three miles to our north-west, on June 9th, where they awaited Hung's report. Just as Hung reached them in the late afternoon, an American light observation aircraft which had been supporting us during the day made a low sweep over Nui Nghe on its way back to Vung Tau. Possibly the crew had noticed a tin roofed hut at the foot of the hill and were investigating it. However, fire from 274 Regiment brought the aircraft down in thick jungle at the foot of the eastern side of Nui Nghe. After discussion with Hung, the commander of 274 Regiment decided that it would be more profitable to ambush the crashed aircraft than to attack us in our defended camp, so the regiment lay in wait for us for the following two days.

However, we had no knowledge that the aircraft had crashed until we received a radio request the following morning from the Americans asking for their aircraft back. Nobody knew where it had crashed and aerial searches produced no evidence as the jungle was too thick. Consequently, the battalion was unable to send out the recovery team to assist any survivors, which would have been sent had the location of the crash been known. Thus the battalion was very fortunate, for had a company fallen into the Viet Cong regimental ambush it would have had a very hard time to hold its own until relief could have been sent to it.

The crashed aircraft was finally discovered by A Company in January 1967. They said that it was invisible from thirty yards away and that it was by chance that the aircraft had been found. The pilot had been killed on impact. He had been shot through the leg and probably this injury had caused him to crash. The observer had been able to climb out and the small pile of empty cartridge cases beside his skeleton testified that he had held the Viet Cong off until his ammunition had run out. They had then shot him through the back of the neck.

The final outcome of this incident was that our occupation of the Nui Dat area was completed without serious challenge, and the Task Force base was rapidly built into a fortification, which even a divisional assault would find difficult to enter. The Viet Cong did not leave us entirely alone however, for two members of D Company were killed and three were wounded on June 11th when a patrol was hit by artillery fire on the south-western side of the Task Force perimeter. But these incidents achieved nothing more than to keep us on our guard and to strengthen our resolve to push the Viet Cong deep into the jungles where they could harm neither the civilian population nor ourselves. Once established in our base, we were free to begin consideration of how we could most rapidly remove the Viet Cong from central Phuoc Tuy and the planning for the next operation was commenced.

4

An Experiment in Night Movement

There is little of the central plain of Phuoc Tuy which cannot be seen from the long level ridge which crowns Nui Nghe. The hill is visible on a clear day from Vung Tau as a small grey bump on the northern horizon, but its six hundred feet of steep, thickly covered slope become greener as one approaches. At Ba Ria it is grey green, at Nui Dat dark green, while in amongst the tangle of bush and bamboo which lead up to it, Nui Nghe becomes a rich mid-green. As the highest piece of ground within a few miles of our base, it seemed fairly obvious that we should investigate it as soon as possible. The area around Nui Nghe had not been cleared during Operation Hardihood, so we had to discover what use the Viet Cong had been making of it.

The first opportunity for sweeping through the area of Nui Nghe arose in early July. The Sixth Battalion, RAR, was engaged from mid-June until early July in searching Long Phuoc and in destroying the great number of tunnels which the Viet Cong had dug there. While the Sixth Battalion was out of the base we had to remain behind in order to defend it and patrol the approaches. One of our companies was always in the vacated Sixth Battalion defences while another was stood by as the Task Force emergency reserve. This situation was reversed when we were out on operations, but it meant that we had to wait until the Sixth Battalion had completed the search of Long Phuoc before we could commence our next operation—Operation Sydney.

Nui Nghe was known to be a focal point for Viet Cong tracks. We did not know exactly where these tracks ran but we did know that the Viet Cong moved between Binh Ba, the rubber plantation village, and the Dinh hills. Nui Nghe lay close to the direct line joining these two places. The main bases of the Hat Dich area lay to the north of Nui Nghe and tracks from these bases joined and crossed the Binh Ba – Dinh hills track. Intelligence reports had indicated that the Viet Cong had established some caches and camps there of an auxiliary nature to support their operations in central Phuoc Tuy and it seemed very likely that the Viet Cong had been observing us from the summit of Nui Nghe.

The Viet Cong forces which we were likely to encounter on Operation Sydney were the guerilla platoon based in Binh Ba and Duc My, the Montagnard hamlet to the south of Binh Ba, and the Chau Duc District Company which operated and lived in western Phuoc Tuy. The possibility of the appearance of the 274 Regiment could not be discounted, for it was located within ten miles to the north of Nui Nghe. Hence, each company would have to take precautions so that it was not ambushed or attacked in an area where it could be cut off from the support of the other companies.

This problem was similar in some ways to that posed by Operation Hardihood. However, the country around Nui Nghe was much less penetrable in the region where the forward companies would be operating. This factor ruled out the possibility of reinforcing by lateral movement of the forward companies and forced us to keep a central reserve which could be sent forward quickly, mounted on the troop of armoured personnel carriers (APCs) which was supporting the operation. Thus the number of searching companies had to be reduced to three in order to provide one company as a reserve to be located at Battalion Headquarters.

Provision of artillery support for the forward companies was another problem. While the possibility of a company encountering one or more battalions of 274 Regiment existed, it was essential that each company's movements were within range of the field artillery. Many of the areas to be searched were at the extreme range of the guns at Nui Dat. Should a company have wished to pursue any Viet Cong to the north or the west of the search areas it would have been forced to move without artillery cover and thus would have been very vulnerable to any Viet Cong ruse designed to lure it out from its protective umbrella of fire. Even if the companies did not move outside the limits of extreme range from the Nui Dat batteries there were many disadvantages in operating at ranges close to the extreme,

4. AN EXPERIMENT IN NIGHT MOVEMENT

such as the greatly increased susceptibility of shells to varying air currents and temperature layers in the air. There was much to recommend that our supporting battery, 105 Field Battery, should accompany the battalion to a new gun position within a few thousand yards of Nui Nghe.

Weighing against this consideration was the need to provide protection for the guns. The Viet Cong have always paid great attention to exposed or vulnerable gun positions in order to prevent the guns from firing by sniping at their crews or to capture these priceless pieces of equipment which they so badly need. Protection of a battery of guns requires at least a company of infantry so the requirements of a central reserve and of protection for the guns were merged by siting Battalion Headquarters at a suitable gun position for supporting the forward companies. This arrangement also made the APCs available for bringing up additional ammunition for the guns.

Several areas were considered for the guns and these were examined by patrols and an artillery officer. It was essential that the area selected was within gun range of the whole of the area to be searched, that APCs could reach it without becoming bogged, that the guns could have hard ground and that water was available nearby. One area which had been selected was rejected forty-eight hours before the operation because heavy rain had made it risky for the APCs. The final choice was the crest of a low hill, one and a half miles to the north-west of Nui Dat, which was code named 'Tennis', a name which was to adhere to that piece of ground, often to be crossed by our patrols, for the following ten months.

Early on July 6th the battalion filed out of the base in company groups. A Company headed off to the west of Nui Nghe, C Company towards the eastern slopes, to wheel south a few days later and come back over the crest of the hill, D Company to the flatter country between Nui Nghe and the Binh Ba plantation and the remainder of the battalion, B Company, the Assault Pioneer Platoon and the Anti-Tank Platoon accompanied the headquarters to Tennis.

We did not wish to let the Viet Cong know that the gun area had been established, for their commanders would have been able to determine the area which we planned to search. Therefore, the guns were moved from Nui Dat to Tennis inside APCs. By exchanging the smaller tyred wheels of the guns of the New Zealand battery with those of 105 Battery it was just possible to fit the latter guns inside the APCs. For five days before the operation, joint patrols of APCs and infantry moved through the general area of Tennis in order to establish a pattern of movement which the Viet Cong might consider to be of minor importance.

During the following ten days the companies wound back and forth, discovering a great number of small camps and huts, some caches and some puzzlingly large diggings. One trench, four feet wide and four feet deep, ran for over four hundred yards. Each company had encounters with small groups of Viet Cong who were living in, or travelling through the area. Lieutenant Hartley's platoon of A Company met a group of several Viet Cong who were much superior in fighting ability to any who had been encountered up to that time. This group wore black uniforms and webbing, their packs were black, they had black turbans on their heads and they were armed with automatic weapons. A heavy fire fight broke out between one of Hartley's sections and this group. By skilful direction during which he exposed himself to danger several times and was wounded, Hartley drove off the Viet Cong, inflicting casualties on what were probably our first main force opponents. Lieutenant Hartley was mentioned in despatches for his leadership in this action.

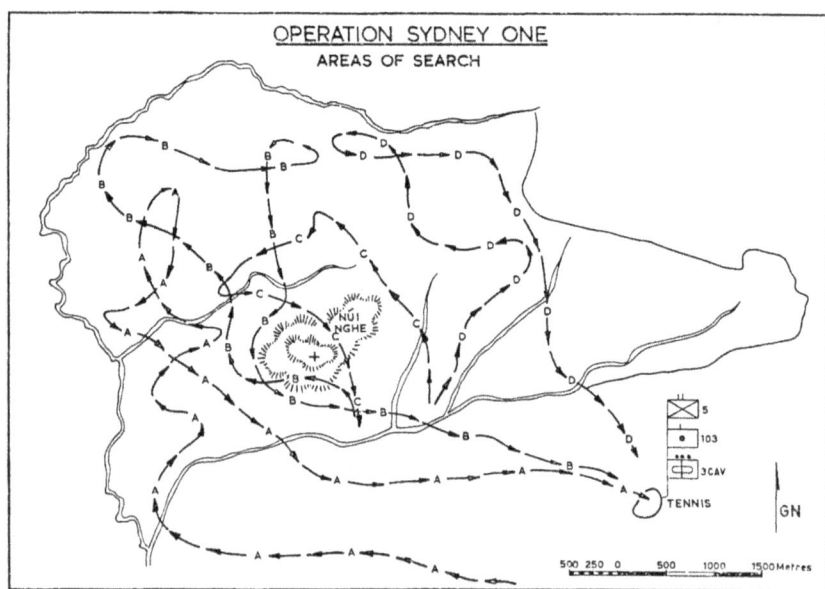

Fig. 9. The company movements during the search around Nui Nghe, Operation Sydney One, 6–17 July 1966.

4. AN EXPERIMENT IN NIGHT MOVEMENT

C Company returned to the headquarters area and their area of search was assumed by B Company. Late one afternoon a patrol from Four Platoon commanded by Sergeant Williams located a small Viet Cong camp on the edge of a clearing. Sergeant Williams had been advancing through thick jungle along the edge of this large clearing when suddenly the patrol heard voices a few yards in front of them. The men went to ground immediately, hoping that their presence had not been detected. The Viet Cong gave no sign of realising that they were being watched. Unfortunately the denseness of the jungle was such that it was impossible for the patrol to extricate itself to test the flanks of the enemy camp without risking noise which would have betrayed the patrol's presence, so the men lay still and watched, hardly daring to breathe, waiting for an opportunity to discover more of the occupants' nature before planning an attack. Sergeant Williams had hoped to lie up until dark and then to withdraw to the clearing where the patrol could noiselessly creep up on the camp and annihilate those inside.

Because of the closeness of the enemy, Williams had not dared to speak into the radio to give his location report so Major McQualter was anxiously broadcasting messages, trying to find out what had become of Williams' patrol. Even the sound of a voice in Sergeant Williams' earphone endangered his patrol, so he had turned the volume of his radio almost completely off. Bruce realised that Williams must have been in some sort of position where it was too dangerous to speak into the microphone, so he asked Williams to press his microphone switch twice if he could hear. The two presses came back to the Company Headquarters set. Bruce then set about finding out Williams' situation by asking questions which could be answered on a yes or no basis—three presses for no and two for yes. This system was sufficient for establishing facts like the number of enemy in the camp, but it was impossible for Williams to give his whereabouts, and so he could not be helped.

As darkness fell, one Viet Cong stepped out into the clearing and, following a hand line of wire, moved out to a small clump of bushes in the centre of the clearing. This was apparently their sentry position and a very good one it was. No one could approach the camp through the jungle without making too much noise to remain undetected, while to step out into the clearing in the amount of moonlight at that time would have attracted the sentry's attention at once. Williams lay and hoped that the moon would go down. Suddenly, after the sentry had been at his post for about forty-five minutes, there was a clashing of cans being struck together. The muscles of the patrol tightened—was this the signal for a Viet Cong attack on them? Another man walked out into the centre of the clearing and the first sentry came back. The signal was for the relief of sentries and the noise went on all night at regular intervals—a most curious procedure which must have attracted the attention of anyone within a few hundred yards of the camp.

Williams had to think of a new plan. He decided to wait until dawn when there would be enough light for aimed shots and then to launch a lightning assault. The patrol lay undiscovered through the night, the men not daring to stretch their cramped limbs, take off their equipment or sleep lest they snore. When dawn began to light the clearing one of the Viet Cong walked out of the sleeping hut to relieve himself. He almost fell over one of Williams' patrols and shouted an alarm. Surprised for an instant, the patrol took a few vital seconds to respond with volleys of fire into the sleeping hut. Although they may have wounded a few of the fleeing enemy, the patrol found no bodies and had to withdraw quickly in case it received a counter attack.

While the battalion had been sweeping around Nui Nghe, Colonel Warr had been thinking about the village of Duc My. Most of the inhabitants of this village were Montagnards who had been gathered together by the Government in 1961 from their isolated huts scattered throughout Phuoc Tuy. This resettlement had been carried out as part of a nationwide programme to complicate the supply system of the Viet Cong. The aim had been to separate the Viet Cong from the people on whose support they depended, applying the successful methods of the British in Malaya. However, the Vietnamese situation was a much more difficult one to control than the Malayan. There were many more people to be resettled, the Vietnamese administration was not as experienced as the Malayan and the forces at the disposal of the Vietnamese authorities for sealing off the villages from the guerillas were neither as efficient as those in Malaya nor as numerous in proportion to the population to be controlled.

In the case of the Montagnards of Duc My, these complications were of vital importance to their behaviour in the following years. They had been taken away from their homes and fields and established in a new area with minimal facilities for the agriculture to which they were accustomed. Consequently, many of the Montagnards were strongly prejudiced against the Government after their resettlement and were highly susceptible to the Viet Cong propaganda which was exerting a growing influence at that time. Gradually the status of the Viet Cong grew in the eyes of these Montagnards to the extent that several men were prepared to join the Viet Cong as guerillas and the majority of the village was ready to assist the Viet Cong with food and shelter.

These Montagnards looked incredibly wild alongside the men from Binh Ba. They were smaller and much darker in skin colour—quite often they were coffee coloured. Instead of smooth, neatly parted hair they had great tousled mops which looked as if they had not seen a comb for months. The Montagnard faces were more lined and craggy, more expressive than those of the other Vietnamese, and their features were more distorted, heightening their appearance of the primitive, their eyes showed wider, whiter and wilder because of the darkness of their skin. Straggly wispy beards sprouted from their chins and several wore a type of black turban. All of these characteristics reinforced the unreasonable prejudiced conception of savagery in my mind, which has its roots in my earliest schoolday reading of tales of imperial adventure set in Edwardian Asia. My first feelings were that these Montagnards were beings of a totally different nature to myself, quite beyond the communicational range of human personality.

They lived in a rambling village of huts built of grass or of teak with iron roofs. Duc My is divided by a swiftly running creek whose waters, some three feet deep and wide, pluck with considerable force at anyone wading across or along its course. Thick tropical undergrowth and trees abound on the luxuriously drenched banks. Behind this line of high vegetation and between the houses lie paddies whose thick black mud clogs and sucks as one walks across them, relinquishing with soft shuddering sighs their apparently desperate attempts to drag the boots off those who have intruded onto them. Dissecting the paddies are the boundary mounds or bunds, often several feet high. Any novice rash enough to persist in the crossing of these slippery sided bunds will probably find himself ejected headlong down the far side before he has gained his balance at the top of the mound and he will then have to extricate himself from a further expanse of ooze. Often the other side of the bund descends a further few feet into a drain which might be filled with stone, slush, or more fortunately, water. Around the paddies lie dense banana plantations, untended for the most part, and choked with grasses high enough to conceal a man standing and so intertwined as to make a pace of six inches fair progress through their tangled growth.

Duc My contained some fifteen Viet Cong guerillas and our presence in the area to the west of the village seemed to offer a good opportunity for capturing some of these men. Colonel Warr had been thinking about the possibilities of first placing a cordon around the village by night so that it would be undetected while it was being positioned and then of searching the village on the following morning with all means of escape to the Viet Cong cut off by the cordon. The major difficulty in such an operation from the tactical point of view was to move the whole battalion at night through strange country over a distance of some miles with precision sufficient for each company to occupy a final position within a few yards of where it was meant to be. The movement had to be executed in complete silence without loss of contact from one man to the next so that individuals and groups did not become separated from the main body and lost. Finally, security of the operation was vital, for the whole battalion was extremely vulnerable to ambush when it was strung out in a number of lines of men moving on fixed paths, close behind each other. Night movement was carried out by very few units on the Government side in Vietnam and consequently the Viet Cong enjoyed all the advantages which the cover of darkness confers. There were many risks to be run, but they did not appear to be insuperable in the light of our training and so Colonel Warr had decided to attempt the cordon and search of Duc My in late July.

The first requirement for his planning was detailed information of the approaches to the village and of its edges. The battalion had to know exactly what sort of terrain it would pass over, what landmarks there were and their location and the time it would take for movement between the assembly area and the final cordon position. In a cordon operation involving the simultaneous movement of several groups, timings must be known down to a few minutes so that the cordon appears in position without any open sides at the required time. In addition, each part of the cordon must know where to locate itself on the ground with respect to the local land marks so that nowhere is there a gap of more than ten yards between men. To achieve this in the case of the join between two companies who have approached the village from assembly areas a mile or more apart demands the most precise knowledge of the edges of the village. Different approaches might suggest themselves and the practical merits of these had to be tested. Enemy activity in the area had to be ascertained. In particular, enemy sentry positions or ambush locations had to be discovered. The amount of movement at night within the

4. AN EXPERIMENT IN NIGHT MOVEMENT

village had to be known. The presence of dogs which might bark, of pigs which might charge about in the darkness, and of buffalo and cattle which could cause casualties as well as betray the movement of our troops had to be determined before the planning of a cordon operation could be completed.

All of this information could be obtained only by a ground reconnaissance of Duc My at night. I was given charge of the patrol which was to provide this information. With the second-in-command of each of the other three companies I was to take two dozen men who were to be the platoon guides for the insertion of the cordon. The route which we had to check led upstream along the creek which flowed out of Duc My. It seemed to offer the advantage of a permanent guide line which could hardly be mistaken. The companies could all diverge from the creek at a dispersal point and move around the edges of the huts to their final positions. On paper it looked a good plan, but as is so often the case with infantry tactics, there were many small factors, all capable of wrecking the operation, which could be discovered only by walking over the proposed route.

I made a preliminary reconnaissance of our route by helicopter on the morning before we were to set out. We wound upwards in a spiral fashion out of the Tennis landing pad and set off to the west rather than flying directly to our objective and hovering over villagers who might swiftly put two and two together. We spent a few minutes over Nui Nghe, a few more over the beautiful and tempting villas of Binh Ba, inhabited by the French managers, then Binh Ba village itself with a good oblique angle view to the south over Duc My. We then took the liberty of a few minutes directly above Duc My, while I made corrections and additions to the map on my knee, peering at the little clusters of houses in bright sunlight 1,500 feet below us. The wind blew coldly in on us for the small Sioux helicopter had had both its doors removed. Maps flapped and threatened to tear out of my hand. I thought how ironical it would be if my new enlargement, complete with guide markings, were torn out of my hand to float down into the curious hands of those people below. Their interest in us suddenly grew beyond the stage of mere curiosity as a shot, harmless at our height, went close to our flight path.

One feature which the air reconnaissance revealed gave rise to some apprehension. This was the presence of a hut about five yards north of the creek on the extreme south-west corner of the village. The map had shown one about ten yards to the south of the creek at that point. This latter hut did exist, so we were faced with the problem of navigating between the two houses that night without alarming the occupants of either. Looking along the creek line I tried to count prominent trees so that we would be able to tell when we were in the vicinity of the houses. Unfortunately the number of trees and the vibrations of the helicopter defeated the resolving power of my eyes and we had to return to the Tennis pad with only an approximate idea of how we would find our way in the darkness.

We set off on the reconnaissance at 4 pm on July 14th, moving out to the north of Battalion Headquarters, across fairly open swampy country, strewn with impenetrable clumps of bamboo which upset navigation through the detours which they compelled. After some forty-five minutes of ploughing through this swamp we entered a plantation of rubber trees. It was cool and dark under their leaves; the long regular rows of tall trunks were like aisles through the white ribbed Gothic arches formed by the intersection of the branches high above us. We could see for long sweeps down the rows of trees. Lanes of uninterrupted vision radiated out all about us, in front, behind, to left and right, and on several diagonals between each of the four cardinals. We could see any small figures in black which moved within several hundred yards of us, but this was cold comfort, for we were equally visible to them. We spread out and kept moving fairly rapidly, reaching the northern edge of the rubber at 5.15 pm—much faster progress than we were to make for the remainder of that day.

We formed a small harbour, all facing outwards around a hollow square, and sent out groups to report on the country to our front and flanks so that we could calculate our exact location. Our navigation for the night march depended greatly on starting from a known point which appeared with precision on the map. I had selected a corner of the rubber plantation from the map and had made the navigation calculations of pacings and compass bearings from it. We were not far away from this corner and so we could settle down and wait for the approach of darkness. An hour of torrential monsoon rain was too much for us to bear with complete stoicism and we roared with laughter at our ridiculous situation for supposedly civilised beings. At 7 pm we moved out through a thickly overgrown banana plantation to its northern edge, arriving just at last light. We sat down in a small square, so that every man was touching his two neighbours for communication, pulled sandbags on over our boots to prevent leaving tracks and let our eyes become accustomed to the

4. AN EXPERIMENT IN NIGHT MOVEMENT

gathering gloom. I reckoned that we should not strike any Vietnamese movement along the creek line after dark, so we waited until 8.15 pm before crossing an open patch of high grass and entering the thick line of bush which bordered the creek. The rain had stopped, but in the inactivity of our two halts our sodden clothes had made us shiver violently with the cold. We grew warmer once we were moving again, shuffling forward with only three feet between men so that we would not lose contact and cause the rear end of the patrol to become lost.

Despite my intention of following along the south bank of the creek, we were forced to cross and recross it several times. As we moved along one bank we would suddenly find a thick patch of bamboo rearing up out of the darkness and we would thus be forced either to skirt it or, if the edge of the bamboo could not be located, to drop into the creek and clamber out up a vertical bank sometimes six feet high.

After two hours of this procedure, our forward scout, Corporal Mulby, noticed a tiny glimmer of light to his right front. About ten feet away from him was the first of the two houses at the south-west corner of Duc My. Hoping that we had not been heard, but rather fearing that we had, we retraced our steps for twenty yards, crossed the creek and formed a small base on the south bank. This point was marked by two tall trees which would enable us to find the area again when we came to meet up after each company group had investigated the ground which its company was to occupy in the cordon.

Captain Ron Boxall and his group from D Company held the base secure while the C, A and B Company groups went out to the western, southern and eastern sides of the village respectively. Each party floundered around in the darkness on the edge of the huts. Fortunately, most of the noise was drowned by another downpour of rain and its accompanying thunder, but the absence of light was so complete that we had to move holding on to each other, for we could not see six inches ahead. This method of movement meant that we fell into more than our fair share of wells and drains, for not only were we virtually blind, but one man falling tended to pull the others down also, all landing heavily on top of him.

We managed to probe the village perimeter without incident, narrowly missing the walls of several huts by feeling as we went. Captain Ron Bade once found himself within the open doorway of a house, but sounds of sleeping people immediately in front of him saved him from completely entering the dwelling. No dogs barked at us and there was evidently, to my relief, no village guerilla organisation waiting to ambush us. During the approach to the village we had been very vulnerable to ambush, for we were moving close together, slowly, and somewhat noisily as we pressed our way through thick bush and grass.

After reassembling at the two tall trees we set off around 3 am, moving some hundred yards away from the creek in case anyone was waiting for us to return by the route which we had taken to approach. I attempted to steer a course to the south-west initially and then due south, but my confidence in my navigation was rudely shattered by Ron Bade who assured me after we had gone a few hundred yards that we had swung around in a huge semicircle and we were heading north-east, back into enemy territory. I made a few checks and guessed that we were heading too far to the west. We then pressed due south, arriving at the northern edge of the rubber plantation by 5 am. After an hour's rest with half the group sleeping and the other half standing to, we moved back through the rubber and the swampy country to Battalion Headquarters.

One of the most significant results of the patrol was the discovery that the creek line was far too tangled with bush for the whole battalion to use for an approach, so Colonel Warr changed his plan. A, B and D Companies would approach along the eastern side of Route 2, through the rubber trees which stretched to the east of the road for over a mile. After crossing Route 2 when they were due east of Duc My, these three companies had from a few hundred yards to a thousand yards to move to occupy their cordon positions. C Company would swing around to the west of Duc My in a wide arc and approach from the southern edge of the Binh Ba plantation. Once the cordon was in position, D Company would sweep through the village from north to south, gathering all inhabitants for checking by the Vietnamese police and security officers.

A further reconnaissance confirmed that these lines of approach were feasible. The date set for the cordon was the night of the 19th–20th July. On July 15th, B and C Companies returned to Nui Dat to assist the Sixth Battalion who were operating around Long Tan. They returned to Tennis on July 19th and received the final orders before the battalion commenced the approach march to Duc My.

4. AN EXPERIMENT IN NIGHT MOVEMENT

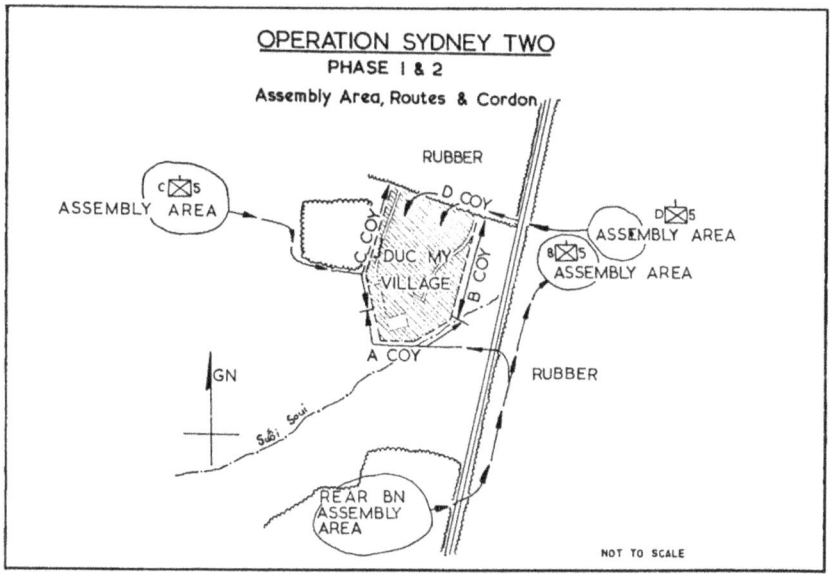

Fig. 10. Placing the cordon around Duc My on the night of 19–20 July 1966, Operation Sydney Two.

One of the main problems to be overcome was the maintenance of contact between each soldier when on the move at night in conditions which made talking intolerable for the security of the operation. Several different solutions were tried by the companies, such as use of each man's rope to fasten himself to the man in front of him, or the manufacture of one long communication cord for the whole company by tying all the ropes of the company together. Useful experiments were carried out with luminous moss worn on the shoulder or on the pack of each soldier. Luminous watches were also of assistance.

Using whatever means it favoured, each of the companies and the headquarters set off from Tennis on July 19th. A battalion harbour was formed in the rubber plantation to the south of Duc My, from which the companies moved to their cordon positions via the planned routes described above. The major incident which occurred during the positioning of the cordon was the disappearance of one man down a well. Private Clark of D Company found himself falling through space at an early hour of July 20th. He had walked into a well in which the water level was fifty feet below the ground. Running across a diameter of the well just beneath the surface of the water was an eight inch timber beam. Clark had the good fortune to avoid striking this beam when he hit the water and so he survived the fall. The problem was to rescue him from the depths of the well without causing too much noise. A long rope was made out of all the individual ropes of the men nearby and Clark was hauled out eighteen minutes after falling into the well, little the worse for his adventure.

The cordon moved forward over the last few yards to the outer houses in the grey light of the dawn. Colonel Warr had arranged for an aircraft equipped with loudspeakers to fly over Duc My at dawn to instruct the villagers to remain in their houses until our troops came through to guide them to a central assembly area. Quickly it became apparent that the cordon had succeeded in surprising several Viet Cong. Armed with rifles, some men dashed out of the houses and tried to break through the cordon by means of sheer speed. Some dived into trenches and attempted to shoot our men down. Some rapid actions overpowered them without loss to the battalion. Lieutenant Carruthers, commander of Four Platoon, B Company, personally captured two Viet Cong at the point of his Owen gun. His knowledge of Vietnamese convinced the two enemy that their best course of action would be to lay down their arms. Another member of Four Platoon, who was investigating a trench was startled by a Viet Cong who jumped into the other end of the trench. A quick draw contest then ensued in which the Australian was the victor. During the afternoon some Viet Cong tried to escape by hiding in the midst of a herd of cattle being driven out of the village. Others hid in the back of ox carts, which were then pursued by armoured personnel carriers in one of the strangest races imaginable. Eventually the situation calmed down and the search was completed. After the interrogation of the villagers it was clear that the night move had been a success. The Viet Cong had been taken by surprise, several of the members of the Binh Ba Guerilla Platoon had been captured and the Viet Cong in all the nearby villages were left to wonder whether it was safe for them to spend the night with their families and friends.

The cordon of Duc My was important also as it brought the soldiers of the Fifth Battalion close to the Vietnamese people for the first time and provided an opportunity to practise the many aspects of civil relations which had formed a large portion of the battalion's training. This opportunity had been looked forward to by most because of the general belief that this was a war for people, rather than for territory. Of particular interest was the attention paid to two Viet Cong who tried to break through C Company's cordon. Members of the company opened fire at the two charging figures, killing one and wounding the other.

The wounded man jumped into a nearby bunker. Colonel Warr ordered that he was to be taken alive if it were possible without endangering our men and Lieutenant Rainer's platoon was given the task. It would have been simple to kill the Viet Cong by lobbing a high explosive grenade into the bunker, but instead a tear gas grenade was thrown through the narrow entrance. A sapper, wearing a gas mask, then took the risk of going into the bunker after the fugitive. All was well, for the gas had overcome the Viet Cong and he was carried out into the open air and resuscitated by Tony White. The episode was swiftly circulated among the villagers and by the end of the day our soldiers were getting along very amicably with many of the inhabitants of this former Viet Cong village.

5

The Reclamation of Binh Ba

Binh Ba was a village which held a strange fascination. Probably this was due to its well cultivated and highly developed appearance which contrasted so sharply with our tents and holes in the ground carpeted by mud at Nui Dat. We had flown over Binh Ba on several occasions and had been tantalised by the acres of smooth green lawn surrounding the French villas, by their gardens laden with exotic flowers, by the cream plastered elegance of the large houses with their flood-lit lawn tennis courts and by the almost suburban character of the village as a whole. The plantation workers' houses had been built by the French in a style far better than any native built village house. Each was constructed of brick with cream plastered walls and roof of red tile. Great brown wooden shutters were hinged back from the windows by day to let the cool air of the rubber plantation blow gently through the rooms. The houses were built in pairs, each dwelling the size of a small Australian suburban house, set in an enclosure of garden which was used both for vegetable growing and for ornamental shrubbery. The whole village was laid out on a strict rectangular pattern of intersecting streets, all of which were lined with green hedges of thick-leaved shrubs which produced red, pink, gold or white flowers at different times of the year.

The village itself was like a delicate piece of impressionist design set within the broad frame of rubber trees, whose regular pattern and even colour served to focus one's attention on the rich reds, browns and yellows of the village. In our early days in Phuoc Tuy as we flew over the village, watching the pits creep slowly across the Binh Ba airstrip, our sense of apprehension that this conglomeration of buildings and people beneath us was controlled by the Viet Cong was heightened by the state of the village's development. The factories, the plantation and the houses were symbols of power—power which had passed in recent years from the Vietnamese Government to the Viet Cong.

The importance of Binh Ba to either side in this struggle was its contribution to the local economy. Not only was the plantation a direct source of wealth, which could be tapped by taxation, but it was a source of good employment for several hundred Vietnamese, and so it was the main source of maintenance for some three thousand persons. Whoever controlled the plantation had the first claim on the services and support of these people. Binh Ba had known many masters over the previous twenty-five years. The French had been displaced by the Japanese in 1941 and had lost the output of the plantation until they were able to resume control in 1946. During the Indo-China war, the French had built a triangular fort, surrounded by a high mound at the western edge of the village. Occupied by a company of Vietnamese troops who were commanded by a French officer, the fortification had maintained French authority until the pressure of the Viet Minh in the north and in the Central Highlands grew too great for the French to be able to afford the men who manned the Binh Ba post. The strongest local influence then became the Viet Minh, who introduced Communism and dissent against the Saigon Government and its local representatives. The ending of the war in 1954 did not bring the influence of Communism in Binh Ba to a finish, for villages like Binh Ba were too far away down the chain of command for the Diem Government to do more than provide exhortation and occasional visits. When the war against the Viet Cong began to build up in the early nineteen-sixties, the old French triangular mound was taken over by Government troops. The people of Binh Ba were compelled to convert their village into a strategic hamlet. They dug a ditch several feet deep around the village and raised a corresponding mound on the inward side of the ditch. Barbed wire obstacles were placed around the perimeter and watch towers were placed in the important corners and at the village gateways. Huge steel gates with spikes were hung from brick pillars to close off Route 2 at the northern and southern ends of the village. But all these works went for nought because the Viet Cong came by night and compelled the people to dismantle the fortifications, and most of the materials which had gone into their construction went to the Viet Cong.

Viet Cong cadres came into Binh Ba in 1961 and began accumulating popular support, both by conducting political meetings and by assisting the villagers with education and agricultural advice. By 1964 the Viet Cong had taken control of the village and they set about intimidating any opposition. They tortured the former head man of the village to death and terrorised the local police and school teachers so that they departed to safer areas. Strangely, the Viet Cong did not take much deliberate action against either the Catholic priest or the French plantation managers. They were well aware that they could not allow the plantation to fall into disuse, for then the village would disintegrate and they would be to blame. Initially, they attempted to humiliate the Frenchmen by making them work as rubber tappers and by subjecting them to some public brutality. The management of the Société Indochinoise de Plantation d'Heveas (SIPH), the group who owned the Gallia Plantation at Binh Ba, decided to attempt to weather the storm, reasoning that whoever was to control Vietnam in the long run would need to keep the rubber industry working. Hence the losses entailed by the interruptions of the war might be offset at a later date. At least there was the possibility of compensation to be paid by a nationalising government if the French owners held on, while to quit their holdings without receiving a cent for their vast investments seemed foolish.

Hence the local plantation managers had to coexist with the Viet Cong as best they could. The French were allowed freedom of access to their plantations through Viet Cong controlled areas, but it was expected of them that they would reveal nothing of intelligence value to the Government. When called upon to provide medical assistance for the Viet Cong sick and wounded they were expected to open their hospital which they maintained for the plantation workers. If, as in February 1966, an Allied force visited the village, the French were expected to give the Americans no co-operation in matters such as permission to use the plantation water supply. While the Viet Cong were the local masters, these conditions had to be upheld by the French, both for their own personal safety and for the health of the rubber trees, which could be quickly ruined by indiscriminate slashing of their bark, should the Viet Cong have desired to put the plantation out of business.

Whether the Viet Cong taxed the SIPH directly through Paris as they did with other firms who were lucrative sources of income for the Communists, I do not know. However, the Viet Cong did not hesitate to take a local tax from the plantation workers, consisting of one day's pay and two litres of rice per month in normal circumstances. At special times, 'acts of patriotic and heroic solidarity' were called for, when the contributions expected were far greater than these amounts. Of course the village had to fill its quota of young men for military service with the Viet Cong. Those who declined such service were required to take a special course to eliminate 'reactionary tendencies'. If they failed to show the desired amount of reformation they were taken off and never heard of again.

Father Joseph, the village priest, was from North Vietnam. He had been able to leave the north in 1956 and he had come to Binh Ba. Although nearly three-quarters of the people of Binh Ba were nominally Buddhist, there were still some hundreds of Catholics to be cared for. The Catholics were not in a strong enough position to prevent the growth of Viet Cong power, but they were sufficiently numerous to represent a special problem to the new controllers of the village in 1964. The Viet Cong knew that Catholic teaching was against them, but they did not attempt to close the church or to get rid of Father Joseph. Probably confident that they could deprive the Church of the support of the youth of the village, they reckoned that they would save themselves a great amount of trouble by tolerating the Catholics, provided that the Catholics did not become too militant towards them. The Catholic Church was placed in a similar position to SIPH—it had to coexist in the hope of better things to come, or lose all that it had built up. Occasionally the Viet Cong carried out measures against the Catholics, such as forbidding services, or preventing Father Joseph from travelling to his bishop at Xuan Loc.

It was fairly obvious that Binh Ba would have to be one of our first goals in Phuoc Tuy. Not only was it the most important village in Viet Cong hands in the province, but it was blocking road access for the Government to the Duc Thanh outpost, and preventing the 5,000 people of Binh Gia, the nearby Catholic village, from getting into the Ba Ria markets. Furthermore, Binh Ba was well sited for Viet Cong aggressive action against the Nui Dat base. Not only could the Viet Cong collect intelligence through the people of Binh Ba, but the village was a useful staging point for any big attack which might be made against the base. The attack of which we had been warned for the night of June 12th had been dubbed by Captain Bob Milligan, second-in-command of C Company, 'the Binh Ba Ten Thousand', and whenever intelligence suggested that an attack on the base was likely, it was sufficient merely to pass the word, 'the Binh Ba Ten Thousand is on tonight', and the appropriate precautions would be taken.

Because it was obvious to the Viet Cong that after our cordon of Duc My, we must have been considering a similar operation against Binh Ba, special precautions had to be taken. They knew that we operated against villages using the cordon technique at night. If the Viet Cong were to lay an ambush on our approach route we could have been in difficulties, so it was vital that the preliminary reconnaissances were undetected. Colonel Warr's plan called for a wide sweeping approach march which went out from Nui Dat towards Nui Nghe, swinging in to the east of the latter hill to enter the Gallia Plantation from the south-west corner, then passing through the plantation on an axis parallel to the airstrip. It was important that no one saw us during the approach or we would find either an ambush or a village empty of Viet Cong when we arrived. Therefore we had to skirt some two miles to the west of Duc My and we could not enter the plantation until after the tappers had stopped work and gone back into Binh Ba. This was likely to be just on dusk so we were faced with a final night move of nearly two miles through the plantation.

An assembly area for the battalion to re-form after the day approach march was selected in the jungle on the south-western edge of the plantation. The battalion would concentrate in this area by dusk and then move out into a forming-up area inside the plantation where the companies could shake out into their final order of march, rope up so that they would stay together, and then get some rest for a few hours before beginning the final movement around 11.30 pm. B Company were given a special approach route which was to bring them into Binh Ba from the east. The other companies of the battalion, together with two companies from the Sixth Battalion (necessary because of the length of the cordon) were to place the cordon in position and remain in their positions on the day of the search, while B Company swept through the village, working towards the west.

The operation, called Operation Holsworthy, required much co-ordination with the Vietnamese authorities, for they had to interrogate the population and supply police to assist in moving people from their homes to the collection point. But because of the danger and consequences of a security leak within any large headquarters, information was kept on a need-to-know basis until the morning of the interrogations. The police and interrogation teams supplied by Colonel Dat reported to the battalion base on the day preceding the cordon. Only then were they briefed on the operation and they came forward in APCs on the following morning. The provincial staff preferred to set up a central interrogation point on the Ba Ria soccer field where they were close to their base, rather than set up a great amount of tentage in the insecure area of Binh Ba for the few days which the interrogation of all males of military age would demand. Consequently, we had to arrange trucks from Vung Tau to come up Route 2 with an armoured escort on the day of the search, in order to take the men into Ba Ria and bring them back again.

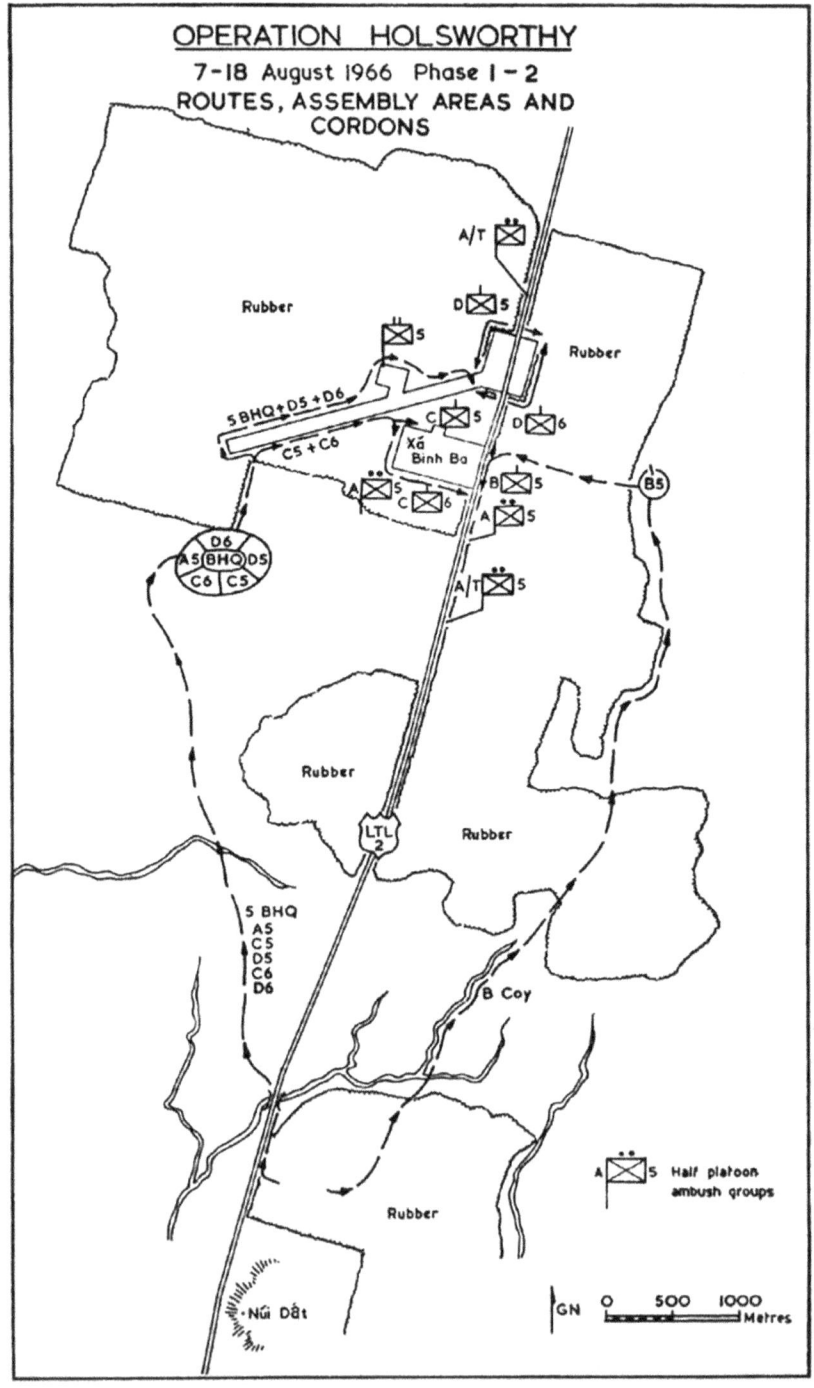

Fig. 11. The cordoning of Binh Ba, 7–8 August 1966, Operation Holsworthy.

5. THE RECLAMATION OF BINH BA

A loudspeaker aircraft was to fly over Binh Ba at dawn, broadcasting instructions to the villagers and reassuring them that they would not be harmed. They were also told to notify the police escorting our soldiers if any person were sick and required medical attention.

This arrangement completed the preparations. Just as we were about to begin the final briefings, Captain Don Willcox, the intelligence officer, was transferred to Task Force Headquarters to replace one of the Task Force intelligence staff who had been taken ill and had had to return to Australia. I was appointed to replace Don on Battalion Headquarters, and took over the running of the Intelligence Section on the morning before we departed for Binh Ba. My first act was to produce what I estimated might have been the Viet Cong provincial leader's operational contingency plan for dealing with an Australian thrust into Binh Ba, so that each of the company commanders would know what forces could be employed against them in the worst instance, and how these forces might be used. Unfortunately the format which I used for this contingency plan was very close to that actually employed by the Viet Cong and one of the American Psywar officers who were working with us mistook it for a captured plan which was going to be put into effect, so he took a little reassuring that we were not deliberately walking straight into a trap.

We left Nui Dat on the morning of August 7th, winding out of the base camp in a long column of companies one behind the other, to lessen the risk of being discovered during the approach to the assembly area. The battalion was strung out over two miles, and would have taken four hours at patrol pace to pass any one point. The companies departed in accordance with an elaborately planned time schedule, which worked surprisingly smoothly, with only short delays as the later companies waited near the start point for the earlier ones to depart.

The column took shape on the first few hundred yards of Route 2 before heading off into the trees to the north-west. The road had become plated with red mud which blended in a harmony of rich colours with the dark green of the rubber trees on either side of the road. The route we took and its accompanying sights were becoming familiar. One felt that the environment was growing more friendly towards us. Certainly we no longer sensed the presence of immediate hostility moving about amongst the rubber and banana trees which we had felt so sharply in that last week in May.

At the bottom of the gentle hill which Route 2 descended from the rubber trees, we crossed the first of the several branches of the Song Cau, passing an enormous tree, which was a graceful study in the transfer of vertical forms to horizontal planes. The trunk rose straight up out of the earth, curving over until it flowed smoothly into one of the several parallel horizontal layers of foliage which made up the character of the tree.

We diverged to the west, moving through the rubber plantation which led up the hill to the wide clearing of Landing Zone Hudson. Every time I crossed Hudson I counted the days back to May 24th and felt a growing difference in my attitude between then and now—not the least of which was the feeling of slight amazement that we had been on operations for one month, for two months, and so on. The next mile of our progress would pass quickly as my mind speculated on the length of the battalion's time in Vietnam and what was yet to be experienced.

On over the undulations of open countryside we wound, around tall whip-like clumps of bamboo, or in between them when it was impossible to do otherwise, across swamps of black mud which the hundreds of marching boots churned to the consistency of sludgy porridge, until we reached the harbour area of thick jungle with small clearings dotted about in which platoons and companies were gathering, resting after the day of marching and eating from tins of cold meat, their first meal since breakfast and their last until the following morning.

The battalion had completed the assembly by 6 pm and in failing light we moved out of the jungle, across a broad strip of turf, and into the plantation. A narrow horizontal strip of light which ran completely across our front separated the convergence of the dark cloud of rubber leaves overhead from the carpet of dark earth beneath. This light filtered through in a pale green swathe from the opposite edge of the plantation. Thousands of thin vertical black lines, the trunks of the rubber trees, linked the horizontal strips of darkness and the dark silhouettes of the assembling soldiers flitted across this static pattern. We sat down, each man close to his neighbour, except for the sentries, who were some hundreds of yards out. Each man tied his rope between his own equipment and that of the man in front, because the first few hours of the night move had to be done in complete darkness as the moon did not rise until after midnight.

5. THE RECLAMATION OF BINH BA

At 11 pm we stood up to move off and the first minor drama of the night occurred. The men in front had not allowed enough time for the men at the rear to put their equipment on before the former began to move off. Max Carroll experienced the anguish of feeling all his belongings whisked from his hands and disappearing into the total darkness which enveloped all, while he had visions of all the secret battalion instructions which he carried for the co-ordination of the operation being scattered far and wide across Binh Ba. Fortunately, the front of the column was halted and most important items were recovered by the several people who had lost them. We abandoned the idea of roping together after that move and relied on hand to shoulder contact for future night moves in the absence of any moonlight.

After an hour of shuffling around rubber trees and over the small banks and bunds which ran through the plantation, light began gradually to filter across our path as the moon rose, and we approached the edge of the airstrip where visibility was much better than in the rubber trees. Moving in front of the line of trees at the edge of the airstrip was like walking beneath a chalk cliff—the whiteness of the trunks and branches in the cold moonlight made them almost scarplike above us.

The cordon went into position close to 4 am and B Company began their search shortly after dawn. Soon afterwards the first groups of Vietnamese began coming into the Battalion Headquarters area for checking, a quick interrogation by myself, and transport to Ba Ria. The first group of villagers was rather bewildered, but a few simple jokes by our jovial regimental police thawed them out a little and they gave us good co-operation. I was surprised at the willingness of the people to go where they were told, for not only had they been predominantly Viet Cong sympathisers, if not active guerillas, but it must have been very inconvenient for them to have to change whatever plans they had made for the day's activities. However, the combination of the Vietnamese police and our soldiers experienced no trouble in handling the villagers and after an hour the curiosity of the children and the generosity of soldiers with their rations had created a fairly warm atmosphere.

I sat in a small hessian screened enclosure to which the Vietnamese were brought one at a time. My two main aims were to find out where the Viet Cong were in the vicinity of Binh Ba and to examine the attitudes of the villagers towards the South Vietnamese Government, the Viet Cong and ourselves. I had never been involved with this sort of work before, and the only way which I knew to get information from people was to be pleasant to them, so I conducted each interrogation accordingly. I used one of our Vietnamese native interpreters when talking to the villagers, not only because I did not speak Vietnamese, but because the interpreter formed a social bridge between myself and the person with whom I was talking. It seemed very important to get each Vietnamese to relax as much as possible and a good Vietnamese interpreter was able to do this far better than any European. This consideration was important not only for interrogation, but for general contact with Vietnamese officials and civilians, for a good interpreter knew the social form, he knew the local area, he could effect the right sort of introduction at the commencement of a conversation, he knew what humour to use, he could warn me if I put a foot wrong and he could suggest something I might do or say to the person with whom we were speaking which would produce a favourable reaction. Vietnamese humour is subtle and it is used in conversation to a greater extent than in western society. The Vietnamese are very perceptive, and those who are educated can express themselves well, not only by speech but by facial expression and gesture. And while most of these Vietnamese were polite enough to make allowance for the more reserved mode of westerners, one obviously cannot generate much warmth if people are always having to make allowances. Thus a good interpreter was one of the most important factors in building and maintaining an intelligence system amongst the Vietnamese. I was fortunate in having several good interpreters who had been supplied by the South Vietnamese Army. Two of them, Sergeants Bic and Chinh, were very good at establishing effective and warm personal relations with people and they were quite indispensable to my work.

The villagers surprised me by the amount which they were prepared to tell concerning the Viet Cong. Quite probably several gave me deliberately false information, but most of what they told me was verified later. The Viet Cong had reduced their activities in Binh Ba shortly after the arrival of the Task Force at Nui Dat. The guerilla unit based on the village had gone into hiding in the jungle and the larger units, such as the main force battalions had not used the village for a few months. However, the Viet Cong had not given up their taxation of the people. The plantation workers were paid around the fifth day of each month and the tax collectors had usually appeared on the seventh. On the night before our cordon had been placed around the village, a team of six armed collectors had come into the village and had begun to collect the August revenue and rice. Some of this team were caught by the cordon and were apprehended by the provincial security police at their interrogation in Ba Ria. This coincidence of operations at Binh Ba deprived the Viet Cong of nearly three hundred dollars (Australian) and one thousand litres of rice.

During the morning we met the French plantation manager, M. Pernes, and his engineer, M. Moro. For their own protection, they were required to come to Battalion Headquarters for checking. We did not suspect them of any friendly inclinations towards the Viet Cong, but we felt that to have given them preferential treatment in front of the villagers would have labelled them too clearly as our assistants and this could have resulted in a swift Viet Cong reprisal against them before we were able to secure the village. They were an interesting pair. Pernes had been born in China and had spent most of his life in the Far East, particularly in North Vietnam before 1954. Moro had been a sergeant in the French Army and had decided to settle in Vietnam in the early nineteen-fifties. I wondered why they continued to accept the apparent risks which they ran in attempting to continue working in war-torn Vietnam without any protection. In fact the risks which they ran were considerable, for they were always at the mercy of some individual Viet Cong guerilla who might have killed them without orders from the Viet Cong headquarters whose policy was to allow the Frenchmen to go about their business. Over fifty French employees of SIPH had been killed by the Viet Cong. But they were both waiting for better times to come and were riding out what they hoped would be only a few more difficult years. Moro's chief joy was big game hunting, but the advent of the Viet Cong around Binh Ba had frightened away many of the animals, including the odd tiger and elephant, and the Viet Cong had forbidden movement into many of the best shooting areas. The difficulties of travelling around the province and the neighbouring rubber plantations, particularly those near Xuan Loc, meant that social life was almost non-existent, except for the odd weekend drive to Saigon. Consequently both men were glad to see us and we got along with them very well. For our part, the presence of some civilised people living a few miles up the road from our base camp was perhaps the chief redeeming feature of Nui Dat. We were careful not to put pressure on the Frenchmen for intelligence, lest they became associated any more than necessary in the minds of the Viet Cong with our activities. There was much to be said for keeping the French in a state of benevolent neutrality.

The presence of the Frenchmen was of paramount importance to the village and this was appreciated by both sides, so a policy of neutrality seemed feasible. However, as time passed, natural affinities began to assert themselves and visits were exchanged more frequently while the activities of the Viet Cong in Binh Ba went into a decline.

Another of those whom I interrogated during the morning was Father Joseph. He was a dignified and gentle man, aged in his mid-forties. He had been well educated in the north and spoke French beautifully without the usual harsh accent of Vietnamese French. His black robes and beret, his fine smooth hands and his rimless glasses lent him an air of authority. His personality was definite, frank and open and he appeared to be well aware of his authority even when cycling, for if dignity is inversely related to speed, *mon Père* was the most dignified figure ever to mount a bicycle. Father Joseph welcomed us to Binh Ba on behalf of the Catholic population and asked that we stay in the village permanently. He said that we would receive little co-operation from the villagers if they felt that we were going to withdraw in a few days' time and leave Binh Ba open to the Viet Cong to return to control of affairs. There had been considerable discontent amongst the people under Viet Cong rule, because of the constant imposition of taxes, conscription and other 'voluntary' labours and the people would welcome the return of the South Vietnamese Government authority, provided that it was on a permanent basis and that the Government could protect them from Viet Cong terrorism.

We made a special effort to ensure that the people knew that they would not be left alone to face the Viet Cong again. The long-term plan for the village was to station a company of Vietnamese Regional Forces troops in the village. However, at that time, no Regional Forces company was available, so one company of the Fifth Battalion was stationed at Binh Ba together with a Vietnamese commando company until the regional troops were available. Captains Boxall and Bade served in turn as advisers to the Vietnamese troops. The company defending Binh Ba faced a particularly anxious time, for there was a definite possibility that the Viet Cong would seek to recover their loss of face by smashing the Binh Ba company with a regimental attack. Of course, support was available from Nui Dat in the event of a major attack, because the Binh Ba post was just within 105 mm. artillery range and the squadron of APCs at Nui Dat could have driven reinforcements to Binh Ba in less than two hours. Nonetheless,

5. THE RECLAMATION OF BINH BA

the garrison of Binh Ba would have had to hold off an attack against ten to one superiority in numbers until a counter attack was launched, so the company could never afford to relax its vigilance.

The provision of this company out of our own resources placed a heavy strain on the battalion, stretching our commitment by almost another third, for there was still the same need to patrol and defend the Nui Dat base and to constantly improve the living conditions in order to weather the monsoon which was due to continue until November. However, the importance of Binh Ba was such that it could not be allowed to slip back into Viet Cong hands and the additional load had to be accepted.

After I had spoken with Father Joseph, I met several of the plantation secretaries. These men were local Vietnamese, who had worked their way up the promotion ladder and occupied the highest positions open to Vietnamese in the SIPH structure. These men had received a secondary education in the plantation school and spoke French fluently. They were in a position of considerable authority over the other plantation workers, their wages were much greater and they lived in larger houses at the northern edge of the village. These men were an interesting group. Their high positions within a capitalist organisation made them obvious targets for Viet Cong propaganda, abuse and victimisation, yet their natural ability and successful careers gave them a position of leadership in a nationalist sense. They were keenly aware of the two pressures acting on them and although they appeared to be very co-operative outwardly and would discuss Viet Cong activities which had occurred outside Binh Ba, they would give no information about the Viet Cong within the village.

This behaviour was also displayed by the third level of village society, the rubber tappers, factory workers, wood cutters and peasant farmers. Quite clearly they did not like the Viet Cong, for they were prepared to give information about affairs which did not have a direct bearing on individuals living in the village, but few gave specific information on happenings within the village. Some asked us to remain permanently in the village and it was apparent that whatever propaganda the Viet Cong had directed against us had not been very effective. I was surprised at these attitudes, because I had expected to encounter a marked degree of hostility and a general conviction that the Viet Cong were the right side to support, for the latter had enjoyed several years of local power when they were able to make the Government look impotent and indifferent to the fate of the villagers. The attitudes of the people of Binh Ba had a profound effect on my approach to the Viet Cong because they had shown me that the Viet Cong had not been any more successful when in authority than the Government and hence there were good grounds for hoping that a stronger Government in the material sense would be successful against the Viet Cong in the long term.

While the provincial authorities were conducting their interrogations in Ba Ria over a period of three days, the members of the battalion were concentrating on meeting people around the village to establish a good image. We, as an operational battalion, could do little by ourselves by way of a civil aid programme except the provision of medical attention and the holding of discussions with several of the more prominent villagers to see what were the best avenues for the provision of more permanent aid under the control of the Task Force Civil Affairs team. In fact, Binh Ba was not badly off for the essentials of life because SIPH ran their plantations with a keen social welfare policy. They provided a school and paid for teachers when they could be obtained, an SIPH doctor flew into Binh Ba every Friday to supervise the village dispensary and to treat serious cases which the medical orderly had not been able to handle, and the plantation authorities saw that the standard of housing was kept fairly high.

However, there was one matter of relative urgency where we could take some action. Route 2 had been closed to all traffic between Binh Ba and Hoa Long since our arrival, because the road ran through the Task Force base for nearly two miles. Until we were properly established in a firm defensive position and could spare the troops to maintain rigid control over all Vietnamese who desired to use the road, it had had to remain closed. Because the people to the north of Nui Dat had been cut off from the Ba Ria market they had been dependent either on their own village markets for commerce or on trade with the more distant Xuan Loc to the north. This state of affairs had to be ended as soon as possible and the occasion of the restoration of Government control to Binh Ba was clearly a good opportunity, for we knew that with Binh Ba under the protection of one of our companies, there could be no large enemy force which could either come down the road from the north, or occupy part of the road in the vicinity of Nui Dat. So a special road clearance operation was carried out to prepare the road for reopening to the people on Saturday, August 13th, ensuring that the Viet Cong did not retaliate with booby traps, mines or ambushes.

5. THE RECLAMATION OF BINH BA

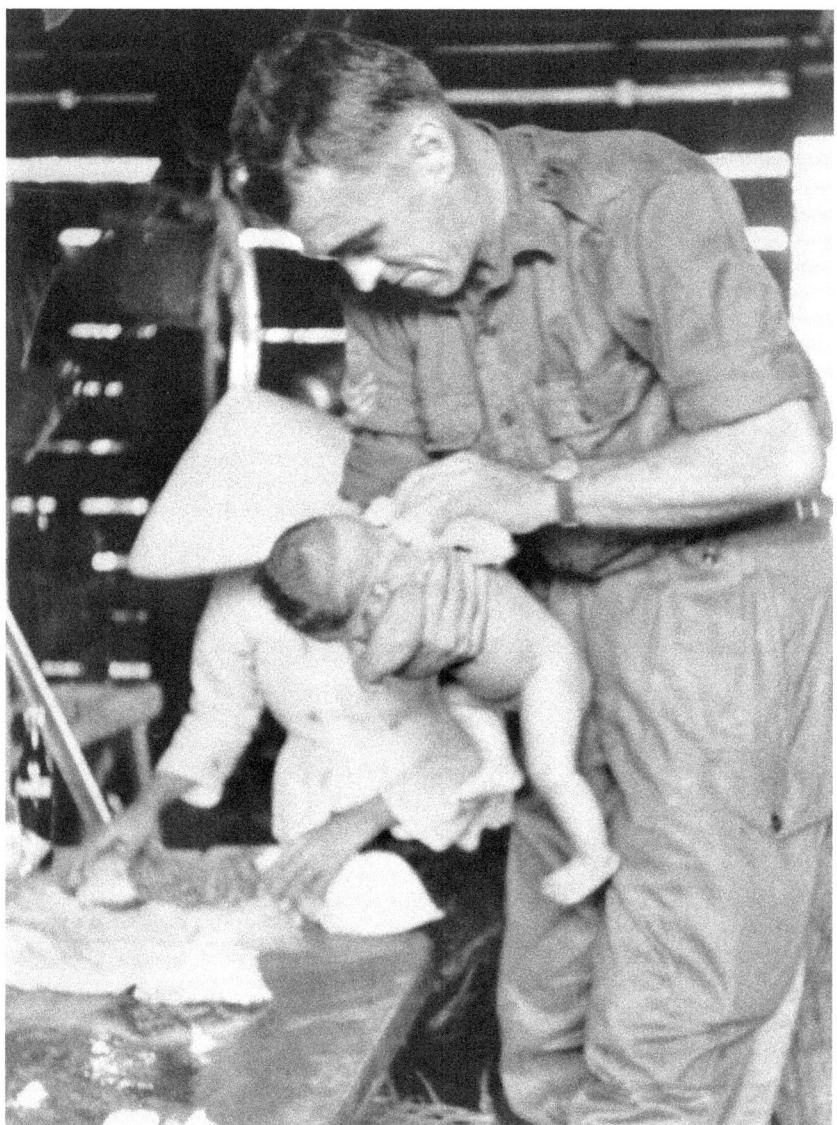

Staff Sergeant Mick Seats, assistant to Captain White, giving treatment to a sick baby. Medical aid was given to the villagers several times each week.

Unloading the guns of 105 Field Battery at Tennis on Operation Sydney, 6 July 1966. They were carried inside APCs (shown in the rear) so that the Viet Cong would not know our strength (see Chapter 4).

Pte. Jerry Bruin of B Company distributing captured Viet Cong rice to the villagers from whom the Viet Cong had taken it in the first place.

5. THE RECLAMATION OF BINH BA

We anticipated that a great number of people from all of the northern villages such as Binh Gia, Ngai Giao, and La Van would swell the numbers from Binh Ba and it seemed sensible to provide as much assistance to the people with our trucks as we could. When the time came for the Vietnamese to board the first truck for Ba Ria, one soldier had been detailed to climb onto the tail board first in order to help the small villagers up. The assistance was useless, for the man disappeared under a flood of seventy Vietnamese who poured onto the vehicle in a torrent, sweeping him to the rear and making his extrication a matter of extreme difficulty. During that first day the trucks moved some fifteen hundred people to Ba Ria.

The opening of the road was of particular importance to the people of Binh Gia for their access to Ba Ria had been severely restricted by the Viet Cong for some years. Denial of market facilities for wholesale transactions had forced up the cost of living in Binh Gia and had reduced the availability of goods, particularly foodstuffs, and so the reopening of the road was greeted with great jubilation. We paid liaison visits to Binh Gia from Binh Ba by helicopter to explain the control arrangements for the road and to make permanent contact with the village leaders. This link proved to be particularly valuable for intelligence of Viet Cong movement around Binh Gia, and so our range of surveillance was extended by many miles for the remainder of our time at Nui Dat. Two weeks after the opening of the road we were surprised to see two truck loads of Vietnamese in their best array drive up to Battalion Headquarters at Nui Dat. We were asked to receive a deputation of thanks from Binh Gia, presented by the entire village council. They presented the battalion with gifts of baskets of limes, bunches of bananas, and several live chickens which Colonel Warr had to hold by their trussed feet at the presentation ceremony. The councillors stopped and talked with us for an hour about the new possibilities in store for the people of Binh Gia now that their isolation had been broken and the danger of their falling under Viet Cong control had receded.

As a result of the eviction of the Viet Cong from Binh Ba, we were able to follow up the cordon of Duc My with some attempt at personal contact with and assistance for the people. The need for civil aid was much greater than in Binh Ba because the administration of SIPH did not extend to Duc My, although many of the Montagnards worked on the plantation. The acceptance of us by the people of Duc My was also surprising. As the battalion civil affairs officer I went down to Duc My with an interpreter shortly after we had arrived at Binh Ba in order to tell the villagers that we had come to stay and that we would help with any problems, such as urgent medical assistance for seriously ill people, transport to hospital in Ba Ria or anything else urgent they cared to request. When the interpreter announced our intentions of permanence in the area the Montagnards broke into a wild burst of clapping. After the talk I was invited into several of the houses to drink tea, eat bananas and have the children presented to me. It seemed incredible that a few weeks beforehand I had been creeping around these houses in the depths of night.

Before the battalion was due to return from Binh Ba, an intelligence report was received that an important local Viet Cong headquarters was located to the east of the Gallia Plantation. Because the battalion was close by, we were given the task of searching the area in which the headquarters was supposed to have been located. Although we spent several days on the search, no headquarters location nor any trace of Viet Cong occupation was discovered. While we were engaged on this search, the first Viet Cong attack on the Nui Dat base was made. In the early hours of the morning of August 17th a barrage of mortar bombs and 75 mm. artillery shells fell on the area around the Task Force Headquarters. Fortunately few casualties were suffered, but the attack had obviously been mounted by a considerable force, and it would have been unwise from the point of view of our future safety to have allowed the Viet Cong to have moved so close to the base without causing them some heavy loss. However, the Task Force Commander, Brigadier Jackson, was not in a position to respond with force for only one of the two battalions was in the base. Consequently, the Fifth Battalion was ordered to return to Nui Dat as speedily as possible with due respect to the completion of the search for the Viet Cong headquarters. The battalion returned to the base on the following day, just after the departure of D Company of the Sixth Battalion for a search of the area from which the mortars had fired onto the Task Force base. D Company of the Fifth Battalion was placed on standby should assistance have been required by the Sixth Battalion and the remainder of the battalion held itself in readiness for instant action to either repel a heavy attack or go in pursuit of the withdrawing enemy.

After we had arrived back at Nui Dat we received notification from Colonel Dat that the cordon of Binh Ba had netted a great number of the Viet Cong cadre and guerillas based in the village. Some of these Viet Cong had been caught while visiting their families for a short period. The cordon had taken them completely by surprise, so all the precautions taken had been effective. Also apprehended were Viet Cong sympathisers who had been giving material aid in unusually large amounts. In all, nearly seventy Viet Cong had been captured without the loss of a single man to the battalion. Two thousand people had been brought back under Government control and road access between the centre of the northern district of Phuoc Tuy, Duc Thanh, and Ba Ria had been re-established. This paved the way for the extension of Government control over another ten thousand people and extended our intelligence net by seven miles. We concluded that we would be unlikely to make such gains so easily again. Binh Ba had been the most significant of the local fruits to be gathered and we now had to ensure that we did not over extend ourselves and allow the Viet Cong to win their way back.

6
A Frustrated Effort

During the afternoon of August 18th D Company of the Sixth Battalion encountered a strong force of Viet Cong just inside the edge of a rubber plantation on the northern side of Long Tan village, a little over two miles from Nui Dat. The right flank platoon came under heavy fire which included mortars, and before the platoon was able to withdraw to concentrate with the central part of the company, Viet Cong infantry launched an attack which compelled the platoon to stand and fight. It soon became apparent that this was no guerilla unit, but main force regulars, as was shown by their high quality equipment, their tactical ability and their numbers. Attacking in waves, the Viet Cong swamped part of the platoon's defences, killing several Australians, including the platoon commander, Lieutenant Gordon Sharp, a national service officer.

The platoon sergeant managed to extricate the surviving part of the platoon and withdrew to where Major Smith, the company commander, had concentrated the remainder of the company. Two battalions of Viet Cong then assaulted ferociously and Major Smith had to hold off odds of ten to one until a relieving force could reach him. The battle began late in the afternoon and there was a possibility that the Viet Cong might be able to isolate the company for the night and whittle it away. Fortunately, the Viet Cong had made the cardinal error of launching the attack within range of the artillery at Nui Dat and they had to cope with the fire of three field batteries and one medium battery. The intensity and accuracy of the defensive fire which the gunners laid around the beleaguered company was of crucial importance to the outcome of the day. The defenders kept their heads and inflicted such losses on the attacking waves that they were able to hold their ground, but the intensity of fire required threatened to exhaust the company's ammunition too quickly. Major Smith radioed for a resupply, which was flown into him by the helicopters of the RAAF whose pilots had to fly low over the heads of hundreds of Viet Cong. The air force was lucky not to suffer any losses that day.

In the meantime, a relief force commanded by Colonel Townsend, commanding officer of the Sixth Battalion, was racing to the plantation in APCs. This force arrived just after darkness had fallen and the APCs began to sweep the battlefield with their headlights on. This was too much for the Viet Cong, who broke off the attack and fled to the east. On the following day the Sixth Battalion, with the assistance of D Company of the Fifth, cleared the battlefield and buried 245 dead Viet Cong. Considering the determination of the Viet Cong to cheat us of statistics by removing their dead under all possible circumstances, this number was extremely significant. Important also was the large number of weapons of all kinds, including mortars and machine guns, which the Viet Cong had abandoned as they fled—weapons which they needed urgently. If at least 245 Viet Cong had been killed it is probable that several hundred had been wounded, so the battle had cost the Viet Cong the operational strength of two battalions for the loss of 17 Australians killed and 19 wounded.

The next problem was to follow up this success as effectively as possible. On August 15th 274 Regiment had launched an attack on a Vietnamese convoy on Route 15 at a point where the road is flanked for some miles in either direction by the Dinh hills. We knew that they had returned to the central northern part of Phuoc Tuy after their attack and it was possible that the regiment was intending to attack our company at Binh Ba. Prisoners from the Long Tan battle revealed that both the D445 Battalion and 275 Regiment had made the attack. Both of these units were seriously weakened and there was much to be said for attempting to pursue them and to destroy their remnants. However, with 274 Regiment lurking in a position where it could attack either Binh Ba or Nui Dat while the Task Force was engaged in pursuit of 275 Regiment, or ambush our pursuing force, the Task Force did not have the strength to act alone and so a combined operation with the Americans was mounted.

Meanwhile the effects of the battle were beginning to be seen throughout Phuoc Tuy. Our stocks rose considerably after the people had learned that the Viet Cong had committed themselves to a pitched battle and had been heavily defeated. The Council of Ba Ria erected a huge banner

5. THE RECLAMATION OF BINH BA

some thirty feet in length across Route 2 where it entered the town. A message in English and Vietnamese, in red letters a foot high on the gold banner, read:

> 'The people of Phuoc Tuy applaud the victory of the Royal Australian Forces and the destruction of the Viet Cong Regiment on August 18th 1966.'

The Viet Cong countered by circulating handbills which claimed:

> '700 Australians killed, one battalion and two companies of infantry destroyed, two squadrons of APC's destroyed.'

This announcement must have stretched the belief of even the most faithful of the Party, for it left but two companies defending the entire Nui Dat base, which for some reason the Viet Cong had neglected to take. Furthermore, we had only one squadron of APCs and these continued to make their presence as obvious as ever on the roads of the province for all to see. We did not dig up the Viet Cong bodies for the sake of exhibition, but Colonel Dat held a display of the captured Viet Cong weapons in Ba Ria to close the debate.

It was interesting to discover that the official report of the outcome of the battle which was sent to Viet Cong headquarters by the Fifth Viet Cong Division which commanded 275 Regiment, was very close to the propaganda leaflet which the Viet Cong had handed out. A few days later we heard on Radio Hanoi and Radio Peking news bulletins which repeated the essence of the handbills. We then wondered whether Ho Chi Minh had any real idea of the true situation in South Vietnam. It is also interesting to note that during our twelve months in Vietnam we were wiped out on four occasions by Radio Hanoi.

The operation conducted by the Americans, in conjunction with the Task Force, was called Operation Toledo. It consisted of a system of sweeps across the likely parts of Phuoc Tuy, designed to force any Viet Cong who were encountered into the arms of several blocking forces positioned to cut off Viet Cong withdrawal. The main problem with this operation was time—would the stable door be closed only after the horse had bolted far into Xuyen Moc district or the May Tao mountains?

A marine battalion landing team went in on the south-eastern coast of Phuoc Tuy, advanced inland and set up a blocking position across the southern edge of the area to be swept. The 173rd Airborne Brigade and elements of the First US Infantry Division were flown in to our north-east with a mission to sweep southwards, flushing any Viet Cong who were still within several miles of us either into the marine position or into a similar block provided by the Task Force.

After two days of searching, small patrols of our Special Air Service Squadron saw some groups of Viet Cong five miles to our north-east. It was possible that these Viet Cong were part of the attacking force which was lying up close to Nui Dat in order to remain inside sweeps and pursuits directed at an enemy who was supposed to be fleeing swiftly. The position in which the Viet Cong were reported was to the south-west of the 173rd Airborne Brigade. All that was needed to surround the area was another force to advance from the south-west. This was obviously a job for the Task Force and the Fifth Battalion was assigned to the mission.

Orders for our part in the operation, which we named Operation Darlinghurst, came through from Task Force Headquarters in the early evening of August 25th. We then began the furious round of planning, preparations, orders and packing which had to precede any operation. We were informed that 274 Regiment had moved out of the area to the north of Binh Ba and had passed through the area to the north-east of Binh Gia, laden for a major operation and moving with urgency. A company of this force was encountered by the 173rd Airborne Brigade to the east of Binh Gia, but an ineffective air strike had allowed the enemy to escape.

We arose an hour before dawn on the 26th of August, so that we could be off at first light. We swung in single file down Canberra Avenue, the Task Force ring road which had been built by the sappers, to meet the APCs on Route 2. No muscles ached for it was much too early in the day for the resilience to be squashed out of our shoulders and backs by our webbing. It was all so easy with the weight of our equipment impelling our tread down the long gentle slope in the crisp early morning air. But underneath this superficial unconcern for things of the moment were deeper pricks of awareness that not all those who stepped off down Canberra Avenue might be coming back. Each operation so far had taken its one or two casualties and one never knew when one was going to strike a massive enemy force which could inflict serious losses.

We mounted the waiting carriers and were soon speeding, jolting and vibrating our way northwards, over the An Phu bridge and up Route 2 to the La Son sector of the Gallia Plantation on the eastern side of the road. We turned in and motored to the eastern edge of the plantation, dismounted, sorted out into our order of march and set off, filing down a track lying deep between two high banks, crested by trees over fifty feet tall. Some of these trees had grown out to the edge of the bank and had supported themselves by growing great buttresses which stretched down and out to the next solid surface some ten feet below. By this distance they often reached a width of three or four feet and several of the larger buttresses had merged together so that two or three trees appeared to be growing out of one flat vertical shaft of mottled wood.

Because of the scanty information available about the enemy to our front, it was not possible to develop a detailed plan for the operation. Our first task was to search the area and then to react flexibly once Viet Cong were found. Colonel Warr's aim was to keep the battalion as concentrated as possible, ready for rapid deployment. However, because speed was important, we were not able to afford the slowness entailed by moving the entire battalion over one route. Furthermore we had to arrive in the area to be searched in such a way that a blocking force could be stationed across one side, while a searching force swept through the area towards the block. The best way of combining these requirements seemed to be a two-pronged approach on parallel lines, one aiming at the northern sector of the search area and the other at the southern sector.

The first of the several hours of movement went by quite pleasantly. The greenness of the jungle was refreshing after the monotony of the rubber plantation. There were twisted trees and trees which wound around each other in weird knotted embraces; trees growing fifty feet or more in height which carried long festoons of vines, and trees growing horizontally across our path which spiralled so that they looked like the threads on giant bolts. Birds shrieked and cackled in peculiar patterns, providing ammunition for a few wits who named each bird in accord with its call after some well-known identity of the battalion. Monkeys whose curiosity had overcome their discretion were occasionally encountered. They ran along branches near tree top height, leaping from tree to tree, pausing to stop twenty yards or so from us and gape at the long column of strange intruders invading their domain.

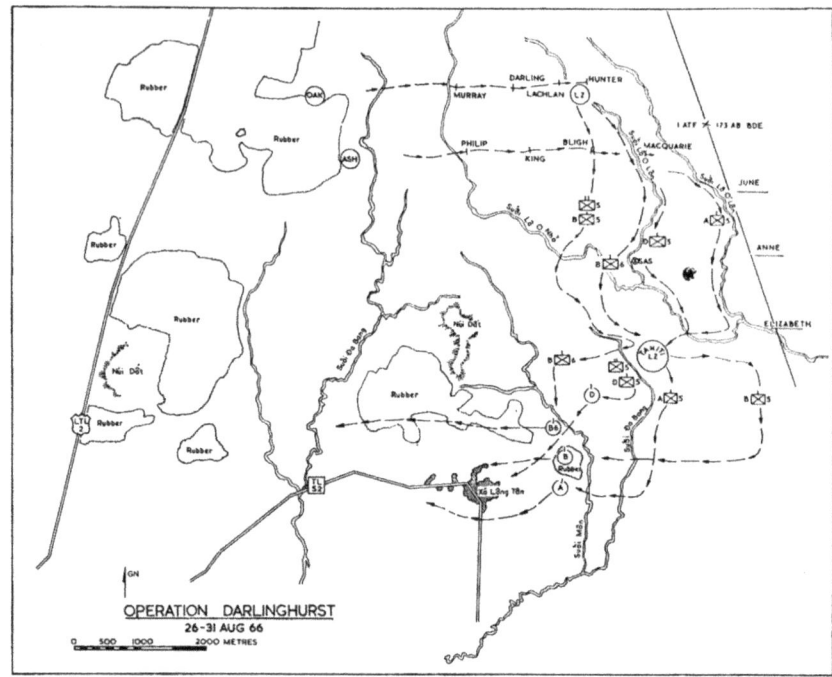

Fig. 12. The search for the Viet Cong who survived the battle of Long Tan on 18 August 1966, Operation Darlinghurst.

After a while our shirts darkened as the sweat from our bodies saturated our clothing. Then our boots became coated with grey mud as the going grew wetter, until we were slopping through ankle deep slush. Surface water began to lie in sheets across the mud, a barely perceptible current saving it from utter stagnancy but not preventing a strong sour stench from rising out of the mud as we stirred it with our passage. At frequent intervals the column would stop while some obstacle in front was carefully checked for the presence of the enemy. Sometimes these halts took thirty seconds, sometimes they lasted fifteen minutes. It took only one or two halts anchored in mud and water to the tops of one's boots to give one the skill to calculate the distance one should keep behind the next man so that when the column halted one would be standing on drier ground on one side or the other of the morass.

Also to be contended with were the creek crossings. Feet can stand up to a lot of punishment and fatigue if they can be kept dry, but when wet they are prey to tinea, blisters and skin complaints nourished by mud particles ground into them with the water. We went to much trouble to keep our feet dry, but were seldom successful. The country across which we were moving was intersected by many creeks and the monsoon was at its height. Every half mile or so we plunged into water. Sometimes it went over an unfortunate individual's head if he stepped into a hole in the river bed. Then there would be a great scramble to pull him out in case the weight of his equipment should keep him under the water. Particular attention had to be paid to seeing that his hat did not drift away on the stream to warn any Viet Cong who happened to be watching further down that the Australians were upstream.

Despite our desperate efforts to dance from rock to rock across rapids, wet feet had to be accepted. Sometimes a quick crossing of a small stream defeated the seeping moisture, but usually one was aware of a gradual feeling of cold across the top of the foot under the boot lacing. This feeling would spread and disappear as the water warmed swiftly to body temperature. Wet socks would grip the inside of boots and slip against the skin so that within an hour or two the tops of the socks which normally came calf high would be down under the insteps, with the greater part of the sock jammed into the toe of the boot, bunching one's toes rather uncomfortably and raising blisters at points where the toes were usually bent. One or two days of wetness merely caused the skin to wrinkle, but a fortnight produced bleached skin, soft yellow toenails and great callouses on the sole. On the earlier operations, when we had thought it unwise to take our boots off at night, it was quite a revelation to see our feet again after a week's captivity.

As we moved quietly on, thoughts became gradually distracted from the round of Viet Cong—home—feet, Viet Cong—home—feet, by a growing weariness in the shoulders and back. Feet would disappear from the cycle as sixty pounds of webbing took its toll of the two-inch wide strip across our shoulders. Sometimes the shoulder ache would dominate all thought patterns, then it would recede, displaced by a lovely long daydream about a home or a face not seen for a long time, or by concern provoked by some needling point in a letter already seven days old when received. It was depressing and frustrating to realise that it would be another ten days before one's attempted solution could be received at home and one wondered what sort of allowances would have to be made for this time lag. With this long period for the passage of thought and answer dared one be anything but mildly and ineffectively pleasant? At this point one remembered the possibility of the little man crouching behind a tree waiting to snipe at passers-by and one tried to concentrate on searching the thick growth to the puny distance of visual penetration. But after a few minutes complete concentration would be eroded by the renewed ache in the shoulders which came flooding through the mind again.

Then a halt would come. Should I sit down and take the weight off my feet, back and shoulders, and chance the effort of having to get to my feet quickly if the column moved on within seconds, or should I remain on my feet with shoulders intensifying their nagging? One of these halts would be followed by the hand signal for lunch. We would then come into a harbour position, capable of providing all-round defence against any midday assault, then we would eat a few ounces of food from a ration pack and gulp half a canteen of warm, heavily chlorinated water.

In the afternoons we forged on freshly for a while before feeling the gradual and sharper return of the pre-lunch aches and lapsing more rapidly back into the old cycle of mental events. However, the afternoon usually brought its own special form of entertainment. Around 2 pm masses of grey cloud would sweep across the sky. Sometimes they poised without action for an hour but never did they depart leaving us dry. A gust of strong wind heralded the first great heavy drops. The pace of the drops swiftly increased until we were walking along in a sheet of driving water. At least it was not cold, but its force impelled the water into the webbing of our packs, into trouser pockets, into wallets and watches, turning money and documents into papier mâché. The great inconvenience of afternoon rain was that the heat of the sun had gone by the time the rain had stopped so that we stayed wet right through the night and for half of the following morning, when we would dry out in time for the next deluge.

On the first afternoon of Operation Darlinghurst the monsoon gave us a respite until the early evening, when intermittent rain both hastened and disrupted our evening harbour making. The afternoon had been uneventful and the battalion was now ready to sweep the area where the enemy had been seen. This area was bounded to the east and west by two creeks. The evening position of the battalion was on the western creek, mostly on the west bank. B Company had crossed the creek and had sent out reconnaissance patrols to see if any enemy were in our immediate vicinity. The patrols trod the jungle gingerly with the prospect of encountering up to a thousand Viet Cong dug in, confronting them. However, nothing was seen and we hoped that our move in and harbouring had been done sufficiently noiselessly to prevent any Viet Cong within a few hundred yards from knowing that we were after them.

5. THE RECLAMATION OF BINH BA

There was a great deal of evidence however, that the Americans were to the north and south. Helicopters buzzed to and fro, light spotting aircraft cruised constantly overhead, and occasional larger aircraft such as Caribous and Mohawks, packed with radio locating, infra red, and photographic equipment moved in leisurely straight lines across the sky in their plotting runs. The size of the American operation necessitated these aircraft, but it must have been fairly obvious to the Viet Cong that they were being sought by a force of such size that they would have been wise to avoid us and withdraw to the east as quickly as possible.

Our sweep began early the following morning with two companies moving slowly up from the south, carefully searching every square yard of jungle. Spirits began to sag as nothing was discovered. For thirty-six hours the battalion had been keyed up to the possibility of a major encounter with the Viet Cong—a battle which could have had a decisive effect on the Viet Cong in Phuoc Tuy. Instead, all we found was dense jungle with no trace of any large Viet Cong force ever having been in the area.

We continued the search, sweeping around to the south to emerge from the jungle near Long Tan. This search took several days and produced nothing—not even a single shot was fired by any member of the battalion during the operation. At Long Tan several extensive Viet Cong tunnels were discovered. These tunnels ran fifteen feet under the surface and some were over one hundred yards long, connecting bunkers, strong points, underground storage chambers, offices and sleeping quarters. At least the battalion was able to ensure the destruction of these installations before returning to Nui Dat.

We had a pause of only two nights and a day at Nui Dat, for the Americans had decided to carry out a similar sweep through the north-western part of Phuoc Tuy and the Fifth Battalion was to act as a blocking force across the southern part of the search area. We termed this part of the search Operation Toledo, the name which the Americans had given to the entire operation. The terrain which we had to cover was familiar to the battalion because we had covered much of it on Operation Sydney in July. Because of this earlier operation we did not expect to find a great number of Viet Cong and it was always difficult to prevent them escaping through the net, but there were several important bases which the Americans could destroy if they found them.

The companies moved out from Binh Ba on September 3rd and occupied base positions from which they carried out intense patrol activity for the following five days until the American sweep had been concluded. Battalion Headquarters and the gun position for 103 Field Battery who were supporting us were located close to each other on the southern edge of the Binh Ba plantation, about five hundred yards west of the village. As events turned out, this was a slightly unfortunate choice of area.

On the morning of Sunday September 4th several villagers wearing black pyjamas appeared and began to dig a large hole in the middle of the gun position. The men said they were digging a grave for a funeral which was to take place that afternoon, but as there was a good chance that these men were Viet Cong intending to bury a box full of dynamite in the middle of our position we had to take a few precautions. Someone would have to make sure that the object being buried was a body and nothing but a body. This would undoubtedly cause distress to the bereaved if the funeral was genuine, but the safety of the hundred odd men in the gun position and headquarters area demanded that the coffin should be opened and inspected.

I suggested to Max Carroll that this was an operational matter and therefore he should inspect the coffin. He retorted that the case was clearly to do with enemy equipment and hence it was my task to inspect the coffin as intelligence officer. I then suggested Tony White as a medical man would be the best fitted to examine a corpse, but Peter Isaacs torpedoed my case by asking who was the civil affairs officer. I was caught and had to prepare myself for a rather ticklish half hour.

When the funeral procession appeared, I explained to the senior relative of the dead woman that we were anxious for the safety of our men and that I had to be sure that there was no bomb in the coffin. When I asked if the coffin might be opened a loud burst of wailing issued from all the women present, but the dead woman's daughter gave her assent with the comment that this was very unusual. The Vietnamese men, who had taken no part in proceedings to that point, sprang to with grinning faces and a few jests and set about prising the lid off the coffin. This took nearly half an hour. Almost one hundred of our soldiers had gathered in a circle fifty yards across to watch events. I stood in the middle, surrounded by a dozen women all shrieking and howling, while I tried to preserve my dignity, appear sincerely regretful and keep a close eye on the activities of the men lest something was slipped into or out of the coffin. The situation would have been funny had it not been so macabre.

5. THE RECLAMATION OF BINH BA

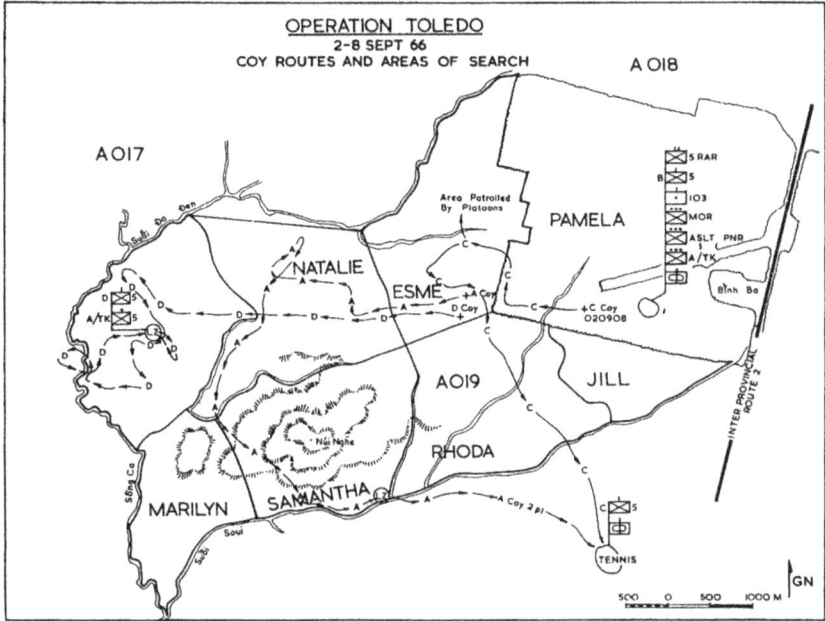

Fig. 13. The blocking operation west of Binh Ba, Operation Toledo, 2–8 September 1966.

The men thanked me for allowing the ceremony to take place and they assured me that they quite understood our problem. They said that the deceased had been ill for three years before her death and that the body was in rather poor condition. They positioned me upwind of the coffin for the climax as the lid was removed. Most of the women were paid wailers and local tradition demanded that they put forth a great noise whenever it was possible that the corpse might hear them. Thus as the lid rose, so did a crescendo of grief. The men then jovially undid the shroud and lifted up the head, the feet, and the middle. There was no bomb. The men were delighted, I was delighted and the women were wailing in excellent voice. The funeral proceeded and everyone relaxed.

We remained in the same dispositions for four days longer, during which we received a visit from the Chief of General Staff, Lieutenant General Daly, as part of his tour of Australian forces in Vietnam. Several Viet Cong attempted to infiltrate through our position and make their escape to the south. Two were intercepted and killed by D Company and the Anti-Tank Platoon and one was captured by C Company. Tony White gave medical attention to the people of Binh Ba and we participated in a combined church service with the Catholic villagers in Father Joseph's church. The Assault Pioneer Platoon spent a busy period building some foot bridges of logs over a river to our west. These bridges were to be used by the Sixth Battalion on their next operation which was to take them into the Dinh hills. Shortly after the bridges were completed we received the order to move back to Nui Dat for a very welcome period of cleaning ourselves up. The battalion had had a fortnight of constant movement, rain, and all the discomforts which go with forward jungle operations. Throughout this time nothing had happened to make the worth of the operation obvious to those participating, apart from some radio equipment found by the 173rd Airborne Brigade which belonged to 274 Regiment. So it was good to put a finish to Darlinghurst/Toledo and to prepare for more fruitful operations.

5. THE RECLAMATION OF BINH BA

Operation Sydney at Duc My, 20 July 1966. In the foreground is the Viet Cong prisoner whose capture is described in Chapter 4. He had just been resuscitated by Captain White (kneeling) and his capture had been controlled by Second Lieutenant Rainer MC, shown standing, centre.

A service in the village church at Binh Ba conducted by Father Joseph, village priest, and Father Williams, battalion padre; attended by members of C Company under Second Lieutenant Neesham (left).

The five Ngai Giao villagers of military age who had no identity cards being guarded by members of D Company under Sergeant Witheridge (standing right), Operation Crowsnest, 3 October 1966 (see Chapter 7).

7
Assistance for Duc Thanh

Attention in September was focused very sharply on the national elections which were held to elect a constituent assembly. This was to draft a democratic constitution preparing the way for the restoration of an elected government in Saigon. The election was regarded as a vital test of the attitudes of the people towards the Viet Cong because the Viet Cong had instructed the people to boycott the election. Government officials were worried that many Vietnamese might not vote, not because they supported the Viet Cong but because through ignorance they may not have understood the significance of a national election and they may not have desired to take the risk of exposing themselves to Viet Cong terrorism. These officials reckoned that a 60 per cent turn out of electors would be about as good as the Government could hope for in the circumstances. The Viet Cong began to exert themselves several weeks before the elections by spreading instructions that people were not to vote, that the candidates were capitalists who would exploit the workers and that Viet Cong displeasure with those who voted would be demonstrated by acts of violence against them. Reports began to come in of local Viet Cong committee meetings which had been planning the terrorism which was to take place on the day of the elections.

All members of the Allied forces were instructed to have nothing to do with the elections and to remain in their camps while the elections took place, so that there could be no hint of foreign interference in Vietnamese internal politics. We remained interested onlookers and awaited the results with eagerness for they would have a vital bearing on the whole conduct of the war, particularly on the confidence with which it was fought. When it was announced that 80 per cent of those eligible throughout South Vietnam had voted our spirits rose, for we had not expected that the Viet Cong counteraction would have been so ineffective. In Phuoc Tuy, 85 per cent of electors voted and no acts of terrorism took place due to the effectiveness of Government against the activities which were known to have been planned. The only act of the Viet Cong in Phuoc Tuy to mark the day was the erection of a barrier across Route 15 between Ba Ria and Vung Tau. Throughout South Vietnam 166 acts of terrorism occurred—only one act per 100,000 people—and approximately thirty persons were killed.

The reaction which these results produced in our thinking was reinforced during September by the local success of the Government Chieu Hoi (Open Arms) policy of amnesty and rehabilitation for any Viet Cong who surrendered himself voluntarily. Thirty-two Viet Cong gave themselves up during August and twenty-two came in during the first eight days of September. These men were sent immediately after their surrender to the provincial Chieu Hoi centre in Ba Ria where they were well cared for and received their first instruction on what the Government policy offered them. In brief, each returnee or Hoi Chanh was taught a trade or a manual skill, given a plot of land in a New Life Hamlet and building materials for a house, and received Government assistance payments until he had established himself.

Particular emphasis was given to the fact that a returnee was to be treated with courtesy and respect from the moment that he surrendered. If a man brought in a weapon or item of military equipment he was paid for it according to its worth. All these points were announced to the Viet Cong by leaflets and safe conduct passes dropped from the air and by loudspeaker aircraft which flew over Viet Cong bases. The Viet Cong reacted very sharply to this programme and decreed death as the punishment for any individual who attempted to become a returnee. Severe punishments were also given to anyone found with a safe conduct pass in their possession or to anyone discovered picking up an air-dropped leaflet. Special squads were stationed near approaches that returnees were likely to use in giving themselves up to a Government post in order to intercept them at the last minute. Several cases occurred in Phuoc Tuy in which these intercept squads then carried out a specially horrible type of deterrent killing in order to discourage other Viet Cong who were tiring of the hardships of the jungle.

Most of the returnees were local guerillas or men from the D445 Provincial Mobile Battalion. These men were persuaded to surrender mainly by their families and they knew that they would not have to face any domestic

7. ASSISTANCE FOR DUC THANH

disruption as a result of giving themselves up. The main force regulars were not subject to the same family influence and they seldom came near enough to a Government post to surrender, except during a battle when it was difficult to make a surrender appear the type which was normally expected of a returnee as distinct from a battlefield prisoner who gives himself up under coercion of arms. The main force soldiers were subject to daily indoctrination lectures and lived in groups of three in which each was responsible for the others' conduct and for reports on their attitudes and behaviour. In addition, if a main force soldier came from a Viet Cong controlled area, or if he was a North Vietnamese, he knew that reprisals would be taken against his family if he surrendered.

However, on September 28th we received a returnee from 274 Regiment. Colonel Warr and I had been visiting Binh Gia by helicopter in the morning to talk to local officials about Viet Cong activity around their village. We had then gone over to the Duc Thanh district compound which lay a mile to the west of Binh Gia, to talk to the newly arrived American adviser, Major Bill Prescott. He had been posted to Duc Thanh shortly after our operation at Binh Ba in order to advise the Duc Thanh District Chief, Captain Nguyen Van Be, and he was swiftly improving the efficiency of the troops who manned the compound. Major Prescott was another important link in our intelligence system for his compound was less than a mile to the south of Ngai Giao, a village which was under Viet Cong control and which lay on the main east-west route which the Viet Cong used in moving between their bases in the north-west of Phuoc Tuy and those in the north-east.

Shortly after our arrival we received a radio call from Warrant Officer King, the Task Force Civil Affairs Unit representative who lived in Binh Gia. A returnee had just come in from the jungle to the north of Binh Gia and had been taken to the house of Father Francis Dinh Quoc Tuy, the priest of the eastern hamlet of Binh Gia, who had sent him the following note:

> Dear Mr. King
>
> Being very happy to propose that we have a glad receiving a V.C. member into the national rank, who now is being in myself. By the reason, please to call to Major Prescott or your Australian Officers if who are now in the village. I gladly invite all to myself.
>
> Yours
> The Vinh-Trung Parisher
> Father Francis Dinh-quôc-Thuy

We immediately flew across to Binh Gia, landing on the broad lawn in front of Father Francis's church. A great crowd of villagers had collected on the broad veranda of his house. We were conducted through the excited throng and in through the wide open double doors of the reception room where a slim figure in a dark shirt and grey shorts was seated. Another throng of household retainers and their friends packed the two doorways which led out of the room at the back so that the whole proceedings had the flavour of a Breughel crowd scene. The young man in shorts who was holding a glass of orange juice in one hand and a new Russian AK 47 automatic rifle with a full magazine in the other was the object of fifty staring faces. Sitting proudly alongside him was a very old, gnarled little man who had been the one to conduct the returnee to Father Francis. The soft mud on both pairs of feet had not yet had a chance to dry and was dripping onto the red-tiled floor.

The young returnee was rather nervous at the centre of so much curiosity and sprang to his feet when we entered the room. We shook his hand and told him that he was very welcome. Father Francis had already seen that he had been given some food and a cigarette, so Colonel Warr then explained to him what would happen to him and asked for his story. He had been born in 1946 in a province from which many of the members of 274 Regiment had come. He had joined the Viet Cong at the age of sixteen because he had believed that the Viet Cong held the best answer to Vietnam's future and because he thought that the Viet Cong would overthrow the Government within a short time. His education had extended only to reading and writing and he had no religious beliefs. Since 1964 he had become disillusioned with Viet Cong methods and with their failure to keep their promises of victory. He disliked the way in which he had had to go about the countryside taking food and money from peasants who were as poor as his family and he had grown tired of the continual surveillance to which he was subjected in his life with 274 Regiment. He had made up his mind to surrender several months beforehand and it had taken him all this time to find the right opportunity for putting into practice what cannot be related at this time for the sakes of others who might be still trying to use the same method. He had been running since early that morning and had obviously been through a terrific strain until he had come out at the edge of the Binh Gia paddy fields, close to where the old man who had escorted him in had been working. The old man had received a fright when this wild looking young man had dashed out of the jungle at him with a rifle. The returnee must also have been

7. ASSISTANCE FOR DUC THANH

under great stress in wondering how he would be treated once he had given himself up. He had heard from others that the Chieu Hoi system was a genuine amnesty but he had no certain knowledge that this was the case. He need not have worried however, for he was paid 1,500 Piastre (AU$15) for his weapon and that evening he was seated in an armchair watching television in Ba Ria and reflecting on the events of the day.

One piece of information he had given us was that one of the battalions of 274 Regiment was moving westwards towards Route 2 around the northern side of Ngai Giao so we decided to keep a close eye on this part of the country. Colonel Warr visited Major Prescott at Duc Thanh on the following morning, Thursday, September 29th and learned that some of the Regional Forces company who lived in the compound had observed two companies of main force Viet Cong seated in open country on either side of Route 2 two miles north of Duc Thanh, eating a meal. This news was particularly interesting in the light of the information given to us by the returnee on the previous day. The area in which this force of Viet Cong were located was on the extreme northern edge of the Task Force's area of responsibility. It had not been searched before and the whole vicinity of Ngai Giao was known to support much Viet Cong activity. They had established several road blocks to the north of the Duc Thanh compound, had completely dug away the road in places for lengths of five yards and had sown the road with mines in several parts. Traffic between Ba Ria and Xuan Loc was taxed at Ngai Giao, and the village was used as a supply collection point by the main force Viet Cong.

Thus time was ripe for a thrust into this area and Colonel Warr obtained permission from Brigadier Jackson to follow up the report received through Major Prescott. Planning occupied Friday, September 30th and the operation, named Crowsnest, was timed to begin on October 1st.

The battalion had been given a troop of APCs in support for the operation by Brigadier Jackson. The area to be searched contained much open field, dotted with clusters of houses and small patches of timber. This fairly clear country extended back from Route 2 to a distance of nearly one mile on either side of the road, so there was much scope for a combined armour and infantry sweep which would cover large stretches of country in which there might have been tunnels or other installations. The clear land was bounded by dense jungle to the east and west and by a rubber plantation to the south. The main group of houses of Ngai Giao lay on the western side of the road at the northern edge of this rubber plantation.

Dotted about the area within a mile of Ngai Giao were the small hamlets of Mo Tin, Huong Sa, Hean and Nang Son. These, together with Ngai Giao, were the obvious points for detailed searches by infantry on foot to uncover any caches, tunnels or bunkers which the Viet Cong had dug. The several clumps of timber also called for infantry searches, but the remainder was suitable for the APCs, with infantry on board to handle any pockets of guerillas who could not be reached by the APCs.

The detailed search to be carried out required at least one company and because we were operating so far from Nui Dat, another company had to be provided to protect 103 Field Battery in a forward gun position at Duc Thanh. The other two rifle companies, A and B, were ordered to remain at thirty minutes' notice to move at Nui Dat. D Company, which had relieved C Company at Binh Ba, was to make the search while C Company was to guard the guns. A skeleton Battalion Headquarters team consisting of Colonel Warr, Max Carroll and myself, our radio operators and an administrative element commanded by Captain Ron Boxall was to move forward and control the operation from the Duc Thanh compound.

The need for haste dragged us out of our beds at 5 am on October 1st to breakfast early, climb aboard the APCs and be off up the road, clattering and clanking through Binh Ba while the early morning mist was still clinging to the tops of the rubber trees. The armoured command vehicle was carefully piloted through the narrow gates of the Duc Thanh compound, a feat which some had declared impossible, while the Vietnamese soldiers and their families who lived in the compound completed their morning washing and breakfasts.

The compound had been chosen as the headquarters site partly because of the invitation of Captain Be, the District Chief, and partly because the security offered by the compound solved the continually vexing question of how to protect the headquarters without taking a company or the support platoons away from forward operations. It certainly proved to be an entertaining choice. The compound was a square with sides of approximately two hundred yards. Hard up against an outer rampart of earth and timber which was crowned by barbed wire, were a continuous row of tin roofed shanties some five feet high, with front walls made from ammunition boxes and cylindrical shell containers. Inside the compound was an inner square of defences which was also ringed by low shanties on its outer side so that all the families of the soldiers, some five hundred persons in all, were grouped in medieval fashion in the outer bailey.

7. ASSISTANCE FOR DUC THANH

The keep was the district headquarters building with its associated bunkers built below ground level. The compound had once been a French fort and the old French style flag pole still stood on top of the low circular platform of the roof of a disused cylindrical concrete bunker in the centre of the inner bailey. A tall Teutonic looking tower stood nearby, some forty feet high, with widely splayed legs of wood. Its square top was capped by a roof which sloped out widely over each side so that there was only a narrow slit some few inches high for the observers in the tower to scan the surrounding area. The wide eaves of the roof protected the men in the tower from view by throwing them into deep shadow and shielded them from missiles like a visor in the age of chivalry—the age from which the tower had been transplanted.

The compound was well protected by belts of barbed wire and minefields. Beyond these obstacles was a broad, flat area of open ground over which any attackers would have to cross. This area was dotted with pre-arranged artillery target points. Route 2 ran close by the western edge of the compound. Two stone blockhouses guarded the adjacent stretch of road from either end of the western wall. A pill box covered with weeds stood by the entrance, half-way along the western wall. The high rectangular gateway could be closed by two large iron gates, and low watch towers stood at the four corners of both of the outer and inner squares.

The families of the soldiers had come from far and wide throughout Phuoc Tuy to follow their husbands and fathers. Small children ran naked or clad only in shirts about the compound, playing in the black dirt and crowding around any parade or other activity of the defenders to stare inquisitively and make their quick chattering comments to each other. The women sat in their doorways, washing pots or children, cooking, smoking, chewing betel nut, conversing, or just squatting on their haunches, staring impassively into space. Some of the men patrolled by day, others did training, while the rest sat about and looked over the fortifications or slept. From midday until 4 pm everyone slept, unless a small local operation was being mounted. When the cool of the evening came the men would play hectic, skilful games of basketball and volleyball before assembling for the evening muster parade, roll call and allocation of duties for the night, for the compound really came alive defensively only at night.

At dusk the outer gates were shut, locking the sentries in each of the block houses on the road out of the compound to face the fates of the night unaided and without means of escape. Men stood in each of the towers around the inner and outer walls. Three men climbed into the high tower to remain there until the dawn, while below ground the switchboard which connected the telephones from each sentry post was manned all night.

It is very easy to point out the faults of this ancient approach to modern mobile guerilla warfare. The company defending Duc Thanh was tied to a static role, its location always known to the Viet Cong, as was the direction from which to attack the compound. The soldiers were severely limited to the type of operations which they could mount on foot from the compound and their situation was beset by many problems caused by the boredom and dullness imposed on the soldiers by this mode of operation. Nonetheless, this post had survived two years of isolation ten miles deep into territory which had been controlled by an immensely stronger enemy. The Government troops had been contained within a tiny area, around which they patrolled to a distance of up to a mile away. They were kept away from all significant centres of population by the strength of the Viet Cong, yet the post had remained in Government hands awaiting the restoration of Government authority and ready to act as a spring board to enable that process to be commenced.

While we were erecting tents and radio aerials in the compound, D Company were moving forward up Route 2, mounted on the APCs to begin the sweep out to the north-east of the compound. Once the company had reached its starting point and was on the ground, a balanced manoeuvre was begun. The company on foot searched the thick areas of bush and wood while the APCs, moving with the Anti-Tank Platoon on board in a cavalry role, swept rapidly across wide open areas to the flank of D Company. The control problems posed by the simultaneous operation of these forces which moved at such different speeds were formidable, for they tended to separate and create areas to which Viet Cong could escape. This made the rapid progress of the combined force along its planned path very absorbing to follow in the battalion command post.

One of our methods of control was the helicopter. I was sent aloft for a few hours to observe our own movement and to look for any enemy attempting to move out of the area. Because D Company had moved into some thick country where I was of no assistance to them, we flew out to the east to see if any enemy could be seen in the country through which

7. ASSISTANCE FOR DUC THANH

they often passed. We climbed to nearly 3,000 feet from which height we could see the entire topography of Phuoc Tuy. Tiny clouds of mist were clinging to the rounded tops of the rubber trees, caught between the joins of the individual tree tops in parallel rows. The greens beneath us looked fresh and soft in the early morning light which was filtering through a layer of cloud in the eastern sky in long slanting rays. We could see far into the distance—much farther than I had ever been able to see before. The Central Highlands of Vietnam rose and fell in a succession of sharp peaks across the horizon. The lesser peaks which crowned the foothills tumbled down in an uneven cascade to the plains of Long Khanh, north of Phuoc Tuy. The conical bulk of the May Tao mountain was silhouetted in the east against white mist from the sea. The horizon to the north and west was broken by the high hills which cross Long Khanh from east to west, by the low hills of the Hat Dich area at the junction of Phuoc Tuy, Long Khanh and Bien Hoa provinces, and by the Dinh hills in western Phuoc Tuy. The broad, flat tongue of the Vung Tau peninsula, terminated by the isolated heights of the Ganh Rai mountains, seemed very truncated when viewed along its axis. Around the southern shore of Phuoc Tuy ran a broad yellow band of sand, edged with the white line of breaking waves.

Urgent reality interrupted my fascination with this scene as the radio earphones reminded me that a war was going on at ground level. Small patches of red earth, recently dug out, could be seen beneath the dark green tree tops. In some places the gaps in the foliage were wide enough to show the unmistakable marks of ox cart tracks. Excitement grew as we saw that these tracks had been used heavily and recently. The long shadows cast by the trees in the early morning hindered us a great deal until we saw a peculiarly regular square shadow cast on part of the track which ran east and west and which had no vegetation to obscure it from the air. A closer look showed that it was an ox cart halted on the track. Its top was camouflaged and the oxen had been hidden to prevent their movement from betraying the presence of the cart.

The pilot, Lieutenant Barron, discussed with me the possibility of directing artillery fire onto the cart. The guns at Duc Thanh were in range so we offered them the target. The white phosphorus smoke-generating shells which were used for ranging were quickly corrected to within thirty yards of the cart and high explosive fire for effect began. Five rounds from each gun in the battery came down in a close pattern of bursts around the cart, sufficient to cause considerable damage both to the cart and to its contents. We then followed the track on which the cart was towards the east, recording the signs of recent use for our own operations and for artillery harassing fire programmes.

Max Carroll was next to use the helicopter. He did several passes over the area to the north of Duc Thanh until he saw a man in black pyjamas running away from our troops at full pelt. He ran into a hut and then vanished. Max indicated the house to D Company over the radio and by hovering over it, almost touching its roof. Troops entered the house and searched it to find nothing. The fugitive must have had some extremely well concealed exit route which had not been visible from the air.

Shortly afterwards the APCs, who were sweeping around towards Route 2 from the east, reported that they were being spied upon by three Viet Cong, one of whom had binoculars. The Viet Cong were on a low ridge line, on the western side of the road. The APCs sped forward until they were halted by a swamp and could proceed no further. The Viet Cong were some few hundred yards away by this time and it was pointless for the Anti-Tank Platoon to dismount and flounder through the mud after them, particularly since the Viet Cong were out of sight on the far side of the ridge. However, two of our 81 mm. mortars were mounted in APCs and they brought down almost instantaneous fire over open sights on the likely Viet Cong line of escape.

D Company's sweep went on during the afternoon, covering some two miles, in which they questioned a number of peasants, examined identity cards and searched huts. All appeared to be very quiet until at five minutes to four a report of a contact with an enemy sniper galvanised all who were within earshot of the Battalion Headquarters command radio. Seconds later another message came through from Major Paul Greenhalgh to say that one of his men had been hit, just as Max Carroll was taking the usual precaution of ordering the Dust Off helicopter at Task Force Headquarters to stand by. The details which Paul gave were: one litter case, priority urgent, landing zone within two hundred yards. The soldier's name was passed in a simple code in order to deny both his rank and name to the Viet Cong who might have been listening to our transmissions. He was Private Warburton, a forward scout of Dennis Rainer's platoon. This news changed the atmosphere and conversation ceased as everyone waited anxiously for more details from D Company and for the familiar rapid thudding of the helicopter.

Private Warburton had been shot by a sniper as he stepped out of some thick bush and stood searching an open patch. The sniper had concealed himself on the other side of the clearing and was quite invisible to Warburton. He fired two shots, one hitting Warburton low in the chest, the other nicking his arm. Immediately the machine gun group of Warburton's section came forward and sprayed the area with rapid fire. They were probably just a few seconds too late. No traces of blood were found when the area was searched, so presumably the sniper had fled as soon as he had fired. This contact emphasised the fact that we were up against a skilled enemy, for that degree of marksmanship indicated a man with better training than a local guerilla.

As soon as news of Warburton's wounding had been passed to Battalion Headquarters, Colonel Warr sent Tony White off to D Company in the light reconnaissance helicopter which we had been using all day. Ten minutes later tension was relieved as the Dust Off helicopter whirred over us at ninety miles an hour and dropped into D Company's area. Warburton's wound was too bad for him to be flown back to hospital on the outside litter frame of the smaller helicopter, so Tony had decided to wait for the larger Iroquois. Tony boarded the Dust Off aircraft as soon as Warburton's stretcher had been placed aboard. Unfortunately the wound was extremely severe and Warburton died while in the air en route for 36 Evacuation Hospital at Vung Tau.

It was now late in the afternoon and D Company began to pull back to a better defensive position to harbour for the night. Inside the compound the hectic chatter of the soldiers' families subsided. The men mustered for their evening parade and those on duty went off to their posts while darkness descended swiftly. The moon was near full when it rose shortly afterwards, making the sky a light background which silhouetted the small sentry towers overlooking the community sleeping inside the security of the barbed wire, the ditch and the rampart. The coming of night and the subsidence of domestic activity concentrated the consciousness of all those remaining awake towards defence, as sentries peered into the gloom to detect any movement out of the trees into the open space which surrounded the compound. The seeming unreality of the evening and the contradictions of the entire war were epitomised by the tinkling oriental music which wafted through the air from a transistor radio belonging to one of the sentries.

On the following morning, October 2nd, C Company went forward to search the village of Ngai Giao which spread out along Route 2 in several clusters over a mile and a half of the road. This search was a difficult one to conduct for the straggling nature of Ngai Giao made it impossible for a single battalion to cordon the village. Fortunately the mobility of the APCs and the presence of a helicopter were some compensation with their speed for pursuing any fugitives observed making for the jungle. The search made good progress and uncovered ample evidence of Viet Cong activity. A large amount of meat was discovered in one house occupied by a woman who said her husband had been absent for a long time. The woman admitted that the meat was to have been collected at night by the Viet Cong. She added that she did not like the Viet Cong but she had to do as they demanded while her husband was under their control. The meat was taken to Captain Be who gave it to the poor Montagnards who lived along the entrance road to Binh Gia in the hamlet of La Van and who could be trusted not to give the meat to the Viet Cong. The major haul of the operation was rice. A large cache of six tons was discovered together with some smaller amounts to make up approximately 15,000 lbs. This was enough rice to feed a complete Viet Cong main force regiment for one week, so its capture robbed the Viet Cong of another useful staging supply to sustain them in moves between eastern and western Phuoc Tuy.

Operation Crowsnest lasted only one further day because of the proximity of an operation to secure Route 15. C Company continued to search Ngai Giao in the morning and they swept around to a hamlet on the north-west of the village, three miles from Duc Thanh. Five men of military age were discovered who did not have identity cards. One of these men was a Chinese who owned a rice shop. He had a large amount of Cambodian money in his possession and kept many pigeons. These men were all suspects and they were taken to Captain Be to explain how they came to have no identity cards. They were later released by Colonel Dat after providing some very detailed information about Viet Cong organisation and activities in Ngai Giao.

Amongst other activities, such as kidnapping people from Binh Gia, the Viet Cong in Ngai Giao had been buying food from the local people at very differing prices. For some commodities such as meat of which relatively small amounts were required, levies were made on the villagers who would receive either a low rate of payment or none at all. However, in the case of rice, fish and salt, the basic ingredients of the Viet Cong diet, the Viet Cong paid the villagers at nearly twice the ruling market prices in order to stimulate the villagers to collect rice from far and wide. The Viet Cong always had plenty of money and paid for the rice in brand new two hundred piastre and five hundred piastre notes. However, penetration of Ngai Giao by this operation had enabled Captain Be to establish control over the amount of rice which could be sold by the shops at any one time and the amount which any individual could have in his house. Both these quantities covered only a few days requirements for a single family so some obstruction was given to the Viet Cong rice collection programme at Ngai Giao.

Operation Crowsnest was the first thrust by Allied or Government troops into this area for several years. Because it was merely a temporary thrust it compelled the main force Viet Cong who had been using the village to vacate the area for a few days only. However we had our hands full with Binh Ba and we did not intend to allow the Viet Cong back into that village by over-extending ourselves. It was sufficient that the people of Ngai Giao had seen that we had the power to operate through their locality and that the Viet Cong could do little about the security of their supplies in an area in which there had never before been any doubt of control by the Viet Cong. These factors are not decisive in a military struggle, but they may be in a political one.

8
Clearing a Mountain

While we had been busy clearing Phuoc Tuy of Viet Cong forces, American planning for the co-ordinated clearance of the entire Third Corps area had progressed to the stage at which a major influx of troops was due to arrive. These men comprised the Third Brigade of the Fourth Infantry Division and they were to land at Vung Tau in the first days of October 1966. Their initial task was to secure the northern sector of Route 15 which lay in Bien Hoa province. They were to operate from a base fifteen miles to the south-east of Bien Hoa city, Bear Cat. This effort was aimed at making Route 15 a 'green' route, one over which Allied traffic could move at will without a heavy armed escort. Once this had been achieved it would be possible to use the developing harbour facilities of Vung Tau to a much greater extent. Large numbers of men and huge amounts of additional material were scheduled to come into the country during the following few months and these would have congested the port of Saigon unduly. Moreover, the Americans were increasing the size of their installations at Bien Hoa and at Long Binh nearby and both of these places were served by the direct connection of Route 15 to Vung Tau.

However, to make these plans possible the hold of the Viet Cong over Route 15 had to be broken. Taxation activities had been very lucrative because of all the wealthy Saigon businessmen who drove down Route 15 to spend weekends and holidays at Vung Tau. Viet Cong attacks on the scattered Government posts along the road had increased during 1966 and it was apparent that the Viet Cong were making a major effort to continue and extend the interdiction of the road. A special point of interest was the village of Phu My, which lay just to the south of the Phuoc Tuy-Bien Hoa boundary. This village was close to the centre of the Viet

Cong controlled sector and was an obvious point for the Viet Cong to concentrate against. Phu My had been occupied by the Japanese during World War II, and they had built an airstrip at the rear of the battalion-sized fort on the northern edge of the settlement. The airstrip had fallen into disuse, but the fort had been well maintained as a matter of necessity. The Viet Cong were able to move forces against the Phu My garrison from either side of the road. On the south-western side lay the Rung Sat with its countless creeks, footpaths and hiding places amongst the mangroves. On the north-eastern side was a thick jungle which covered a network of tracks leading down to Phu My from the Hat Dich base area.

During August 1966, 274 Regiment had made attacks on Phu My, harassing the post with mortar fire and ambushing reinforcement and supply convoys on their way to the fort. We knew that the commander of 274 Regiment intended to wipe out the Government force at Phu My as soon as he could and so there was some urgency in dealing with the Viet Cong along Route 15. The Americans had stationed a brigade of the First Division at Bear Cat to begin domination of the northern sector and to pave the way for the Third Brigade of the Fourth Division.

The safe passage of this brigade from Vung Tau to Bear Cat required the establishment of temporary control over the whole length of the road for several days. The convoys were a tempting target to the Viet Cong, so the force protecting the road had to be strong enough to counter a Viet Cong attack of battalion strength at any point and also had to be capable of rapid redeployment to meet a regimental attack. Of course the Viet Cong did not have to elect to take massive action, for they could have cut the road and done considerable damage by the use of mines and booby traps, perhaps covered by a few snipers hidden in the jungle nearby.

Four battalions were provided to secure the road—three from the 173rd Airborne Brigade and one from the Australian Task Force. Because the Sixth Battalion had just completed an arduous sweep through the Dinh hills, the Fifth Battalion was assigned the task and Colonel Warr was warned for the operation in early October. The battalion was to be responsible for the southern sector from Ba Ria to Phu My while the 173rd Airborne Brigade took the sector to the north of Phu My.

The southern sector was threatened from two areas in differing ways. Bordering the road on both sides were strips of coastal plain from one to several miles wide, linking the mangroves of the Rung Sat on the south-west with the hills on the north-east. These flat areas were covered mostly with a low scrub which gave protection to any ambushing party. The scrub terminated within a hundred yards of the road for much of its length, and was sufficiently thick to give cover from air observation so that withdrawal routes for the ambush party would be difficult to locate. Hence it was important that these areas were regularly patrolled to a distance of several hundred yards back from the road.

The second area from which the road was threatened was the long spine of hills on the north-eastern side. These consisted of the Dinh hills which ran for six miles along the road, and Nui Thi Vai and Nui Toc Tien. This latter pair were joined by a pass which climbed to five hundred feet about the plain which lay close to sea level. The Dinh hills had just been cleared by the Sixth Battalion and close surveillance had been kept over the access routes which led into them from the Viet Cong base areas. Hence we could be fairly certain that danger would not come from the Dinh hills. However, the northern pair of hills, Nui Thi Vai on the north-west and Nui Toc Tien on the south-east, presented a more difficult problem because neither had been cleared before.

Nui Thi Vai rose to over fifteen hundred feet and commanded a particularly long section of Route 15 because the road swung around the base of Nui Thi Vai to change its direction from north-west to north as one proceeded towards Phu My. Nui Toc Tien was fourteen hundred feet high, but its position to the east of the taller Nui Thi Vai robbed it of much of its view over the road. Nui Thi Vai was a rectangular mountain with straight, steep faces to the north, east and west and a long ridge running out in a series of lesser peaks to the south. Because of this rectangular configuration, the easiest lines of ascent lay up the spurs on the north-west, the north-east, the south-west and the ridge from the south. Therefore these points were likely places for finding any Viet Cong who happened to be on the mountain. The southern ridge included two peaks of five hundred feet, separated by low saddles. The more southerly of the two was crowned by twin peaks separated by three hundred yards and a drop of sixty feet in between. From here, the ridge ran down steeply to sea level at the foot of another hill, Nui Ong Trinh, 750 feet high. Nui Ong Trinh approached to within a mile of the road while most of Nui Thi Vai was within 81 mm. mortar range of the road. Mortaring was the chief method of attack which the Viet Cong could use with relative impunity against the road. From positions up on Nui Thi Vai they could correct their fire by direct observation of the bomb bursts. They could then retreat from our counter bombardment in an instant into caves or tunnels and be ready to emerge again when the next likely target appeared on the road. Not only could a Viet Cong force with mortars on Nui Thi Vai have damaged road traffic but they could have seriously threatened any troops down on the plain who were patrolling near the road.

Nui Toc Tien did not present such danger because it did not command very much of the road. Not only was it masked by Nui Thi Vai, but its configuration, a long ridge with five main peaks, ran parallel to the road and none of the high ground was sufficiently close to the road to be within mortar range. Of course it was possible for the Viet Cong to set mortars up anywhere on the flat country along the road, but it would have been much more difficult for them to have achieved accurate fire than on the hills and their positions would have been less secure than in the rocky caves which the hills offered.

Several Viet Cong track systems ran through the area, and these were important because of the possibility of finding some base camps which formed part of their supply channel between the Rung Sat and the Hat Dich area. A broad track, the size of a two lane highway ran through the main pass, between the Dinh hills and Nui Toc Tien. Another track, although for foot use only, ran up over the pass between Nui Toc Tien and Nui Thi Vai, and then for several miles through jungle to intercept the main track which ran between the Hat Dich area and the Dinh hills to Ba Ria. Several tracks ran around the western side of Nui Thi Vai from different points on Route 15 between Phu My to the north-west and the village of Ong Trinh to the south-west.

The jungle-clad slopes of Nui Thi Vai rose steeply from the plain with an average gradient of one in three. From the relatively bare summit one could see individual vehicles moving along Route 15 for ten miles. From this vantage point the Viet Cong could learn the composition of military and civilian traffic using the road, taxation points could be controlled and, in the particular cases of bridges and culverts which had been mined by the Viet Cong, the right instant for detonation could be seen. Increasing Allied pressure on the Viet Cong in September had prevented them from making extensive use of the hills during the weeks before our operation, and we did not expect to find more than a company of Viet Cong on Nui Thi Vai, although it was always possible that the security of the American intentions to send a brigade along Route 15 had not been perfect and that a main force regiment would be tempted to strike at such a prize.

8. CLEARING A MOUNTAIN

The area was mostly uninhabited. The people who lived in the roadside villages on the plain were forbidden by the Government to move more than one thousand metres to the north-east of the road. On the north-western side of Nui Thi Vai, a few hundred feet below the summit was a Buddhist pagoda, a red-tiled building of grey granite sited on a wide ledge which afforded a magnificent view over miles of jungle, the wide loops of the estuaries in the Rung Sat and the plains beyond which stretched to Saigon. It was a splendid reward to those who had made the steep climb for the sake of contemplation. A number of houses ran up the western face, lining a rough track which led to the pagoda. At the foot of this track was a large rectangular clearing through which the main track to Phu My ran. Several more houses were gathered at the eastern edge of this clearing. Intelligence reports indicated that the Viet Cong had been making use of these houses and that they also had a camp on the south-western spur of Nui Thi Vai.

An important complication with this operation, Operation Canberra, was the time limit imposed by the requirement to be stationed along the road when the American troops drove through, commencing on October 11th. We returned from Operation Crowsnest on the evening of October 3rd and to have launched the battalion into another operation without two days of preparation was undesirable. The most important piece of ground to be searched was Nui Thi Vai. The companies could search their area of plain alongside the road in a day's work so there were five days available for clearing Nui Thi Vai.

The area which had to be examined was one and a half miles from east to west and three miles from north to south. Obviously the battalion would be much better balanced by advancing on the narrower front and this would also enable a closer search to be made. The choice of movement was thus reduced to sweeping to the south from the north or vice versa.

A sweep to the south had the advantage of interposing a blocking force between any Viet Cong on the mountain and their main base positions to the north. The Viet Cong would then be driven towards the road and their escape from the area could be made extremely difficult. The chief disadvantage with this direction of sweep was the inaccessibility of the area to the north of the hills. This area could be entered only on foot or by helicopter. The approach by foot was very long and exhausting and would require some days to complete. To land by helicopter at the foot of Nui Thi Vai would have made it perfectly obvious to every Viet Cong soldier in the area that we were looking for them.

The approach from the south presented most of these points in converse. Any Viet Cong on the mountain would be driven back onto their well-known routes to their base areas, but troops could be introduced into the area from many points along Route 15 without making it obvious that our intention was to move on Nui Thi Vai.

The shortage of time and the importance of keeping the Viet Cong guessing led Colonel Warr to adopt the latter course and forced us to accept the possibility that we might not cut off any Viet Cong who were still active on the mountain.

Provision of fire support to cover the area of Nui Thi Vai was a problem. The gun area had to be established near a road for ease of access and for ammunition resupply, and the area had to be secure. Because the companies would later be deployed along Route 15, this gun area had to be located close to the centre of the length of road for which the battalion was responsible. However, adoption of a gun area on Route 15 compelled us to take the battalion mortars up into the hills with us because they could not cover enough of the hills from the road to effectively support the searching companies.

The normal security demands of protection of Battalion Headquarters and the gun area cut the number of companies who could operate forward to three. It was the turn of D Company to act as palace guards, and one platoon was detached from this company to protect the gun area with the Anti-Tank Platoon. The routes of A, B and C Companies were then planned to bring these companies around to the north side of Nui Thi Vai by the afternoon of October 10th, ensuring that the most obvious re-entrants and slopes were examined. I spent much of the 4th and 5th of October making aerial reconnaissances of the area from a light helicopter. Unfortunately I was compelled to observe the area from a considerable height so that our intentions were not made obvious to the Viet Cong. The main air lane from Vung Tau to Saigon ran to the south of the hills and an auxiliary lane used by helicopters flying between Nui Dat and Saigon ran to the north of the hills so there was a reasonable chance of concealing the purpose of these flights.

8. CLEARING A MOUNTAIN

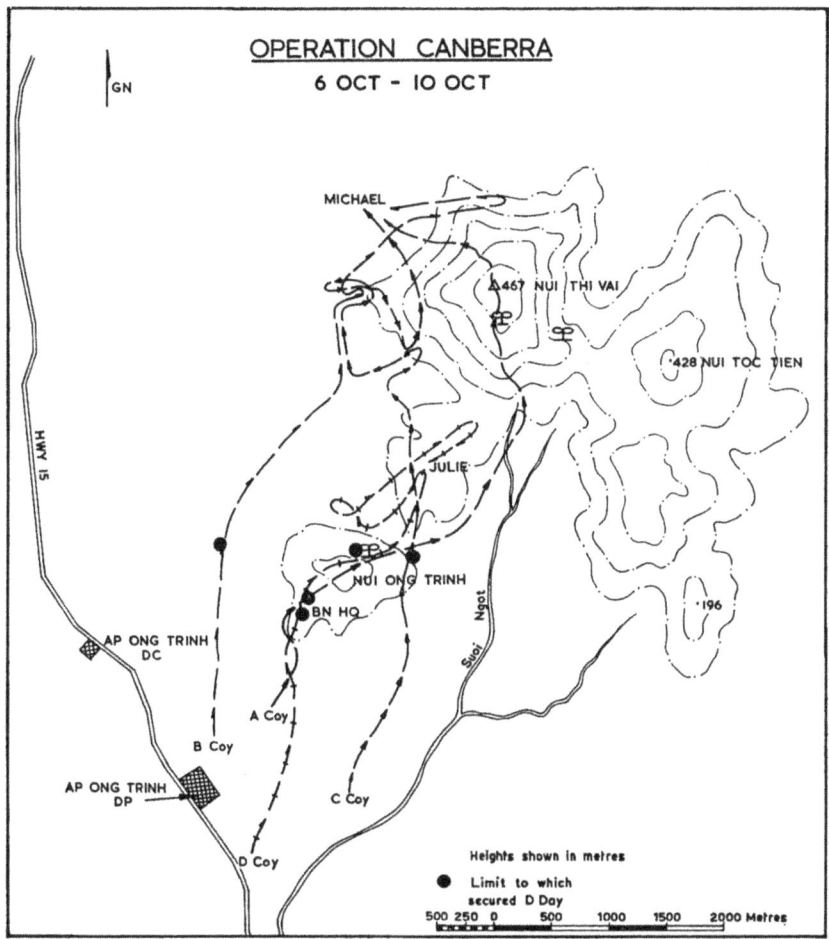

Fig. 14. The company movements during the preliminary clearance of Nui Thi Vai to secure Route 15, Operation Canberra, 6–10 October 1966.

October 6th was a fine sunny day of the period which begins the transition from the monsoon to the dry season. The long rambling ride around to our starting point south of the hills was rather pleasant. At intervals of one or two miles along Route 15 were small villages of brick houses with cream plastered walls and red-tiled roofs. Around the outskirts of several of these villages were grass huts, some of which were inhabited by refugees who had come from Viet Cong controlled territory further to the north along the coast. Some villages supported the Viet Cong, some were neutral and others were opposed to them, but these complications made no difference to the children who ran to the road in crowds to dance up and down and wave at the passing soldiers.

123

During the year the provincial police had been making progress in weeding Viet Cong out of these villages and a great deal was known about enemy activities along the road. The greater availability of Vietnamese manpower conferred by the rising tide of American support had enabled the stationing of some regional force companies along Route 15. Once these companies had established control over the few miles around each of their posts the task of the Viet Cong in attempting to oust them would be greatly complicated.

We left the APCs at Route 15 because it was difficult to move them off the road over the marshy ground on the north side. Captain Brian Ledan lightened the atmosphere by measuring his length in the first inundated area we had to cross. We had not gone more than ten paces when we had to commence wading—a bad omen for the operation. Brian tripped and went straight into a foot of water. The weight of his equipment prevented him from struggling to his feet for several seconds and he was thoroughly saturated. Our hilarity was sobered by the thought that within a few hours we would all be saturated if the climate lived up to its usual record.

The battalion fanned out and pushed through some miles of thick scrub in marshy ground to reach the foot of the hills. B Company went around to the western side of Nui Ong Trinh, C Company went to the east, and A Company followed by D Company and Battalion Headquarters began to climb the southern slope of Nui Ong Trinh. The day was uneventful as far as contact with the Viet Cong was concerned and we camped amidst rocks on a steep ridge leading to the summit of Nui Ong Trinh.

On the morning of October 7th the central group completed the ascent of Nui Ong Trinh. From the summit Battalion Headquarters had excellent radio communications with the forward companies and we could obtain a fine view over the country to be searched later that day. The final objective of Battalion Headquarters was the next hill which had been nicknamed Julie for want of a better name. The valley we had to cross was extremely steep so we surveyed the top of Nui Ong Trinh anxiously to see if a helicopter landing pad could be found. Alas, it was a fruitless search. A Company took a long time to find a way down into the valley from the summit and time threatened to defeat our efforts to gain the next summit before nightfall. Just as we were starting on the descent, Major Paul Greenhalgh appeared to say that he had found a landing pad a little further down the hillside. Greatly cheered, Battalion Headquarters set off after D Company. However in the thickness of the bush the forward scout

8. CLEARING A MOUNTAIN

of the headquarters party did not notice where D Company had diverged from the track made by A Company as they made their way to the bottom of the hill, with the result that we found ourselves in the midst of thick jungle at the bottom of the valley watching D Company fly out to the top of Julie several hundred feet above us with the greatest of ease.

Swearing terrible revenge, the headquarters plunged off through the bamboo and lantanas to begin the next ascent. Julie was a much easier proposition than Ong Trinh and within an hour we were at the top. D Company occupied one of the twin peaks and the pioneers cut a landing pad which fitted the Iroquois machines like a glove in the saddle which led to the other peak. Battalion Headquarters went on to this second peak to make a balanced defensive position. We all dug in vigorously for we knew that the Viet Cong could not only mortar us from nearby but they could easily observe us from the summit of Nui Thi Vai which dominated the northern horizon.

Late on the morning of October 8th the peaceful atmosphere of the tree covered hilltop was shattered by the rattle of firing followed by the reverberations of explosions. C Company had swung around to the north-west, crossing the summit of Julie the evening before and were now searching the southern slope of Nui Thi Vai. The forward platoon had found a track which it was climbing when it encountered two Viet Cong trail watchers. The platoon was fired upon and the men leaped off the track to take cover. However, the Viet Cong had booby trapped the likely areas of cover and several of our soldiers were wounded by explosions as two of the traps were sprung. The Viet Cong made their escape while our men were attending to their own wounded. Mortar fire from the helicopter pad on Julie and artillery fire from Route 15 was brought swiftly onto the likely Viet Cong withdrawal routes while C Company prepared a landing zone for the Dust Off aircraft.

One amazed witness to the morning's events was a young Viet Cong prisoner who had belonged to one of the units which had been stationed on Nui Thi Vai. He had been captured by Vietnamese troops and taken to Ba Ria and thence to Bien Hoa some months previously. He had told his captors that he knew where a large cache of rice was hidden near the foot of Nui Thi Vai and had offered to guide us to it. My expectations had fallen somewhat when I had met him on his arrival by helicopter at our pad. He looked rather dazed and bewildered and was clearly a very simple peasant lad. With my interpreter I took him back up the hill and we sat on a group of rocks.

One of our chaps heated up a tin of food and made a brew of coffee for him. His dazed state was complicated by his lack of any notion of his location. He had not been on the southern part of the mountain before and the helicopter flight had thoroughly confused him. Like so many Viet Cong soldiers he could not read a map. All he could do was to guide us from the camp he had lived in to the cache and until we reached the site of his camp he was of no help. We were not due to cover this ground for another two days so the practical side of our conversation came to an abrupt halt.

However, an opportunity to talk with a Viet Cong prisoner was a rare one and so I turned my questioning to wider matters, such as why he had joined the Viet Cong, how he had joined, how he had been treated, what he thought of us, and so on. He was aged 19 and had lived near Ba Ria. One day two years before he had gone into the jungle to attend a Viet Cong political rally. He, together with the other young men at this meeting, had not been allowed to return to their homes and had been enlisted as soldiers in the Viet Cong. He had not wanted to join the Viet Cong although he had felt that they were rather exciting as a band of Robin Hood types. But once he was in the Viet Cong forces, political surveillance was so intense that he had no choice but to try to be a good soldier. Treatment had been rough and he had had an unhappy and arduous time. The conflicts between his desires to return to normal living and the impossibility of doing this had induced in him a state of acute depression and all he wanted to do was to withdraw from conflict. He had no idea of whom we were—he said he thought we were French.

I persevered in trying to get through to him, to see if there were some sort of spark which could be struck out of his sagging personality, and to give him some inkling that we were interested in his personal well-being for his own sake. Evidently the political angle was not going too well so I tried to be a little more basic. He replied that he liked drinking beer so we dug around everyone's packs and turned up a can of Fosters. I then left Xuan and Bic, the two interpreters, with our guest to give him the first informal companionship with his own nationals that he had had during the previous weeks. When I returned half an hour later he was smoking a cigarette and had taken his shoes off. He seemed less bewildered but by

8. CLEARING A MOUNTAIN

no means fully alert. The required therapy seemed too deep for my means. We put him back onto a helicopter and this strange sad product of the war flew out of our presence but not out of our minds for he was the essence of our problem.

While Major John Miller was organising the extraction of C Company's wounded by helicopter, the platoons of B Company were swinging around the base of the south-western spur of Nui Thi Vai. Their route lay eastwards across the crest of the spur. By early afternoon they had begun the ascent when the forward platoon came on a group of forty Viet Cong. The forward scout of the platoon concealed himself within feet of the Viet Cong and counted them. Major McQualter immediately sent out reconnaissance groups and ascertained the locations of the flanks and rear of the enemy. The Viet Cong were grouped around some huts and were preparing to make their departure, thus speed was vital if they were to be prevented from escaping. Colonel Warr gave Bruce approval to deal with them himself and he then arrayed his platoons around the Viet Cong position with particular attention to the high ground so that one platoon was looking right down onto the enemy position and could deliver decisive small arms fire onto them while the others blocked the escape routes.

Yet this apparently perfect plan for overcoming the most significant Viet Cong force which the battalion had encountered never went into effect. While B Company were creeping into position around the Viet Cong, a fascinating drama was taking place in the battalion command post, two parallel slit trenches dug amongst the granite rocks which covered the summit of Julie.

As we were debating the enemy situation and means of obtaining more information, Major Alex Piper, the senior intelligence staff officer on Task Force Headquarters, arrived by helicopter to say that he had reliable information which indicated that a considerable number of Viet Cong were on Nui Thi Vai and that they were commanded by the deputy commander of 274 Regiment. This news seemed to be decisive. If B Company became involved in heavy fighting only C Company could assist them and C Company had been depleted by the casualties of that morning. Both A and D Companies were too far away from B Company to move to their support quickly. Any aggressive move by B Company could be very dangerous and contact with the Viet Cong should not be opened until some new factor appeared or until the information brought by Major Piper could be shown to be a pessimistic assessment of the enemy situation.

Just at this moment Bruce McQualter called on the battalion command net to announce that he had the group of forty well covered and that he was about to move in on them. Colonel Warr was faced with the classic dilemma of command. He had to decide within seconds whether to let B Company go ahead with their attack or to pull them back. Was it worth the risk? Forty Viet Cong eliminated from the war would be a most successful afternoon's work and would offset the losses suffered in the morning. The mettle of our men was roused and they were not in a mood for caution. Yet this could be the beginning of a heavy reverse for us. We knew not what lay beyond this group and we had been told that they were not alone. All these thoughts were flashing through Colonel Warr's mind—to seize the opportunity and risk the losses or to be cautious and perhaps lose the opportunity forever. Fractions of seconds dragged by as we waited for his decision.

He reached for the microphone and ordered Bruce to halt his action and to move out of the area to the west. The course for the next twenty-four hours was set.

B and C Companies pulled back to safe distances from the Viet Cong location and artillery fire began to pour in. Our own mortars which were right alongside Battalion Headquarters opened up and the re-entrant between the south-western spur of Nui Thi Vai and ourselves resounded with the thunderous roars and crashes of the bombardment. Then came the gun ships of the American light fire team which was in support of us. They wheeled slowly and deliberately over the target area to familiarise themselves with the exact locations which were to be hit. Minutes later they were loosing volleys of rockets on their unerringly straight paths into the hillside. Heavy ground fire hit back at them from the Viet Cong as they followed through over the target, with their door gunners spraying bullets at the black-clad figures running about on the ground.

In the meantime an air strike was being called in to take care of any Viet Cong who were still in bunkers. First came the light Cessna aircraft of the forward air controller which buzzed slowly over the target area looking for points to be hit, while Captain Bob Supple, the Assistant Adjutant, briefed him from the ground. Then a high pitched scream announced the arrival of the F100s overhead. They began their terrifying ritual of circling the target for several minutes while the forward air controller explained the details of the targets and the exact locations of our troops to them. All attention was focused on the howl of their engines as they swooped and soared on their path around the hill with intense purposefulness. Their sharp, pointed noses were complemented by the needle points of the bomb pods held under their steeply raked wings. Once they were thoroughly familiar with the target they commenced making trial bombing runs across the hill, diving in at a furious speed in a straight line towards the hillside, then climbing swiftly to avoid collision with the slope. These approaches were made from the west and lay right across our field of vision as we stood on a vantage point just by our helicopter pad. The re-entrant in which C Company had struck the booby trapped area was directly in front of us, its far side only a thousand yards away.

On the first runs the jets loosed two five-hundred-pound bombs each. We watched the bombs drop away from the aircraft in pairs and dive on their long parabolic trajectories into the target area and we felt the shockwave of their explosion crack through the air around us. The next weapon to be loosed into the enemy position was CBU—a large bomb which exploded above the ground to scatter a large number of smaller canisters widely through the surrounding jungle to detonate on impact. We saw the long CBU pods loosed, guided into the target by the path of the F100s and by their own aerodynamic shape and tail fins. There was a dull thud as the outer case exploded and then we saw the bursting flashes of hundreds of small explosions scattered in a long swathe across the steep slope, sending a polyphony of crunching cracks reverberating around the rocks and through our heads.

The aircraft then began to alternate their lines of attack, swooping in from the east through the low saddle between Julie and Nui Thi Vai to let a burst of destruction fall in a horizontal path across the slope. The dramatic effect of the strike was greatly heightened by the wave of sound emerging from the jet as it hurtled before our eyes at our own height and only a few hundred yards away. After their heavy ordnance had been expended the jets then dived low over the target area strafing it with bursts of machine gun fire whose sound ripped through the air like the tearing of a giant cloth as dozens of rounds left the guns every second.

The first strike wave pulled off and the Americans had offered us a second. Our mortars continued the bombardment in the meantime so that there would be no respite which would allow the enemy to escape. The second wave came overhead at 6.30 pm, just as the sun was setting and light was beginning to fail. The first stages of this strike were similar to the previous one—the soaring, plunging encirclement of the target with the ominous punitive wails of the engines, followed by the shattering explosions racing across the valley. But in the climax there were two variations on the first strike. In the growing dusk the F100s swooped in on a southerly approach path directly above our heads and about one hundred feet above the top of the hill on which we were standing, their exhausts glowing and spurting flame against the dull background of the darkening sky, their shrieking rising in an ear splitting crescendo. Then there was the napalm. From where we were on the hilltop, directly behind the line of flight, we watched the aircraft streaking towards the hillside at a speed which seemed to make it inevitable that they should spear straight into the rocky slope, yet at the last instant they were saved by a sharp banking swerve to the left which brought them just clear of the south-western spur of Nui Thi Vai. We could see the direct line of the napalm pods as they dropped on their long glide to the target. A brightly glowing orange and crimson ball appeared at the point of explosion, puffing up rapidly to tear apart into a hundred flaming drops of heavy jelly which hurled across the darkening slope with menacing brilliance and a dull whoomp as the furious combustion sucked all the oxygen out of the surrounding air to leave a great cloud of suffocating vapour.

The time taken to produce all this firepower had consumed the remaining hours of daylight and a rapid exploitation of the bombardment by our troops was out of the question. This break gave the enemy the hours of darkness in which to make their escape. We attempted to make this withdrawal as hazardous as possible by a continuous bombardment of the hill and of likely escape routes through the hours of darkness. For this bombardment we were forced to depend entirely upon our own 81 mm. mortars, for the field artillery could not obtain the tremendous amount of ammunition needed to sustain fire across Nui Thi Vai all night. Colonel Warr had ordered one thousand rounds of mortar ammunition to be flown in during the late afternoon and this amount was now waiting on the mortar line at the bottom of the landing pad. We then pored over the map, pinpointing known enemy positions and tracks and estimating where his withdrawal would take him during the night.

Colonel Warr passed these requirements over to Lieutenant Trevor Sheehan, the Mortar Platoon commander, who produced the fire plan. Only four of the battalion's six mortars were with us because we always had to leave two back in our base area with the skeleton defence force while the bulk of the battalion was out on an operation. These four tubes fired 960 rounds during the night. When we attempted to sleep however, we began to regret bitterly both the extensive fire plan and the proximity of the mortars as we were shattered every few minutes by the explosions of the bombs being fired from the tubes and the crashes when they hit their targets. After a few hours we became accustomed to the noise and slept fitfully, but it was an edgy group of men who sat around the pits of the battalion command post at stand-to on the following morning.

The companies moved back onto the slopes of Nui Thi Vai as soon as they could on the morning of October 9th, but the Viet Cong had disappeared and had taken with them any casualties they had suffered from the bombardment. By this stage the operation had developed into something different from the original intention. Instead of clearing through the area in a rapid sweep of five days, we had been held up by a sizeable encounter and had had to make a substantial enemy group move out of the area. There were only two days left for us to sweep the remainder of Nui Thi Vai and this would mean racing through many tempting Viet Cong installations, overlooking much of value which the Viet Cong would be able to recover after we had moved back to Route 15. However we were committed to support the American convoy and there was nothing else to be done but to find as much as we could as quickly as possible, go down to the road and return to Nui Thi Vai as soon as we were released from the road.

A Company had moved up under the eastern crest of Nui Thi Vai and were in a good position to sweep across the summit and dominate the feature. This they proceeded to do and they moved across the top and down to the pagoda on the north-western spur just a few hundred feet below the summit. On the evening of October 9th, some members of A Company discovered a strange individual lurking about the pagoda. He had the appearance of a hermit monk, but appearances were apt to be misleading where the Viet Cong were concerned and so he was captured as a suspect.

Early on the following morning he was sent to Battalion Headquarters so that I could question him. He stepped out of the helicopter looking just as puzzled as our previous Vietnamese visitor. Bic, the interpreter, brought him up the hill and sat him down on a rock. The monk was a frail little figure, wearing a long brown tunic and trousers and a plum coloured woollen skull cap pulled down over his ears. His feet were bare. In his hands he clutched a transistor radio and a small bag of medicaments. He told us that he was a Buddhist monk, his name was Nguyen Van Xe and he was thirty-seven years old. He had been a monk for eighteen years and had spent six years tending the pagoda on Nui Thi Vai. I told him that he might be able to help us and that he had nothing to fear provided that he did not try to escape or to mislead us. As events turned out these admonitions were quite unnecessary, and he must have thought that our outlook on life was rather serious.

The first questions which I put to him were purely military. He said he was not a member of the Viet Cong and denied having given them any assistance. He lived in a cave two hundred yards away from the pagoda. He had seen very little of the Viet Cong on Nui Thi Vai because they had told him not to wander more than two hundred yards from his cave except for use of the main track which led up to the pagoda from the foot of the hill. He frequently saw some five or six Viet Cong on the mountain. He obtained his food from people who came up to the pagoda from the villages along Route 15 and from Ba Ria, supplemented by fortnightly journeys to his monastery at Thu Duc, between Saigon and Bien Hoa. He added that two nuns also visited him once a fortnight. This was confirmed by the discovery of some nylon night attire in his cave. Very few people had come up to the pagoda during the previous two years because the Viet Cong were using it as a shelter. They had been based in the area of the pagoda for over three years. As far as he knew there were no Viet Cong still on the hill, for he had not seen any for ten or twelve days. He thought that they had all gone into the jungles on the plain to the north side of Nui Thi Vai.

This information was naturally of little value. It seemed to be a consistent and credible story and he had several photographs of himself in saffron robes, together with a number of certificates accrediting him with various monastic qualifications. As there seemed nothing more of immediate value to be gained from questioning him I retired to consider this negative information.

8. CLEARING A MOUNTAIN

Pte Shoebridge and L/Cpl Bryan supporting Pte Riik after a booby trap explosion had wounded several members of C Company on Nui Thi Vai on 8 October 1966, during Operation Canberra (see Chapter 8).

Members of C Company after clearing a helicopter pad on the slopes of Nui Thi Vai to evacuate the men wounded by booby traps on 8 October. Major Miller is standing bottom centre without hat.

Second Lieutenant Deak MC, Reconnaissance Platoon commander, at Phuoc Hoa during Operation Hayman in November 1966 (see Chapter 11). The platoon soon established friendly relations with the people.

B Company after dismounting from APCs in the Binh Ba rubber plantation before patrolling an area crossed by tracks used by the Viet Cong. Pte. Barney Gee is the forward scout.

If it were true, it suggested that the information which we had received through Major Piper on the previous afternoon had been exaggerated. On the other hand, there were many parts of the hill which Nguyen Van Xe never visited and so his information counted for little. Had he been one of the Viet Cong then he could have been of tremendous value for most Viet Cong talked very freely once in our hands—something very surprising for a group of people supposedly so dedicated to their cause.

The pace of the operation was rather tedious during the morning of October 10th because the operation was being rounded off and the companies organised for extraction by helicopter and APC. Tony White and I spent a couple of hours therefore in talking with the monk and in trying to grasp some of the fundamentals of his thinking. Unfortunately this made for a one-sided conversation consisting of the monk's lengthy answers to our questions. Everything spoken had to go through our interpreter which slowed the monk's rate of delivery a great deal for he was rather expansive. He spoke in the peculiarly soft voice of educated Vietnamese, in a tone which conveyed a humanity quite inexpressible in English.

His basic philosophy was to help others to achieve happiness. The most important thing in life was self-purification which could be accomplished only with the assistance of much study and meditation. Politics was a field which could be left to others. He did not approve of the activities of Tich Tri Quang, the Buddhist extremist leader who had been causing much political trouble earlier in the year. As a contemplative rural monk he paid no attention to what happened in the outside world. He used to spend his time on the hill reading scripture, tending the pagoda gardens and listening to classical Vietnamese music on his radio. He did not particularly care who ruled Vietnam, as long as it was not the Viet Cong for that would mean the end of religion as he knew it. He told us that it was predicted in scripture that there would be a great battle between the Americans and the Communists in four years' time, that the Communists would win with Buddhist assistance and that the Americans would depart. The Vietnamese people would then absorb the Communists to decommunise them. Any Communists who would not change would be driven out of the country and in twenty years time Vietnam would be peaceful and free again.

Nguyen Van Xe had no idea of our nationality. He thought that we were either American or French, probably the latter because we were different from the Americans and he had seen others of our soldiers at Bien Hoa during the past year. He said he had heard of Australia but he did not know where it was. After we had talked for an hour we offered him some refreshment. He said that he could not eat anything with meat in it because it was wrong to kill anything living, but he would like some biscuits and some hot water with sugar added. These demands were easy to meet and we envied his appetite for army biscuits.

We could not release him for he had no idea of where he was and he might have been killed by a shell during the following two weeks, so we sent him back to Task Force Headquarters for transfer to the provincial authorities in Ba Ria. We dug up a few more packets of biscuits for him and some jam and sent him off, hoping that someone would be kind to this rather helpless unworldly soul. Two of his thoughts remained with us in crystal clear form. The first was that all religions are good and the second was that he could comment on the characters of only those men whom he knew personally.

During these two days, C Company had been making some very useful discoveries in the re-entrant in which they had suffered the casualties on October 8th. They had found a major Viet Cong base camp which consisted of a hospital, a training camp, and a booby trap factory. Other finds included Chinese Communist ammunition, tools, clothing, web equipment, several hundred tubes of penicillin and other drugs, surgical packs, beds, four anti-tank mines, nineteen anti-tank rockets, many grenades and ten tons of rice. Several sacks full of documents were also retrieved, which included reports of traffic movements on the road, tax collection records, weapons registers, roll books for the company which had administered the base, food issue registers which showed both the units and numbers which had passed through the Nui Thi Vai base in recent months, and a great number of training pamphlets, Viet Cong news sheets and local orders. The most important find was a Viet Cong map to the scale of 150,000 which showed the complete Viet Cong track system for western Phuoc Tuy. Also indicated were several base camps and fortified areas. This map provided us with the basis for several successful ambushes in the following months and was of great use to the gunners in planning their harassing fire programmes which went on day and night right through the year.

8. CLEARING A MOUNTAIN

On the afternoon of October 10th we flew out of our hilltop position, one helicopter load at a time, soaring down in a smooth, swinging, curving path to our intended positions along Route 15. We left the hills with considerable regret, for the discovery of the base camp indicated that there were many other Viet Cong facilities within our grasp. We consoled ourselves with the hope that it would not be long before we were back on Nui Thi Vai to finish the job.

9

Securing Route 15

No sooner had we arrived at the new location for the Battalion Headquarters opposite the village of Ong Trinh North than we encountered several acts of hostility. Clearance of Route 15 for mines and booby traps began on the afternoon of October 10th and the first mines were soon found. Unfortunately one of the sappers who were making the first search with mine detectors was blown up by a booby trap. A mine laid close to the verge of the road blew a track off an APC—the second APC to be disabled that afternoon, as one had been similarly damaged on the track between Phu My and the foot of Nui Thi Vai while bringing A Company back to Route 15. The most serious incident was the crash of our light reconnaissance helicopter. A sniper had fired at the pilot, Lieutenant Bill Davies, when Davies was flying at low altitude. The bullet had hit Davies in the head and the helicopter ploughed into telephone wires at the side of the road, turned over on its side and crashed straight into the bitumen, turning over and over as the tremendous momentum of its rotating parts expended itself.

Our medical officer, Tony White, had been waiting some eighty yards from the crash point for the helicopter to collect him. His immediate presence on the scene resulted in Davies being flown direct to the American Third Field Hospital in Saigon for emergency brain surgery which could be carried out only by the specialists at that hospital. This snap decision saved Davies's life for his condition was extremely grave. Later Davies made a complete recovery and was able to return to flying within six months.

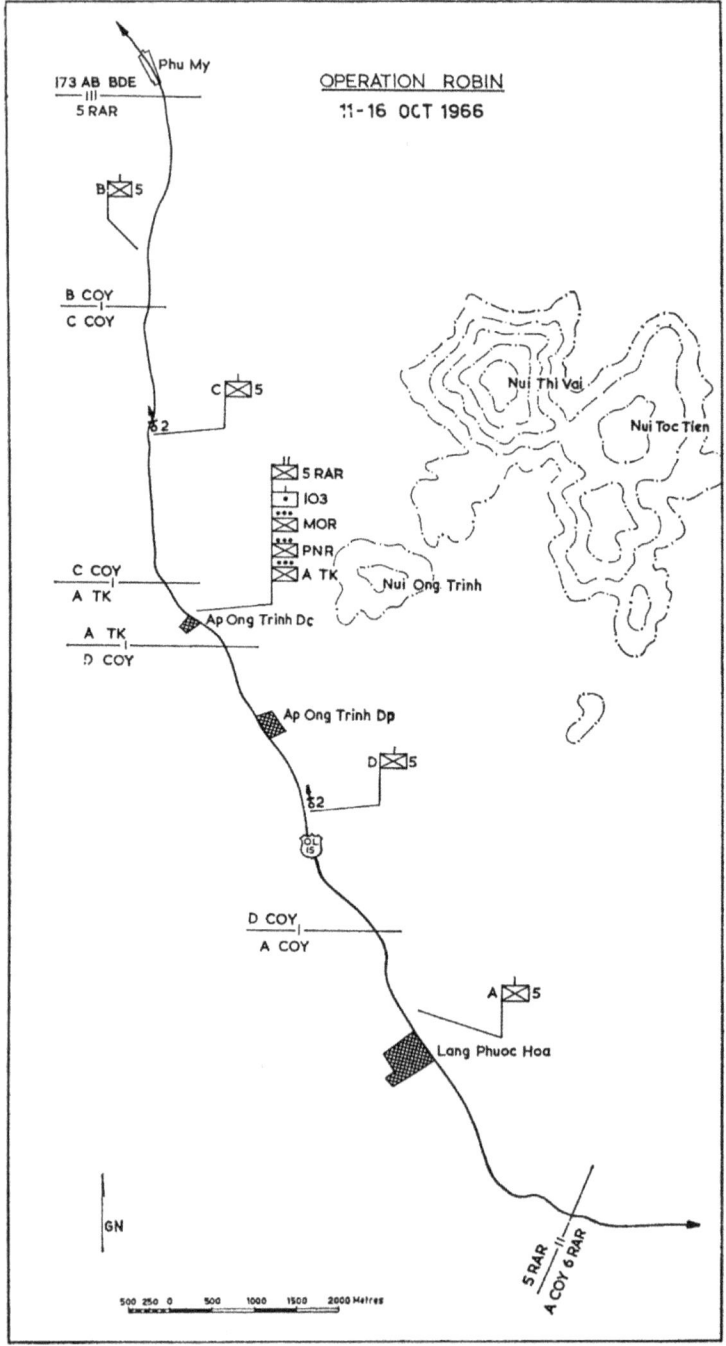

Fig. 15. The company dispositions while the American convoys were using Route 15, Operation Robin, 11–16 October 1966.

9. SECURING ROUTE 15

Davies's passenger had been Staff Sergeant Mealing, Quartermaster Sergeant of B Company and it was to our great loss that Mealing had to return to Australia as a result of this accident. He was fortunate in that his injuries were not serious for he had seen the crash coming as soon as Davies had been hit, he had relaxed as the aircraft went into the road and his safety harness had saved him even though the helicopter itself was a wreck. Mealing had served in Korea where he had been seriously wounded and he had also fought for a year in Malaya during the emergency period. Fortunately he made a good recovery from this accident.

On the following day, October 11th, the companies set about clearing their individual stretches of road. Each company was assisted by sappers with mine detection equipment and no further casualties were caused by mines. Each company sent out clearing patrols at dawn to examine the road and it was patrolled at frequent intervals throughout the remainder of the day. Patrols also pressed back into undergrowth which could have concealed snipers and APCs cruised up and down the road, ready to assist the infantry with their speed and firepower and occasionally taking patrols through to the muddy reaches of the mangrove fringe to search for Viet Cong hides and caches.

Several of the villages along Route 15 derived most of their livelihood from the production of charcoal, and clusters of long low mud ovens were scattered along the roadside on the few pieces of dry ground available. Drainage from the hillsides had made the flat country along the road into a shallow swamp and most areas on which houses had been built had been raised and surrounded by drains. There were few places from which to choose the Battalion Headquarters site and it had to be placed amongst the charcoal ovens opposite the village of Ong Trinh North. This location immediately raised a security problem because the villagers had to have constant access to the ovens and Viet Cong infiltrators could have concealed explosives in an oven by masquerading as villagers. However this risk had to be accepted and precautions were taken by detailing men to watch the activities of the villagers as they went about the ovens.

The people who burnt the charcoal were extremely poor—quite the poorest we had encountered in Phuoc Tuy. We learned from them that many were deeply in debt and that they existed by borrowing on their next batch of charcoal to pay for the labour which went into the present batch. Thus they were always at the mercy of the charcoal wholesalers who came down from Saigon to buy their produce at low prices. One would expect that these circumstances would produce people who inclined naturally towards the Viet Cong. However they were remarkably friendly to us and this attitude was inconsistent with people who were known to be Viet Cong supporters. The villagers allowed their children to play around the outskirts of our position and to join in splashing under the showers which our Assault Pioneer Platoon had erected by means of a pump, a well and a few pieces of piping.

While most of the villages along Route 15 had been lived in for many years and were composed of Buddhist South Vietnamese, two were of recent origin and were inhabited by Catholic refugees from North Vietnam. These villages were Ong Trinh South and Long Cat. Each of these was surrounded by well maintained defences and the houses inside looked much tidier than those of most of the other villages along the road. Both villages also provided their own defence force which guarded the outer perimeters at night and were always ready to repel a Viet Cong attack.

Because these villages were known to be friendly and to harbour no Viet Cong it was an easy matter for us to pay a courtesy call to each without taking any elaborate precautions. In this type of village, social structure is simple for everything revolves around the priest. He is usually the only man who has had a tertiary education and so he is the fount of much of the local knowledge on everything from economics to electricity. He is usually the person whom the villagers rely on to handle their negotiations with outside authorities, particularly the Province and District Chiefs. He maintains the spiritual cohesion of the village in the broadest sense of the word by his attitude to vital questions such as the Viet Cong, education, village growth and planning and self-defence. Although each village administers itself through a village council elected by the people, the councillors look to the advice of the priest in most matters which fall outside the day to day experience of a peasant farmer. Consequently the whole character of a village depends on its priest. Where he is energetic and concerned about his people the village is independent, it does not lack for many fundamentals and the people are in good spirits. Where the priest is indifferent to his people, the village lacks identity and is neglected both by the people who live in it and by the outside agencies who are there to improve the standard of village life.

Consequently the first person whom we contacted in visiting a Catholic village was the priest and he was almost always the man who could give us the clearest idea of how we could be of assistance to the local people and how the Viet Cong could be countered. The priest at Long Cat received us with joviality and welcoming hand gestures. We had arrived while workmen were still building part of his house so we sat around a table and drank a tea made from local flowers while plasterers clambered about overhead on flimsy bamboo scaffolding with amazing agility. Our host gave a broad smile and told us in French that his village was much happier now that Viet Cong pressure had been taken off it. In 1965 the D445 Battalion had attacked Long Cat in order to punish the villagers for their total rejection of the Viet Cong. The village had managed to hold the attack off due to the stout fight put up by the self-defence force, but the people were afraid that a regiment might overrun them one night.

When Colonel Warr asked how we could be of assistance while we were in the vicinity of Long Cat, the priest asked for a visit by our doctor and a dentist and showed us part of the outer fence of the village which had been cut by the Viet Cong. These requests were easy to answer. Tony White and one of the dentists from the Task Force dental unit spent a day treating the villagers and Colonel Warr sent down some coils of barbed wire for the fence.

The situation at Ong Trinh South was similar, except that the Viet Cong had not launched a heavy attack on the village. The priest was an older man and did not speak French so we had greater use for the services of Bic. It was fascinating to watch the priest and Bic in conversation for so much seemed to be communicated or emphasised by their eyes and eyebrows. It is difficult to imagine how more facial muscles could have been brought into play during conversation. Again, medical and dental aid was provided for a day and some urgently needed defence stores were given.

After each visit to the priests we met the commanders of the village defence units and some of the leading men of the village. They said they had been very sorry to leave North Vietnam and they realised that there was no other refuge for them so they were resolved to stop the Viet Cong or go under. They were at their last ditch.

On October 12th the American convoys began to pass through. Twice daily, columns of over one hundred vehicles would stream past. The convoys were preceded by APCs and gun jeeps with machine guns mounted on swivels behind the front seats. Overhead flew a command helicopter and to the sides flew a team of gun ships at low altitude, ready to engage any snipers or detonators of electric mines who attacked the convoy. Twelve hundred men were ferried through to Bear Cat on each of four days, seated in three-ton trucks from which they keenly regarded the country which had occupied most of their training and thinking for the past few months.

It was a warming experience for we who watched them go by because it brought home the realisation we were not fighting the war alone but were a small part of a huge effort. How this was comforting I don't quite know for the presence of another American brigade did not mean that we were exposed to any less danger from the local hazards, but it was certainly a welcome sight.

While we were stationed opposite Ong Trinh North, the regular visits of Brigadier Jackson which we received every few days during all operations became more frequent as plans were discussed for the return to Nui Thi Vai. Glad though we had been to see the Americans, we were also glad when the last convoy had rumbled past, ending the tedium of patrolling familiar stretches in the fierce heat from which there was not the protection of jungle or rubber trees. We felt that the Viet Cong would put up a hard fight for the hills and so tension and excitement at the prospects of the next phase began to mount.

10
Return to Nui Thi Vai

The decision to return to Nui Thi Vai was not taken automatically. When the original clearing operation had been launched we had not expected to find such extensive Viet Cong use of the area which we had cleared and so special plans had to be made to follow up the initial success. These special plans determined the whole operational programme for the Task Force for as long as we remained out of the base and so a lengthy extension of our operation required some serious consideration by Brigadier Jackson. Several intelligence reports which we had received from various sources indicated that the Viet Cong were still installed on Nui Thi Vai and that there were more bases to be discovered with possibilities of the capture of further documents, equipment and supplies. Brigadier Jackson was convinced that the operation was worth continuing and gave his approval a few days before the convoys were due to finish so that our planning could proceed.

The most fruitful area of Nui Thi Vai seemed to be the western and northern sides. A great number of tracks ran around to that part of the hill and the derelict houses on the north-western spur were the sort of shelter which the Viet Cong liked to use. Also, the western side of the hill offered the best view over Route 15 while the natural withdrawal routes from the hill lay to the north. Colonel Warr decided to move the battalion in around the northern and western sides so that two companies could advance up the western side of the hill, one could clear the ground immediately to the north of the hill and the fourth company could lie in ambush positions on the approach routes to the north of the hill, a little further out. This company could prevent Viet Cong movement both toward and away from Nui Thi Vai if the Viet Cong used the track systems which we had discovered from the captured map. This task was assigned to D Company, B Company was to be its neighbour on the north, A Company was to search the north central sector of the western slope, C Company was to search the remainder of the western slope, while Battalion Headquarters, protected by the Assault Pioneer and Anti-Tank Platoons was to advance up the track to the pagoda and install itself in an area where good radio communications with the companies could be ensured. The Sixth Battalion assisted by providing one company, D Company, to protect the gun area.

It must have been fairly obvious to the Viet Cong on Nui Thi Vai that we would return when the convoys had stopped, so we had to take a few deceptive measures. In these we were both hindered and helped by the excellent visibility enjoyed by the Viet Cong over our movements along Route 15 from their observation posts on the hill. This visibility could be exploited, for the Viet Cong might imagine that they were secure until they saw us concentrate the battalion and begin the long move back to the base of the hill.

The jungle which covered most of the plain between the hills and Route 15 afforded cover from observation. Once we had disappeared into it without attracting enemy attention, the Viet Cong would not know where we were until we emerged right in front of their positions. The main problem was how to disappear into this jungle without the Viet Cong seeing. Two of the companies, B and C, could move directly from their positions along Route 15 to their areas of search, but A and D Companies had to come up from the southern sector of the road so that they could move by reasonably short routes to Nui Thi Vai, and so that their paths would not intersect the routes of the other companies for this could have caused an accidental clash between our own forces.

D Company was moved from its position to an assembly area south of Phu My in small groups who travelled in closed down APCs, mounting and dismounting under cover. The movement was spread out over the whole of the last day of the convoys. The APC movement was quite normal for armoured patrols had been running constantly along the road ever since we had begun securing it. A Company and Battalion Headquarters were moved at dusk in closed APCs to an assembly area midway between B and C Companies so that both these sub-units could advance straight to the east to strike Nui Thi Vai near the foot of the track which led up

10. RETURN TO NUI THI VAI

to the pagoda. The tents and installations of the Battalion Headquarters site on the road were left erected and some of the Sixth Battalion men moved into them so that the area was not deserted. The gun position was completely unchanged and the Sixth Battalion company was introduced carefully into the area amongst the daily resupply convoys.

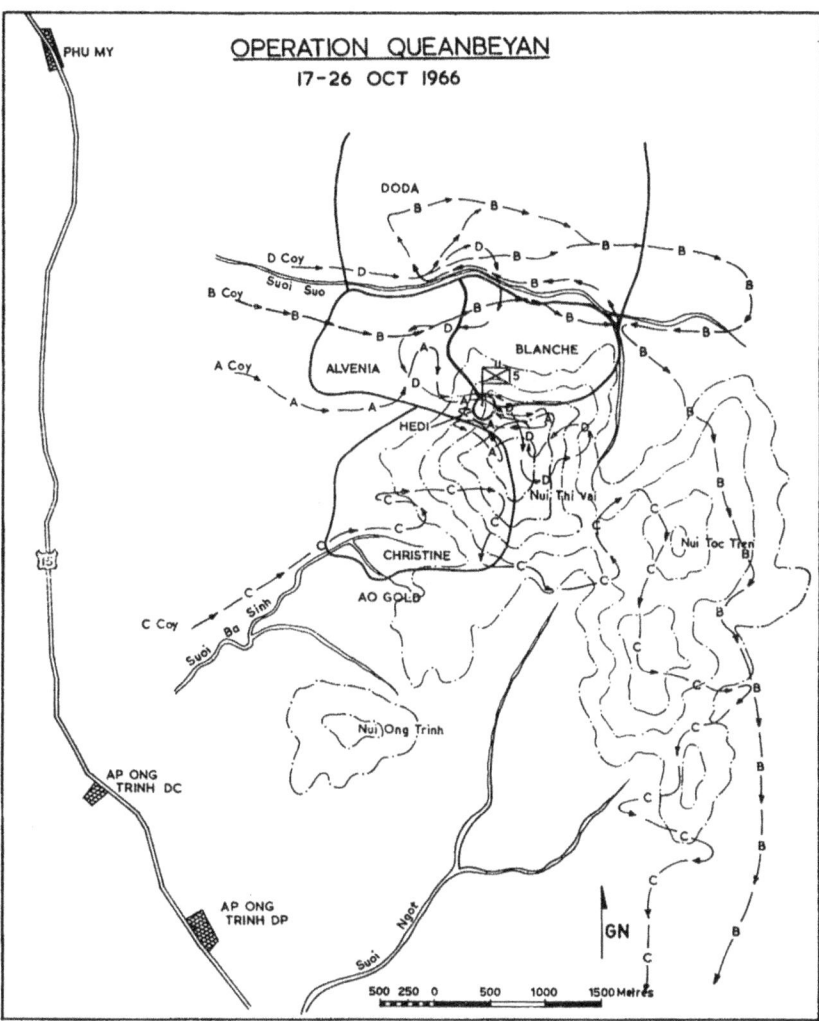

Fig. 16. The company movements to dislodge the Viet Cong encountered on Operation Canberra from Nui Thi Vai, Operation Queanbeyan, 17–26 October 1966.

Each of the companies was to cross Route 15 and the open ground to the east of the road in the early hours of the following morning, October 17th, so that they would be at least a mile into the jungle by first light.

These moves were completed smoothly. Battalion Headquarters had harboured a few hundred yards away from a Buddhist shrine beside which stood a white marble Buddha nearly twenty feet tall between two lotus covered pools. We moved out into the darkness at 3 am, having silently put on our equipment which had been carefully packed the evening before and left undisturbed save for the use of our mosquito nets which were an essential precaution and had to be used every time we slept.

Our progress through the jungle once we had crossed Route 15 was accompanied by the booming of gongs and the ringing of a deep noted bell. These sounds wafted through to us clearly and lent a totally unreal atmosphere to our slopping progress through the half mile of water which lay alongside the road. We had not been close enough to the shrine to have been seen by the monks so we presumed that these sounds were as innocent as they purported to be. Captain Ledan, who commanded the Battalion Headquarters party while it was on the move, led us onto a wide sandy track running through trees which protected us from view. We were glad to have a couple of hours of rest in another harbour area some way along this track.

At dawn we moved off into taller trees which arched over the straight sandy track to allow only tiny patches of sunlight to strike the ground. The track was heading in the direction we wished to follow so we kept to it, moving rapidly. At an intersection with a similar trail which crossed the one we were following at right angles, we were puzzled to find a sign, written in English, warning that danger lay ahead. My first reaction on seeing the sign was to pinch myself. To encounter a well made, printed sign in English in the middle of a Vietnamese jungle was not something we had expected that morning. The sign was not booby trapped and it had been made at least six months previously. There was no Vietnamese translation to accompany the English so it must have been intended either for an American force or for ourselves. Its purpose was hard to fathom for all it did was to make one aware that Viet Cong were active in the area and, shortly afterwards, A Company who were leading the advance found a well constructed Viet Cong camp, equipped with trenches and cover from artillery, sited with roughly one company on either side of the track. A booby trap was tripped just by this camp, but it exploded without

10. RETURN TO NUI THI VAI

harming anyone and we continued on, realising that this explosion must have made the Viet Cong suspicious although they may have put the noise down to a pig which had run into the trip wire.

After passing through the camp we came to the first of the houses which lay at the foot of the hill. Some of them had been well built of brick and reinforced concrete. Several bore signs of Viet Cong occupation and it was evidently going to take A Company at least a day to search them. A Company then began to spread out to secure the area and have a brief rest while the Battalion Headquarters group, which had to get up to the pagoda twelve hundred feet above before darkness, continued on up the track.

The path began to ascend steeply after leaving the houses. The sandy track became a series of rock steps which were sometimes very rough, but often had been carefully hewn and fitted by hand or set in concrete in difficult parts. We climbed to about two hundred feet and waited for the Anti-Tank Platoon, who were leading Battalion Headquarters, to clear the next stretch of high ground dominating the track. While we stood on the rocks it began to rain in swift heavy drops. It was already past midday but we did not want to pause for lunch before climbing Nui Thi Vai because of the effects of exhaustion on a full stomach. The path ascended extremely steeply and we were looking forward to being at the other end of it.

A huge rock was discovered a little further up the track. It was like a large triangular prism resting on one of its edges, leaning on and supported by some huge trees. It was some fifty feet long and thirty feet high, with a roughly horizontal top of approximately the same dimensions. There was plenty of shelter under one side of the rock so we gathered in out of the rain, sharing the cover with a few sleepy bats which had suspended themselves upside down from the rough stone ceiling.

After some twenty minutes the Anti-Tank Platoon radioed that they were approaching the crest of the north-western spur. Then three shots cracked through the air high above us. The platoon had seen one Viet Cong disappearing behind a rock to the side of the track. The enemy was pursued for a short distance but was not found.

Brian Ledan then asked Colonel Warr if he could push on up the track with the reconnaissance group of Battalion Headquarters so that he could get the headquarters laid out on the ground at the pagoda before the main body arrived. Colonel Warr assented, adding a warning about the enemy sighted further up the track. Despite his awareness of the possible dangers lying in wait for his small party, Brian made an optimistic reply and bounded off up the rocks holding his Owen gun in his right hand at full arm's length to balance his rapid movement.

Ten minutes after Brian had departed the remainder of Battalion Headquarters moved off up the track. We were strung out over one hundred yards of the steep slope. This meant that there was a long interval between the different individuals making up the headquarters, and therefore all comunications between the groups which comprised the headquarters had to be by radio, with the double disadvantage of one-way traffic at any one time and the broadcasting of our thoughts to anyone listening in on our frequency. For a headquarters composed of several groups which were required to command and co-ordinate the numerous diverse activities of several hundred men, from tactical deployment to ammunition resupply, direction of air strikes and the helicopter evacuation of casualties, we were not in an ideal situation. However we had become accustomed to this sort of inconvenience by dint of experience and Max Carroll had even become cynical enough to hold that fate decreed enemy contacts when Battalion Headquarters were on the move, it was raining and we were hanging onto a rocky precipice by our fingernails. His cynicism seemed fully justified by events on this afternoon of October 17th.

Shortly after setting off we heard a few shots crackling around the rocks above us. They immediately aroused our apprehension because they were clearly not from one of our own weapons. A strong volley of Australian fire replied. A few minutes later, Brian Ledan's radio operator reported that the reconnaissance party was under fire. Brian had been hit and was pinned down by the Viet Cong behind a rock so he could not get to the radio to give the details of the enemy's location and number. The Viet Cong had evidently recognised Brian as the commander of the group and had fired at him first. Despite the fact that he had been wounded, Brian had been extremely lucky. The sniper's bullet had hit his Owen gun on the safety slide, missing his body by a fraction of an inch. The bullet had smashed the safety slide and jammed the gun, preventing Brian from returning the fire. It had ricocheted from the Owen gun and had passed into his chest on the right side making a deep gash which took months to heal, but which caused no serious injury.

10. RETURN TO NUI THI VAI

Further firing at our reconnaissance party continued. RSM Foale and CSM Hughson were both fired at when they attempted to move despite efforts to neutralise the enemy by directing a machine gun at the general area from which the fire was coming. However, the attack came from many points scattered about in the rocks which covered the slope to the right hand side of the track and all of the enemy were out of sight in caves or in hides built amongst the rocks so that they commanded the only access route to the top of the ridge. Either the Anti-Tank Platoon had crept unnoticed past the Viet Cong except for the last man or they had thought that only a small patrol was on the hillside and hence they could ignore it and remain in their positions.

By this time the Anti-Tank Platoon had reached the top of the spur. They cleared the immediate area of the pagoda, checking particularly for booby traps, and then saw that the slope which ran up to the summit of Nui Thi Vai was free of Viet Cong. They caught a glimpse of several Viet Cong in the central part of this slope, but the Viet Cong withdrew swiftly. However, it was very advantageous for the whole of the Battalion Headquarters group that the Anti-Tank Platoon had reached the top of the spur for they could manoeuvre from the high ground to make an attack on the Viet Cong who were holding up the reconnaissance party. Without the Anti-Tank Platoon in this position, the Viet Cong could have held up our advance for a long time because their positions covered all the approaches to them from the lower slopes of the hill.

The area in which the encounter had taken place was an abrupt slope strewn with boulders up to fifteen feet high. Thick bush and large trees grew amongst the rocks, limiting vision to about ten yards in many places. The narrowness of the track permitted only one man at a time to advance. Although there were boulders at frequent intervals behind which one could shelter, most of them were isolated so that once in their shelter it was impossible to move without exposing oneself to fire again. The area which the Viet Cong had selected for their position was amongst a huge rock slide —a pile of boulders extending for most of the way down the hillside, covering it to a depth of over fifty feet. Within this rock slide the Viet Cong had many shelters and tunnels so that they could move from one fire position to another without exposing themselves to view. They exploited this position with skill and it was not until we had captured their equipment that we knew whether we had faced a dozen or fifty men. The position of those who were trapped by the Viet Cong fire was rather terrifying because of their impotence to fight their way out of the area and, while they were safe from the fire which came from the right hand side of the track, they did not know if anyone was creeping up on their left side to fire on their unprotected flank.

The Anti-Tank Platoon commander, Second Lieutenant Mick Deak, was ordered by Colonel Warr to move down onto the enemy position and to flush them out. The platoon was rather weary as it had just climbed over 1,300 feet, heavily laden, so Deak ordered his men to take their packs off and leave them at the top of the spur in a central dump. Deak's problem was to get his platoon across a sharp gully which ran between the path on which the reconnaissance group were located and the beginning of the rock slide where the Viet Cong were. Most of this gully could be swept by fire from the rock slide.

Deak ordered his Second Section under Corporal Womal to cross the gully while the First and Third Sections covered their movement by firing onto the Viet Cong positions from further up the slope. Womal's section advanced widely dispersed into the central part of the gully, dodging from rock to rock, without receiving any Viet Cong fire. But as they were about to climb out through the rocks on the far side, a shot rang out and Corporal Womal fell, yelling that he had been hit. A bullet had passed through his neck. He had fallen onto the top of a large flat rock and continued despite his severe wound to control the fire and movement of his section. He was out of the sight of the remainder of his platoon and it took a short while for Deak to establish Womal's location in order to commence to extract him from the danger zone and attend to his wound. Womal continued to give directions to his platoon commander and also directed the fire of his machine gun group to cover the movement of the platoon down towards where he lay.

The Anti-Tank Platoon had taken the pressure off the reconnaissance group and Brian Ledan was able to reach the radio. We were tremendously relieved to hear him speak and to hear his description of the situation, for we had known very little of the exact disposition of the Viet Cong and how Deak's platoon was progressing. Tony White had dashed off up the track to give attention to Brian as soon as he had been hit and by this time he had almost reached him. The wound was quickly dressed and Brian began to move back down to the main body of the headquarters for he required immediate evacuation to hospital. In the meantime, directly after the contact, Max Carroll had organised the Dust Off helicopter to come forward to the gun area on Route 15, three miles away.

10. RETURN TO NUI THI VAI

The officers of the Fifth Battalion in January 1967.

From left: *rear* — 2/Lt. L. O'Dea, 2/Lt. M. Roe, Lt. D. Rowe, Capt. R. Milligan, Capt. W. Molloy, Capt. J. Taske (on exchange with Captain A. White), 2/Lt. T. Sheehan, Capt. R. Bade, Capt. R. O'Neill, Lt. R. Wainwright, 2/Lt. R. Gunning, 2/Lt. D. Lovell, 2/Lt. H. Neesham, 2/Lt. E. Pott; *standing* — Capt. R. Shambrook, 2/Lt. J. Carruthers, 2/Lt. M. Deak, Padre J. Williams, Mr J. Bentley (Salvation Army), Capt. R. Supple, Lt. G. Negus, 2/Lt. J. McAloney, Capt. K. Mallinson, Lt. R. Thompson, Capt. B. Ledan, 2/Lt. D. Rainer, Capt. R. Boxall; *seated* — Maj. P. Cole, Maj. J. Miller, Maj. A. Carroll, Maj. I. Hodgkinson, Lt. Col. J. Warr, Capt. P. Isaacs, Maj. B. McQualter, Maj. P. Greenhalgh, Maj. R. Hamlyn.

Four members of the Intelligence Section by the model of An Nhut which they prepared in early February 1967 before Operation Beaumaris (see Chapter 14). From left: Pte. Colin Ross, Pte. Noel Clare, L/Cpl. Colin Bruce, Cpl. Bob Williams.

Second Lieutenant Bob Askew, a helicopter pilot of 161 Recce Flight, who performed outstanding feats of flying in support of our operations.

Major Maizey—a historic photograph of the second-in-command.

The most pressing problem at Battalion Headquarters was to find a landing zone for the aircraft. The nearest clearing was at the foot of Nui Thi Vai, several hundred yards away over ground which would have made stretcher bearing painfully slow. At that point the top surface of the large rock which we had just left suggested itself. It was roughly horizontal, it was easy to climb onto from the uphill side and its breadth was sufficient to allow a small Sioux helicopter to sit near the centre without its rotor blades striking any trees. The chief complication was to find a line of approach for the helicopter. The machine had to come in and depart on an angle gentle enough for it to acquire sufficient forward velocity to keep lifting once it had passed over the edge of the rock. The surface of the rock was important in enabling the helicopter to lift off because the helicopter needed the support derived from the upward thrust of the direct draught of air sent downwards onto the rock by the spinning rotor blades. This support, called ground effect, was important until the helicopter had reached a speed through the air of twenty knots, when it could derive all the vertical lift needed from its forward motion. Once it had flown out across the edge of the rock, the helicopter would have lost most of its ground effect and a great deal of skill would be demanded of the pilot to keep the machine flying. Fortunately there was an appreciable air current flowing up the hillside which had the same effect as if the helicopter had been flying horizontally through still air at the speed of the air current, so hovering was made easier. But despite this current, the angle of ascent possible for the helicopter was still very gentle.

There were tall trees all around the edge of the rock. The only feasible line of approach was from the western or downhill side because of the steepness of the hill. The Assault Pioneer Platoon scrambled around to the western side of the rock and chopped down the obstructing trees. Now it was up to the skill of the pilot. It was still an extremely difficult landing zone to use for there was only one line of approach and this was just wide enough to take the main rotor blades of the aircraft, permitting the tail rotor only a few degrees of swing from side to side. To get out again, the pilot would have to fly backwards off the edge of the rock, climbing as he went until he had achieved enough height to turn the tail of the aircraft around to the east so that he could fly forwards over the falling slope of Nui Thi Vai, picking up speed as he went. It was a very severe test and there was no way of foretelling its outcome.

The Sioux which was equipped with stretcher frames on the outside could then fly the casualty out to the big clearing below us and transfer him to the Dust Off aircraft, a larger Iroquois, which could provide immediate medical attention while it was flying the wounded man back to Vung Tau.

The Sioux aircraft which was directly supporting our operations came overhead within minutes of the trees falling and began to attempt the landing. Lieutenant Bob Askew, the pilot, made a few preliminary passes over the rock to estimate the difficulties of the approach. It was an acid test of his judgement because once he was committed to the landing it was not possible to pull out at the last moment without grave risk of crashing. However, like all of the pilots of the 161st Reconnaissance Flight who had flown so much for us since we had been in Vietnam, often up to eleven hours a day, we knew that Askew's judgement was to be relied upon.

Captain Bob Supple guided the aircraft in. An additional danger which the pilot had to face was the risk of being shot down by an enemy sniper from the group further up the slope. While on its final approach, the aircraft was virtually a sitting duck and the pilot had no protection apart from a flak jacket. The surface of the rock was saucer shaped with a high lip on the eastern side, the side from which we could climb up onto it. The rotor blades cleared this lip by about two feet so no one could approach the aircraft while its blades were still spinning, and Bob Supple had to bring the helicopter right in alongside him to avoid decapitation.

A few minutes later, Brian Ledan came walking down the track. He was wearing only trousers and boots and looked quite unruffled despite the large blood soaked shell dressing tied across his right chest. We chatted on top of the rock after Brian had climbed into the aircraft and Askew began the start up procedure. The signals course at which I had first worked with Brian in 1961 seemed strangely distant. It looked as if he was going to be all right though he must have been in considerable pain. We kept our fingers crossed that he was not bleeding internally. The helicopter lifted a few inches off the rock and began to reverse outwards, taking great care not to back the tail rotor into one of the trees which were close behind. This feat was delicately accomplished, the pilot swung the machine clockwise to the west and sped off down to the clearing and the waiting Dust Off aircraft.

10. RETURN TO NUI THI VAI

Some minutes after Brian Ledan's departure came notification by radio of Corporal Womal's wound. The Sioux was recalled to take Womal out and the landing procedure was repeated. However the extraction of Womal to a safe area was presenting some problems to his platoon on the spur above. The snipers knew where Womal lay and could shoot anyone moving to his assistance. Although the Anti-Tank Platoon could neutralise the Viet Cong by covering fire for a short time it was doubtful if they could keep the fire up for long enough to extract Womal.

Despite Deak's orders to the contrary, the platoon stretcher bearer, Private Fraser, began to crawl forward to Womal, under fire. He reached Womal and proceeded to dress his wound, placing his own body between Womal and the enemy in order to shield Womal from further fire. The snipers opened up again, missing Fraser by inches. In the meantime, the stretcher party which Lieutenant Deak had organised was moving forward under the direction of Sergeant Calvert and protected by the covering fire of the remainder of the platoon. By this time, the enemy had learned to recognise the voice of Deak as that of the leader. Each time he shouted orders bullets flew over his head from the snipers.

The boulders were imposing severe difficulties on the stretcher party. In places they had to lift the stretcher head-high to get through the rocks and they were exposing themselves continually to fire. Each time they had to expose themselves like this, Sergeant Calvert called down covering fire and they managed to cross the killing ground in both directions without being hit, although the volume of enemy fire made movement extremely slow. However, the extraction was successful and the stretcher party struggled back to the cover of rocks behind the positions occupied by the remainder of the platoon.

Tony White had taken the risk of moving forward to the platoon position and was waiting to dress Womal's wound when the stretcher party arrived. He saw very quickly that Womal had little hope of survival for the bullet had severed several major blood vessels in his neck. A few moments later Womal died and we had lost both a very fine man and an outstanding section commander. The stretcher bearers clambered on down the wet rocks to place Womal's body onto the helicopter. Shrouded by a groundsheet, he was placed onto the aircraft and flown out to Vung Tau, while the impact of his death settled over all those left behind on the hillside. The stretcher bearers laboured back over the rocks with tremendous weariness and dejection.

The next problem was to extract the section which was still trapped in the gully by the Viet Cong fire. It seemed unwise to attempt to dislodge the enemy by further movement of this section because of the difficulties of the ground. Also they had done such a good piece of work in providing prolonged covering fire for the extraction of Womal that they were running low in ammunition. The whole platoon was experiencing a similar shortage, although to a slightly lesser degree. Some way had to be found to neutralise, or preferably, to dislodge the Viet Cong by fire support without endangering the men who were trapped in the gully.

Major Peter Cole, commander of A Company since September, radioed from the bottom of the hill, two hundred feet below, that he could see exactly where the Viet Cong were located on the steep slope six hundred yards from him and he could smother their position with machine gun fire from his current location. Also available were the two gun ships of the American light fire team which was in support of us. It was impossible to use artillery or mortars because our men were too close to the Viet Cong for their own safety, but both A Company and the gun ships were capable of hitting the Viet Cong position without risking casualties to the Anti-Tank Platoon.

All of us on the hillside began to mark our locations with coloured smoke and soon four plumes marked the Anti-Tank Platoon, the two groups of Battalion Headquarters and the Assault Pioneer Platoon. While the gun ships were brought onto station, Colonel Warr gave the order to A Company to open fire.

Soon the air above us was filled with the peculiarly sharp cracks of bullets heading in our direction but passing over us from A Company to the Viet Cong position. In a few minutes the gun ships came overhead and circled slowly over the target area, picking out likely caves to fire into. Soon the double thumps of the firing and the explosion of their rockets reverberated around the hillside. The aircraft expended their rockets and then poured machine gun fire into the position. From their altitude, the gun ships, which were simply elevated gun platforms using mobility as their main protection, were able to fire down into the cave mouths which were unreachable from below. Many of the rockets were fired on trajectories which were almost horizontal. These rockets roared straight in through the cave mouths, blowing up inside.

This combination of strafing was effective in making the Viet Cong withdraw. They retreated to the south, moving quickly through tunnels in the rocks which gave them protection from both observation and fire as they went. After the gun ships had completed their fire missions, the Anti-Tank Platoon edged forward to examine the results. They soon found that the Viet Cong had departed, leaving blood-stained bandages strewn about behind them and taking their casualties with them. The Anti-Tank Platoon discovered a great number of holes and tunnels amongst the rocks which had enabled the Viet Cong to dash from one position to another without exposing themselves to danger. As they proceeded they found that the caves had been extensively booby trapped and it looked like being a very slow operation to clear them. It was still possible that the Viet Cong had withdrawn to lower levels of the cave systems to await the cover of darkness before re-emerging to escape or to attack us.

This action had consumed the whole afternoon and by this time it was 5 pm Battalion Headquarters could not stay where it was, in such an exposed and indefensible position. If we moved back to the foot of Nui Thi Vai we would concede the day's gains in the advance to the enemy and would probably have to repeat the entire procedure the next day. In addition, the Viet Cong would know to set booby traps higher up the track, particularly around our goal, the pagoda at the top of the spur.

Colonel Warr decided to press home our advantage and move on up the mountain, hoping to reach the pagoda before darkness. It was going to be a close thing. Everyone trod that track rather anxiously lest the snipers should reappear. The Anti-Tank Platoon went back to where they had left their packs, hoping that the area around the pagoda had not been booby trapped already by the withdrawing Viet Cong. Soon exhaustion replaced apprehension as we climbed rapidly, but the opening expanse of view over the surrounding jungles was a pleasant distraction as we caught our breath at short halts on the way up.

Darkness was falling as we passed through the stone gateway at the edge of the pagoda garden and bats flitted through the archway and the branches of the trees overhead, or dived under the wide eaves of the pagoda. Just before we reached the gateway, we passed the mysterious cave of the hermit monk of our earlier encounter, Nguyen Van Xe. The growing gloom prevented us from seeing anything within the wide arched mouth.

The pagoda was a large low granite building, rectangular in plan, and with a red-tiled roof. Grey stone swastikas looked down on us from beneath the eaves. The front section of the pagoda, facing the west, was in ruins. It had been shelled by the Vietnamese artillery from Phu My when they discovered that the Viet Cong were based there. At the back of the building we found a large kitchen and several shelters which the Viet Cong had been using recently. At right angles to the main building, another rectangular building ran out to the north from the rear of the former. A courtyard was formed by these two buildings and some outhouses on the northern side. A swiftly flowing stream ran into the south-eastern corner of the courtyard from the hillside to the rear of the pagoda. This stream was confined between beautiful rock-lined banks and ran into a large concrete cistern which fed a piping system supplying water to the houses near the foot of the hill. A stone bridge with a covered walk linked the two buildings. Ornamental trees and shrubs combined with the stone walling of the banks of the stream and the raised stone platforms on which both buildings had been erected to give the courtyard great natural harmony. Some level ground ran out towards the north and west for twenty yards but the hillsides came down sharply to the east and south of the pagoda. Dark green jungle approached the pagoda closely on all sides and the garden in front of the main building had become overgrown.

We were very glad to find that the pagoda and its environs had not been tampered with by the Viet Cong and we settled in rapidly. Battalion Headquarters was set up in the rear of the main building where it could enjoy the unaccustomed luxury of working from a table and stools. The Administrative Section, this time commanded by Captain Ron Shambrook, went into the other main building and the two platoons spread themselves around the outside of the pagoda complex to give complete protection on all sides. We did not dare risk showing a light to any Viet Cong who may have been lurking nearby, so we established ourselves in darkness. Fortunately we heard no more of the Viet Cong that night. Each of the companies had harboured securely in their planned locations. Major Neville Gair, commander of 103 Field Battery, produced a fire plan as usual for every halt that we made so that we were well prepared for an attack by the Viet Cong. Colonel Warr spoke to each of the company commanders by radio to pass on co-ordinating instructions for the following day, and then we were very glad to get what sleep we could between shifts of command post duty or sentry duty on one of the perimeter machine guns which were all manned constantly.

10. RETURN TO NUI THI VAI

On the following day, October 18th, the clearance of the caves had to be commenced, not only for our own safety as we moved around the hill, but also to render them useless to the Viet Cong for as long a period as possible. The caves were protected by numerous booby traps so the Assault Pioneer Platoon, our booby trap specialists, were assigned to the task. One important tool for cave clearing, flamethrowers, had to be flown in from Nui Dat. Once they had arrived, the platoon set off to return down the hill to the caves with two guides from the Anti-Tank Platoon and three sapper captains as observers. The whole party was under the command of Lieutenant John McAloney, commander of the Assault Pioneers.

They approached the caves warily, positioned sentries on the track, above and below the area in which the platoon was about to work, and located a machine gun in a dominant fire position overlooking the area immediately to the front of the caves in which the Viet Cong had been located on the previous afternoon. McAloney told the guides to lead him to the cave where the booby traps had been found. Taking a radio operator and a sentry with them, the small group set off, clambering over and around the great boulders which had to be negotiated for the one hundred yards between the track and the furthest caves.

The cave in question was quickly located, and sentries were posted to either flank and uphill and downhill of the mouth. McAloney then entered the cave and began to search for booby traps. The first trap did not take long to find for it was just inside the entrance, below a large rock. The trigger mechanism had attracted John's attention. He lowered himself to inspect the workings of the trap so that he could disconnect it. Just at that moment a shot cracked across the rocks, narrowly missing the sentry below the cave mouth, Private D'Antoine. John climbed back out of the cave, told D'Antoine to crouch down and take cover and to indicate the area from which the shot had come. He ordered the machine gun and one section to move down the slope and locate the sniper. Another shot was fired, D'Antoine moaned and lay silent. John was already on his way across to D'Antoine and was able to approach to within twenty feet. D'Antoine did not answer his name when John called to him.

The machine gun group was ordered by John to fire into the area in which the sniper was hidden while he crossed to D'Antoine. He had to halt the fire however, because ricocheting bullets were passing dangerously close to him. Corporal Burge, commanding the fire support section, then fired a single shot at a Viet Cong who had peered out at McAloney from the cave entrance. The head disappeared. Burge was certain that his aim had been true. McAloney then heard a scurrying tumbling noise through a passage in the rocks beneath him. D'Antoine's legs were hanging over the edge of the rock and it was difficult for John to pull him back into shelter. The platoon medic came to John's assistance and despite the appearance of death on D'Antoine's body set to work with the application of mouth to mouth resuscitation and dressed D'Antoine's wound. The bullet had passed through his back and out through his chest. They found a faint heart beat and evacuated D'Antoine immediately on a stretcher which had been hurriedly prepared. During this interval the Dust Off helicopter had been requested and by the time that D'Antoine had been carried the three hundred yards to the nearest landing zone, the helicopter was on its way. Once again rapid evacuation was of no avail, for D'Antoine died during the flight to Vung Tau.

John McAloney returned to the cave and crawled up to the mouth to begin clearing it of any further Viet Cong who may have been inside. This procedure was particularly hazardous because our men had no idea of the numbers and whereabouts of the enemy and they were unable to clear any one cave without exposing themselves to danger from several others. Despite this, Macaloney personally led the clearance of the system into which the sniper had disappeared.

John began the clearance by throwing grenades into the mouth of the cave. No reaction from inside was observed and so a flame thrower was brought forward. Before it was used, John noticed D'Antoine's automatic Armalite rifle lying in front of the cave. He called in covering fire and began to crawl out to retrieve the weapon. The covering fire was of necessity extremely close as it had to penetrate the mouth of the cave in front of which John was crawling, but nevertheless, he felt more comfortable with it than without it—until a bullet ricocheted from the cave mouth and struck him in the right temple, causing a good deal of bleeding but not a serious wound. He grasped the Armalite and crawled back to safety remarking laconically that it seemed a pity to waste it.

John then led the flame throwing party forward towards the mouth of the cave. First they squirted fuel from the high pressure nozzle right into the cave, saturating all exits from the first chamber, all holes, nooks and crannies. Then they made a rapid assault on the mouth of the cave by dashing forward from the cover of the rock where they had been in partial shelter. When they were standing at the centre of the cave mouth they poured fuel right down the main cavity under the cover of small arms fire from the left flank. They ignited the last burst of fuel and drew back as flame engulfed the cavities and passages into which the sniper had fled. The preliminary saturation had been so effective that the sentries higher up the slope could see flame billowing out of several rear exits to the cave system. By the time that the flaming had been completed, darkness had begun to fall and the small group withdrew to the track, regrouped and virtually ran back up the hill.

During the following several days, teams of men from A Company, the Assault Pioneer Platoon, and the First Field Squadron of the Royal Australian Engineers from Nui Dat entered the caves and searched them. A Company had moved to a position half-way up the hillside to the vicinity of the caves from where they covered the north-western side of Nui Thi Vai with patrols. When they entered the caves, the men discovered that the system of tunnels was very complex for it contained several levels. Often the passages from one level to another would be very hard to see. It was pitch dark in many of the caves and passages, so the searchers had no idea of what a cave might contain until they were standing in its entrance with a torch in their hands. The tension of the search was heightened by the danger of booby traps. A great number of these were encountered. Often they were found first by the patrols from A Company who would gingerly enter a new cave or a lower level in the darkness and begin feeling their way delicately for the threads or the moving rocks which could trigger an explosion at a touch. Once the booby traps were located, Sappers or Pioneers were called in to dismantle them. So proficient had the men become that no casualties were suffered during this nerve-racking time.

The caves had been the permanent base for up to a company of Viet Cong who maintained the observation posts on the hill and transported supplies along the track system which passed the foot of Nui Thi Vai. The caves had been well developed. Most had planking beds in them, with small stoves built out of rocks. They had a piped water supply which had been tapped off the conduit which ran down the hill from the pagoda. Water storage and filtration facilities were provided deep under the surface so that the Viet Cong could have stayed underground for long periods without showing themselves. Some of the cave entrances called for amazing agility, for their only access was through chinks in the rocks of just over one foot in diameter. Some caves were too difficult for any but slightly built Vietnamese to enter. Others had been improved by building walls of rock across openings, leaving only loopholes for firing from. As the search went on the complexity of the system revealed itself, with the discovery of the succeeding levels. Each of the caves had several escape holes. One was discovered of particular ingenuity. A counterbalanced rock was poised on the edge of a vertical shaft down which a fugitive could jump. Once at the bottom he could tug a rope which released a beam supporting the rock at the entrance. With this support removed, the rock would tumble over and mask the entrance to the shaft. The fugitive could then escape through a low level passage which led to an exit on the uphill side of the caves.

The area bore many signs of a rapid abandonment. Apart from a foul stench of considerable strength, the searchers discovered large amounts of personal equipment and papers. It appeared as if the Viet Cong had been forced to flee with their weapons only. Their bedding, clothing and packs were still by their beds and cooked food was ready for eating in several of the caves. The greatest discovery of the operation was the radio station of the deputy commander of 274 Regiment, Nguyen Nam Hung, together with some vital documents, including his diary. The radio was found carefully hidden on the third level of the caves on October 21st by A Company. It was a recent model Chinese Communist transmitter and receiver—one of the few which have ever been captured from the Viet Cong. For a piece of equipment such as this to have been abandoned indicates that the Viet Cong were in desperate straits before they fled, and we must have just missed capturing Hung and his party.

Hung's diary was very informative for he had begun each day's entry with his current location, so that we were able to follow his movements for the whole of the first ten months of 1966. A great number of valuable deductions were derived from this study which occupied a great part of my time for the following three months. He also left other notes which related to the future activities of 274 Regiment so that we were able to formulate a detailed picture of what we would have to guard against during the following months.[1]

Amongst the equipment finds it was interesting to see that the Viet Cong were equipped with Armalite rifles and that they had left 125 lbs. of Chinese Communist explosive. Several Chinese Communist Claymore mines were captured whose diameter exceeded that of any others we had

---

1   Hung apparently did not report these losses as the plans were adhered to.

10. RETURN TO NUI THI VAI

previously encountered by twenty per cent. The quantity of equipment which came out of those caves was such that it took eight pages of closely typed foolscap to list everything.

While A Company spent seven days in searching the caves, C Company had been patrolling through the south-western part of Nui Thi Vai where they had found further Viet Cong bases and huts, and a sow with litter, all of whom had been carefully camouflaged. The huts and other installations were blown up and the company moved on over the southern ridge of Nui Thi Vai and onto Nui Toc Tien. Despite intensive patrolling over this hill, nothing more than dense jungle was discovered.

B Company examined a number of buildings which the Viet Cong had been using on the northern side of Nui Thi Vai before moving out into the jungle to take over the ambush role from D Company on tracks further to the east. After a few days of intense alertness to the extent of lying motionless for the greater part of every day, ready to fire with accuracy at a split second's notice, eating silently without heating food and forgoing smoking, B Company began a sweep around to the north of Nui Toc Tien, to emerge on October 26th on the main track which ran to the north in the gap between Nui Toc Tien and the Dinh hills. This sweep discovered a small group of Viet Cong and more was learned of their movement patterns in the area.

After three days of fruitless ambushing, D Company was ordered to ascend to the summit of Nui Thi Vai to search the upper slopes and the eastern side of the hill. On October 21st Lieutenant Dennis Rainer's platoon crept down into the pass between Nui Thi Vai and Nui Toc Tien. Some alert observation by Lieutenant Barry Campbell, the forward observation officer from 103 Field Battery who was accompanying this patrol in case it ran into trouble and needed artillery support, discovered some huts on the western slope of the pass. These huts had been very carefully camouflaged and were in extremely thick bush. Further investigation showed not only that they were surrounded by a belt of mines and booby traps but also that they were occupied by a group of Viet Cong who were inside one of the huts. During a complete reconnaissance around the huts, the entrance path was found. By the path was a notice written in Vietnamese, displaying a scarlet skull and cross bones. The notice warned that the reader was passing through a minefield and requested that he ring the bell which was close by. Rainer's men did not stop to observe this formality and crept up into the immediate vicinity of the huts. After stealthy movement and careful deliberation, Rainer launched his platoon into a surprise attack. Out of the eleven Viet Cong in the camp, ten were killed and one escaped for the loss of no casualties to our men.

In the camp the platoon found all the weapons of the former occupants, together with their ammunition and equipment. The survivor fled through the jungle for several days and gave himself up at the Duc Thanh district compound. He had been convinced that the day of the Viet Cong had passed in Phuoc Tuy since he had been finally tracked down in a hiding place deep in the jungle, even though his unit, the Chau Duc District Company, had not been engaging in offensive operations for some months. He verified that Rainer's attack had completely wiped out that particular post of the company.

As the days went by it became apparent that we were reaching the end of what was to be found on Nui Thi Vai and we prepared for departure on October 26th. However, we were certain that the Viet Cong would send replacement garrisons back to the hills once we had left, so we did what we could to deny the use of the area to the Viet Cong for some months. By spreading tear gas crystals in the caves and tunnels it was possible to create fumes which would linger for up to six months and so the last days on the hillside were spent in treating the caves. We were able to blow up all of the surface installations and huts but nothing could have demolished that great mass of fallen rock which contained the caves.

This operation had proved unexpectedly successful in view of the captured radio and diary and it had also been extremely difficult. These two factors combined to give the battalion a great feeling of mutual confidence amongst its members. Although it had not been as significant in terms of the long-term aim of our presence in Phuoc Tuy as the cordon of Binh Ba, it had the strongest impact on the spirit of the battalion and Nui Thi Vai became one of the most vital sections of the battalion's tradition. For bravery and leadership in this operation, Military Crosses were awarded to Lieutenants Deak, Macaloney and Rainer, the Military Medal was won by Private Fraser, and Corporal Womal was posthumously mentioned in despatches.

11

The Western Approaches

While we were operating along Route 15 in October, we were able to form a detailed picture of Viet Cong activities along the western coast of Phuoc Tuy. This area was important for two types of Viet Cong operations. First a significant quantity of traffic from the Mekong Delta came into Phuoc Tuy via the Rung Sat. The Viet Cong in Phuoc Tuy needed both supplies and men and these were available from the heavily populated rice-producing areas within the Fourth Corps area. They could be loaded onto small sampans which could pass swiftly and inconspicuously through the maze of narrow channels which led to the Phuoc Tuy coast. Second, the Chau Duc District Company was active along the western coast and on Long Son island to the south. This company had been recruited from the island and from several of the villages along Route 15 and so one of its main functions was to exert as much control over these areas as possible. Another important function was to assist with the transfer of supplies which had been brought from the Mekong Delta from the landing points to the bases inland close to the hills. Now that we had struck at some of these bases, it seemed opportune to attack these landing points and harass the activities of the Chau Duc District Company.

Long Son island was situated near the junction of several sea channels, some which led into the Rung Sat to the west and two channels which led into the Phuoc Tuy coast. Thus the island was a natural staging post and a small landing jetty had been built at the north-western tip, Ben Da. Most of the population of the island lived on the eastern shore, in a well constructed village which nestled at the foot of Nui Nua, an abrupt, but smooth-sided grassy hill rising to six hundred feet and dominating the island. Three-quarters of the island lay to the west of Nui Nua and the

Viet Cong had converted this area into a training and rest area controlled by the platoon of the Chau Duc District Company which was stationed on the island. The area between Nui Nua and Ben Da was a plain, two miles long by one mile wide, broken by a long ridge which ran north-south a little to the west of the half-way point between the western coast and Nui Nua. The ridge ascended to two hundred and fifty feet and was covered by low scrub. Officially no people lived to the west of Nui Nua for the Government had ordered all the inhabitants to live in the main village which could be kept under some form of control by the local Popular Forces platoon. However, some inhabitants of the island had not complied and had remained in the area used by the Viet Cong. This defeated the Government programme for making the western end of Long Son island into an area in which any persons sighted from the air could be engaged by artillery or strafing, on the grounds of their being in a prohibited area and hence aiding the Viet Cong, if not actually Viet Cong themselves.

The eastern settlement, Long Son village, housed several hundred people in white plastered brick houses which lined narrow sandy streets. Most of the houses were set in yards and amongst trees which gave the village an appearance of softness and coolness. In the centre of the village was the largest pagoda in Phuoc Tuy. Much of the pagoda had been built in the mid-nineteenth century, before the arrival of the French in the south. Steep red-tiled roofs descended to curling eaves which swept upwards in semicircular curves. Bright blue porcelain dragons breathed fire and arched their backs from the crests of the roofs. Small chapels rose above each other in low towers linked to the main building by high gangways. The interior of the pagoda and the market bore witness in their construction to the former importance of the island as a holy place and to the wealth which had thereby flowed into the island. The main part of the pagoda contained several small chapels, each with altars of teak, inlaid with mother of pearl, and decorated with candle holders and vases of hand worked silver. Huge tables with tops of polished teak planks two inches thick stood by the walls beneath paintings of local scenes. The market was a vast structure, approximately one hundred feet by forty, with a high, steeply pitched roof supported on columns of teak. The red brick floor blended well with the weathered teak of the columns and the teak beams of the roof. These two buildings were to us the most impressive in the entire province.

11. THE WESTERN APPROACHES

Running forward to the east from the village was a long narrow spit over a mile long. A deep drainage canal with high banks ran for a few hundred yards along the northern side of this spit, linking the village to a sickle-shaped arm of the sea which curved on through half a mile of mangroves. Fishing boats and sampans were moored in the canal, which formed the main harbour of the village. At the mouth of the canal a special landing point served the Government outpost which stood on the spit at the head of the channel to the open sea. The outpost was a small quadrangle of fortifications, surmounted by a tower and distinguished by a flagpole flying the gold and red flag of the South Vietnamese Republic. The quadrangle was surrounded by several fences of barbed wire and by minefields set amongst flooded ground from which occasional mud banks protruded. Thirty village men defended the fort and endeavoured to exert the authority of the Government over the island.

The Viet Cong had not been seriously threatened by this smaller force and had established a machine gun post and observation point on the summit of Nui Nua. From this point they watched over the activities of the village and the Government platoon. If these men attempted to patrol around the northern or southern sides of the hill, they were fired on from the summit. Provided that they kept to within close proximity to the village, they were not molested. In the face of superior forces, the Government platoon could do little else but comply with this policy of divided control of the island.

We began to consider the possibilities of an operation on Long Son island in August, but the priorities of our other commitments had compelled postponement of the idea until November. However, the months between August and November were very useful for conducting several aerial reconnaissances of the island, without arousing direct suspicions of our intentions because the reconnaissances could be conducted from the heavily used air corridor from Vung Tau to Saigon. After a few flights over the island, it was possible to select sites for the Battalion Headquarters, and search areas for the companies and helicopter landing zones. Close liaison with the Vietnamese naval patrols which worked around the island in small boats in the hours of darkness enabled us to know the degree of use which the Viet Cong were making of the island and the points at which their sampans usually called.

In order to catch the Viet Cong on the island before they had time to disappear into the surrounding mangroves, the whole battalion had to be landed on the island within a very short space of time and at widely separated points, so that the companies could spread out and cover the whole of the Viet Cong area. At the same time, a seal had to be placed between the village and the remainder of the island so that the Viet Cong could not disappear into the village. The only way to get troops onto the island was by air for a sea approach would have been slowed down by the mangroves around the island. However we could obtain the services of only one American helicopter company of ten aircraft which could lift seventy men in one load. To have lifted the battalion direct from Nui Dat to the island would have taken twenty-five minutes for each seventy men, thus spreading the concentration of the battalion over several hours, allowing for refuelling pauses. This would have robbed the operation of any surprise and the Viet Cong would have been given sufficient time to flee from the force which had made the first landing and so escape. Alternatively, it was possible that the first men onto the island could encounter superior Viet Cong forces, if they happened to arrive at a time when a Viet Cong battalion was resting there. Thus the delays in reinforcing them from Nui Dat were also unacceptable.

Consequently the battalion had to be assembled at some point on the mainland as close as possible to the island, from which it could be flown in, taking less than ten minutes for each round trip of the helicopters. The next problem was how to concentrate the battalion on the mainland opposite the island without making it perfectly obvious to the Viet Cong that the island was our goal, long before we had begun to land on it. This difficulty could be overcome by commencing the operation with a cordon of a village on Route 15 which was conveniently situated with respect to the island. The battalion could concentrate after the cordon, and instead of flying back to Nui Dat or to some other part, descend on the island.

One of the major Viet Cong tracks into the interior of Phuoc Tuy was the one which crossed the low ground between the Dinh hills and Nui Toc Tien. This track began at Phuoc Hoa, a village of five hundred people, on Route 15, and very close to Long Son island. Phuoc Hoa possessed one of the best harbours on the western coast and it was known that the village played an important part in the Viet Cong supply system. We had specific information concerning the identities of several of the Viet Cong who lived in Phuoc Hoa and so a cordon of that village seemed to be a worthwhile project.

11. THE WESTERN APPROACHES

In September we received indications that the Viet Cong were expecting us to go to the island in the near future. Some bar girls in Vung Tau had been asking our men when we were going to operate against the Viet Cong on the island. It was known that some of these bar girls were in the pay of the Viet Cong so the girls represented a ready made earpiece through which we could feed misleading information to the Viet Cong. Because the Viet Cong had some idea that the island was possibly one of our goals it was important to attempt to give them the notion that although we might be operating near Route 15 in the near future, these operations would not involve the island. Four seasoned members of the battalion were chosen to go to Vung Tau and to spread a cover plan by discussing the plan discreetly yet somewhat unguardedly amongst themselves in circumstances where barmen or waitresses might overhear. The men went in pairs at different times and moved at random through several bars which were thought to be suitable for our purpose. According to the cover plan the battalion was going out along Route 15 and from there was striking north into the western part of the Dinh hills.

Colonel Warr's plan for cordoning Phuoc Hoa was to move the battalion out to Long Cat on Route 15, one mile south of Phuoc Hoa, then to walk inland into the cover of scrub where a harbour area would be formed. Once night had fallen, the battalion would then move in an arc around to the west to meet the cart track which ran back into Phuoc Hoa from the gap between Nui Toc Tien and the Dinh hills. This cart track was an excellent navigational aid and the battalion could then move onto and surround Phuoc Hoa in the cover of darkness. Unfortunately the sea front of the village could not be covered by a land cordon, but the assistance of the Third Special Air Service Squadron in supplying men in assault boats made a sea cordon possible. After the cordon, the battalion was to move off towards the Dinh hills, stopping for the night at the edge of a large clearing from which we could fly to the island at dawn on the following morning.

The cordon of Phuoc Hoa, Operation Yass, was scheduled for the night of November 6th–7th, and the landing on Long Son island, Operation Hayman, was to be on the morning of November 8th. By fortunate coincidence, the Chief of Long Le district, Captain Kim, in whose district the island lay, was making a visit to the Popular Forces platoon on November 4th in order to pay them for the month. This visit offered an excellent opportunity for finding out at first hand about recent Viet Cong activities and strength on the island. Kim had invited me to go with him but I was troubled by the possibility of my presence on Long Son arousing the suspicions of the Viet Cong so soon before an operation, for they could easily disappear to the mainland for a week if they thought that my visit presaged the anticipated Australian landing on the island.

Fortunately a cover plan was available. On November 4th we were to receive a visit from Sir Wilfrid Kent Hughes and as one of my functions was to brief and escort visitors to the battalion I was detailed to show Sir Wilfrid around the area of Nui Dat and whatever Government-controlled parts of the province he wished to see. If I were to visit Long Son as escort to Sir Wilfrid and we were to ask a few casual questions while we were on the island, there seemed a good chance that not even the local garrison nor Captain Kim would connect the visit with a possible operation in the near future. I put the problem to Sir Wilfrid and he agreed to help us, so we set sail with Captain Kim and a platoon of his troops from a naval station on the Vung Tau peninsula on the afternoon of November 4th.

We travelled in two medium sized landing craft of the Vietnamese navy which churned along through the broad channels between the mangroves at twelve knots. Each craft was armed with several machine guns mounted on the gunwales behind armour plate shields. The trip was considered to be perfectly safe, but no chances were taken lest an ambush had been laid along one of the narrower channels which were used to avoid the detours made by the wide meanders of the broad reaches. After nearly two hours on the water we wound our way into the narrow curving arm which led up to the island landing point by the fort.

The local soldiers were a curious sight for their religion required them to wear their hair long and fastened in a bun behind their heads. This long hair and the smoothness of their skins confused my determination of their sex for a few moments. Instead of green uniforms they wore long black robes, rather like cassocks. They were in good spirits for not only was it pay day, but the Viet Cong had only some twenty men on the island at that time and so they felt reasonably secure. The Viet Cong had sent a few bursts of machine gun fire into the fort from the top of Nui Nua a few days previously as a type of psychological warfare, but they had hit no one. No main force battalion had used the island for a rest centre since our arrival at Nui Dat and so it was unlikely that our landing would meet with any substantial opposition.

We had to wait for an hour while the American medical team which had accompanied Captain Kim attended to the villagers. The monks at the pagoda were keen to show us around when they learned that an Australian VIP was visiting, so we passed the time in going from chapel to chapel, ascending and descending dark teak staircases, and walking apprehensively along the high gangways which spanned the chasms of tiles between the upper chapels. Captain Kim departed late in the afternoon, at a time which afforded us some splendid views of the setting sun behind the island and of crimson reflections in the long reaches of dark water which settled quickly to a calm after our passage.

On the afternoon before the cordon, while travelling along Route 15, Major Miller noticed a portable wire barrier, festooned with grenades, standing by the main gate of Phuoc Hoa. If the APCs hit this barrier as they drove into Phuoc Hoa at dawn on the following morning some casualties might have been caused. However, it was possible that the barrier was not placed across the gateway at night and so Major Miller paid a visit to the village chief just at dusk on the pretext of announcing a visit by an Australian medical team on the following day. He saw that the gate was not blocked by the barrier and so the APCs were able to enter the village the next morning without any hindrance.

The movement into the cordon position at Phuoc Hoa took place smoothly. There were no attempts to break out of the cordon and when A Company entered the village at dawn after our interpreters had broadcast instructions, the collection of the villagers took only a few hours. During A Company's search of the village, a few young men tried to make a break for cover into the surrounding paddy fields but they were speedily apprehended by the cordoning companies. The men and women of Viet Cong military age, i.e. from 12 to 45 years, were taken by truck into Ba Ria for questioning by the provincial security teams. The deception plan of moving inland from Long Cat must have been effective for five Viet Cong and eleven suspects were picked out in Ba Ria, together with several deserters and draft dodgers.

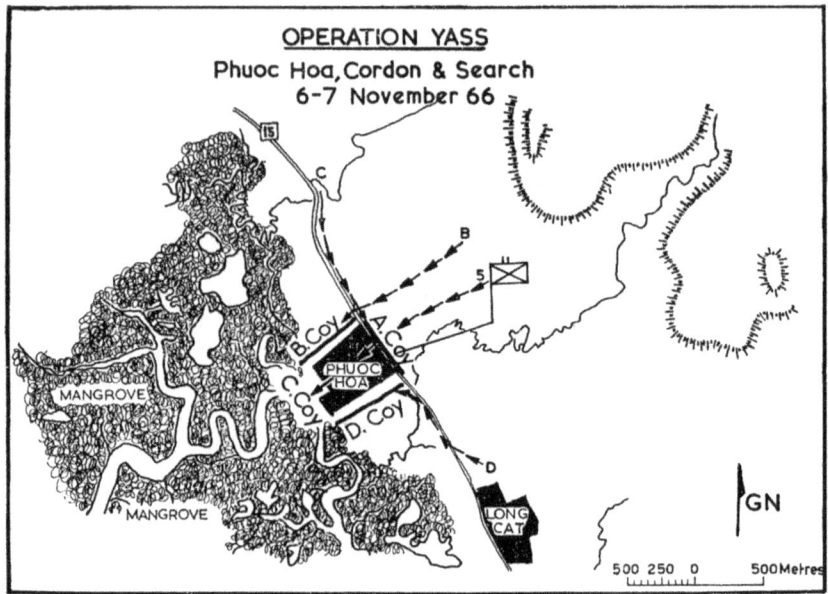

Fig. 17. The cordoning of Phuoc Hoa on the night 6–7 November 1966, Operation Yass.

In the late afternoon, the battalion moved off by companies to form a harbour area one mile to the west of Phuoc Hoa. We had not left much time for this move and we ran into difficulties in finding the correct landing zone for there were several very similar areas close to each other. The situation was not helped when some of the APCs who were accompanying us to assist with the defence of the harbour area became bogged in thick black greasy mud. The vehicles had broken through the dry crust of several inches covering a vast plain of mud caused by the water flowing off the Dinh hills which had not had time to drain away.

We made a hurried camp for the night and stood to at dusk by shell scrapes sufficient to give minimal protection in the event of a mortar bombardment or an attack from the hills which overlooked us. After half an hour of darkness, we stood down and the normal night routine of sentries on all the machine guns took over our protection until the battalion commenced the morning stand-to, half an hour before first light. We had to be ready to move at first light for the helicopters had been arranged to lift the battalion onto the island before the inhabitants had time to move out of their houses and see us coming.

11. THE WESTERN APPROACHES

The landing was preceded by a short artillery bombardment of the areas which threatened the landing zones. B, C, and D Companies were to land on the crest of the southern ridge of Nui Nua and then spread out so that C Company covered the south central part of the island, B Company covered the north central part and D Company went into the village and searched it. A Company was to land near the north-western tip of the island to prevent any Viet Cong who were near Ben Da from escaping to the mainland. Battalion Headquarters was to land on the eastern side of the ridge across the western part of the island. The size of the operation had grown since the original conception for C Company of the Sixth Battalion landed with us, and the Special Air Service Squadron surrounded the island in small assault boats to cut off any escape by sea for the Viet Cong and to search the mangroves for hiding places. Because of these additional units which were not part of the Fifth Battalion, Brigadier Jackson decided that this would be a good opportunity to deploy the Task Force Headquarters in a forward role for the first time. After the Battalion Headquarters had flown in, several large Chinook helicopters lifted in the Task Force Headquarters which occupied an area immediately to the north of the Battalion Headquarters.

The bombardment of the landing zones was planned by Major Gair and carried out by the gunners of 103 Field Battery, during the several minutes before the helicopters were due to land the troops. The helicopter commander had made a reconnaissance of the island from the air with Colonel Warr several days previously and they had agreed on a flight path for the helicopters landing on Nui Nua which would sweep around to the east in a wide curve so that they would not cross the line of fire from the guns at Long Cat when they were firing the preparatory bombardment. It was fortunate that the whole landing and bombardment was being controlled from a command helicopter containing Colonel Warr, Major Gair and myself, for the first flight of helicopters flew straight across the path of the shells which were still being fired. Major Gair immediately stopped the bombardment and no mishaps occurred. Colonel Warr discussed the problem with the commander of the helicopter company who was one of the pilots of our helicopter and further danger was averted.

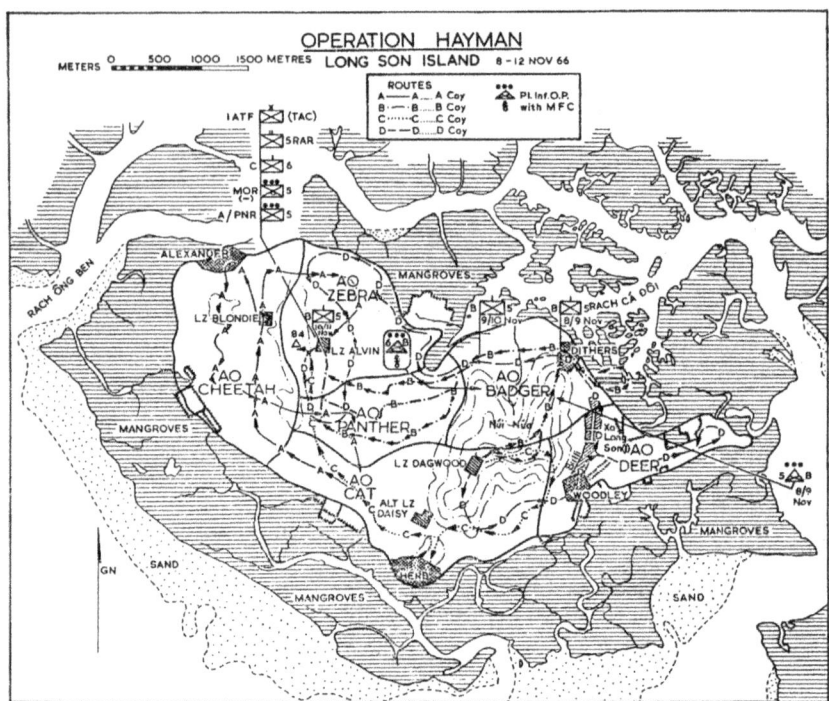

Fig. 18. The clearing of Viet Cong from Long Son island, Operation Hayman, 8–12 November 1966.

As soon as the first troops, most of B Company, landed on the long ridge they came under machine gun fire from the summit of Nui Nua. One of the helicopters had the misfortune to strike its main rotor blades on one of the large rocks which were strewn over the steeply sloping landing zone. The rotor shattered and the turbine burst into flame. No one was seriously injured but the helicopter was a wreck. It was particularly difficult for the Americans to salvage because the main rotor shaft had been completely shattered. When a helicopter had to be recovered after a mishap the normal method of lifting it out was to use a Chinook with an attachment which grasped the main rotor shaft to lift the disabled aircraft. However, they were determined not to leave it behind and after much trouble it was suspended from slings around and through its body and lifted out by one of the larger helicopters.

While D Company was searching the area of the village, the other companies had several minor contacts with Viet Cong. B Company moved forward on the enemy machine gun post on the hilltop, but the Viet Cong made a swift retreat and escaped to the thick bush of the central

11. THE WESTERN APPROACHES

plain. C Company encountered several enemy in the south-western part of the island, and A Company found many installations which had been used by the Viet Cong for living and storage of supplies. There were several indications that some Viet Cong were trapped on the island and so a series of co-ordinated sweeps was organised to gradually flush them into the open.

These sweeps were controlled by Major Stan Maizey who was filling Max Carroll's place as S3 while Max was taking his five days leave in Hong Kong. This was one of the few opportunities which Stan had had to escape the administrative cares which made up the greater part of his work as the battalion second-in-command. He had commanded several forces of two companies which had been mounted by the battalion for special operations, namely assistance for the Sixth Battalion when they were doing the first search of Long Tan and then road clearing operations to the village of Long Hai. This village on the eastern coast of Phuoc Tuy looking onto the Vung Tau peninsula had been a resort used by the Diem family. Stan had also been in command of A Company during Operation Holsworthy at Binh Ba when Major Cassidy had been ill. However, these were small compensations for the months he had spent in the base. Furthermore, he was due to leave the battalion in January to take over from Major Richard Hannigan at Task Force Headquarters as the senior operations staff officer, so it was important that he had had the experience of controlling the operations of one of the two battalions which would shortly be under his direction.

As the pressure of the searching companies on the Viet Cong increased, several enemy attempted to hide in the mangroves or to get to the mainland in motorised sampans. Clashes involving chiefly B and D Companies on the northern side of the island took place. Combined manoeuvring of the men in the assault boats and the men on land, directed from helicopters, resulted in the deaths of ten Viet Cong and the capture of three for no casualties to ourselves. However, when B Company began to move back to the south to link up with C Company, a Viet Cong sniper killed Private Watson, a member of Four Platoon. Snipers had been bothering the headquarters on a few occasions, but their fire was so wild that no casualties were caused. It was simply a matter of one man creeping up towards the perimeter which was manned by the Support Company platoons, hurriedly loosing a few rounds without taking careful aim before he dashed away to avoid the return fire from the perimeter.

The operation finished with the closure of the sweeps on November 12th. We did not eliminate all the Viet Cong on the island, but the process had been begun. Several families who lived on the western side of Nui Nua had to be resettled back in Long Son village so that the western side of the island could be fired on occasionally to discourage the Viet Cong from attempting to rebuild their destroyed buildings and re-establish the island as an important link for supplies coming in from the west. The most significant indication of the degree of success of the operation was received a few days after we had gone when the remaining thirteen Viet Cong on the island crossed to Vung Tau in sampans and gave themselves up to the Vietnamese police. It seemed that Long Son island was now at peace.

12

An Isolated Outpost

While most of our operations in 1966 took place in central and western Phuoc Tuy, we had been paying close attention to one of the main problems of the eastern district—the isolation of Xuyen Moc. This village contained approximately 1,500 people and was defended by two Government companies of infantry, the one a Regional Forces company, the other a Popular Forces company. We had become interested in Xuyen Moc for two main reasons—first to see if we could do anything about relieving its isolation and second to expand our intelligence net to the east to cover an area of heavy Viet Cong activity.

The village of Xuyen Moc was situated centrally within the district of the same name. It was a large district and the village was seven miles from the coast and twelve miles from the nearest village in central Phuoc Tuy. Government control was non-existent in the area between central Phuoc Tuy and Xuyen Moc village, and it was far from strong in Dat Do, the main village on the eastern edge of central Phuoc Tuy. Consequently, the Viet Cong were able to range freely over the whole of the province to the east of Dat Do. The next province to the east, Binh Tuy, was sparsely populated and defended by very few Government troops and so the Xuyen Moc district formed part of an immense zone of unrestricted movement for the Viet Cong. Much of this movement tended to concentrate on routes through the Xuyen Moc district because it was close to the current location of Viet Cong fighting and because several roads ran through the district, leading to the chain of Viet Cong bases in the north-east of Phuoc Tuy. These bases needed access to the sea coast for receiving supplies brought in from the north by small ships and junks, they required roads over which the Viet Cong could drive trucks and ox carts laden with rice from central Phuoc Tuy and they needed frequent access to the bases close to central Phuoc Tuy from which the Provincial Mobile and District Company activities could be sustained.

The network of roads which had been built through Xuyen Moc district in earlier times served each of these three needs very well.[1] Route 23, the main road which linked Ba Ria, Long Dien, Dat Do and Xuyen Moc provided good communications for the Viet Cong from central Phuoc Tuy to the western part of Xuyen Moc district. They were not confined to using the road itself for there were many ox cart trails which ran in the same general direction as the road and offered the advantage of cover from view, because they ran through thick scrub and low jungle. Running north and south throughout the length of western Xuyen Moc district was Route 328, a well made earth road which bore the main weight of Viet Cong traffic to the coast and to central Phuoc Tuy. Route 328 was a prolongation of Route 330, which ran southwards from Route 1, swept around the western side of the May Tao mountain, crossed a jungle covered plain where the road became Route 328, and ran due south to Route 23 past the former Viet Cong model village of Thua Tich and the junction with Route 327, which ran due west to Binh Gia and Route 2. After travelling westwards on Route 23 for half a mile, Route 328 swung off to the south again, passed through the village of Phuoc Buu and then ran south-east to the coast at Cape Ho Tram. Wide beaches ran along the coast for several miles on either side of the cape and so it was a very suitable area for landing supplies from small ships.

When we arrived in Phuoc Tuy, Route 328 was one of the best maintained roads in the province, in sharp distinction to Route 23. As one flew eastwards from Dat Do along Route 23 one saw a succession of blown up bridges and culverts which had been dug away and which could be crossed only on single planks, reducing the capacity of Route 23 to that of an ox cart track—or worse in those places where travellers were not permitted to use the Viet Cong controlled fords. Route 328 had a broad, smooth surface of red earth. All its banks and culverts were in good order and the bridge over the Suoi Cay Gia near the junction with Route 23 must have been the only road bridge intact in Phuoc Tuy, east of Dat Do.

After passing the junction with Route 328, Route 23 turned to the north-east to run into Xuyen Moc village. In the centre of the village, the road turned at right angles and left the village running south-east. After a mile it

---

1   The roads described are shown in Fig. 1 (p. 4) and Fig. 22 (p. 259).

12. AN ISOLATED OUTPOST

turned to the east to link several hamlets in its last ten miles within Phuoc Tuy. After entering the Ham Tan district of Binh Tuy the road continued to run eastwards until it converged with the coastline and inclined to the north once more. From this eastern section of Route 23 several other important Viet Cong roads branched to the north and south. From the centre of Xuyen Moc village in prolongation of the north-easterly direction of Route 23 ran Route 329. This was nothing more than a broad ox cart track, but it appeared to have been properly laid out by a surveyor and so it was capable of carrying more traffic than the normal winding narrow ox cart track. This route led into the southern part of the May Tao mountain and met several tracks of varying capacities, including Route 331, which ran along the Binh Tuy border to Route 23 and to the coast.

All of these roads and tracks, except for the area within two miles of the Xuyen Moc intersection, were heavily used by the Viet Cong. Consequently, the Viet Cong were anxious to dislodge the Government forces from their last foothold, but while the Government outpost continued to exist we were provided with an excellent listening post for detecting Viet Cong movement on the road system leading into the main bases of the Fifth Viet Cong Division.

The Viet Cong had always held a strong influence over the Xuyen Moc district, for since the time of the Viet Minh, it has been a base area for the Communists. For this purpose the district was well suited because it contained few people to observe the movements of the Viet Cong, it was relatively close to Saigon and it linked the sea coast with the May Tao mountain and War Zone D, further to the north. Ever since the early nineteen-sixties, the garrison had been confined to the immediate locality of the village because of the superiority of local Viet Cong forces, particularly the D445 Provincial Mobile Battalion which had its bases to the north of Route 23, between Xuyen Moc and Dat Do, centred about the Song Rai. This battalion mounted several attacks on the garrison but suffered such losses in doing so that it seemed better to be content with having isolated the garrison from the provincial administration.

Because they were unable to take Xuyen Moc by force, the Viet Cong began to use means which were slower but which could have been just as decisive. They set up several tax points along Route 23 which the villagers had to pass through when they went to Dat Do. Xuyen Moc village was not self-sufficient in important foodstuffs such as meat, fish and rice, so the people had to make frequent journeys to Dat Do to sell their fruit, wood and hand-made articles and to buy the foods which they could not produce. Consequently the Viet Cong had an inescapable grasp over the lives of the villagers by their control of Route 23, and a sure means of local income. The taxation points were spread out over a wide area of country on either side of Route 23 in order to catch people who tried to walk around the tax collectors. The rate of taxation varied up to as high as forty per cent of the goods being carried, and thus it imposed a considerable burden of poverty on the people of Xuyen Moc.

The village grew poorer and poorer. The people were faced by an acute dilemma—they either had to move to the central part of the province and abandon their homes and land without recompense or they had to endure the continual loss of a major portion of their income until Government control over Route 23 could be re-established. Had the people left Xuyen Moc, the Viet Cong would have won a significant success in demonstrating to the people in other outlying villages in Phuoc Tuy that the Government could not protect them and that the Government was still the weaker of the two contenders for control of South Vietnam.

The Government attempted to assist the people of Xuyen Moc by supplying their needs by air. Every few weeks, several American C123 aircraft flew to Xuyen Moc to drop rice, medical supplies, ammunition and equipment for the garrison. The strength of the garrison was maintained at two companies despite reductions elsewhere in the province, and it was provided with two 105 mm. field guns and a platoon of artillerymen. However, the scale of Government support available for Xuyen Moc did not meet its needs and so the fundamental problems of the people were still present.

The village was fortunate in its garrison commander, the District Chief, Captain Duc. Duc was a lithe man and when one saw how well maintained his compound was and how effectively his troops went about their duties it was obvious that Xuyen Moc was under the leadership of an outstanding man. Duc had been at Xuyen Moc since 1961 and had been confronted with the serious problem of maintaining the morale of the people over a long period. When we first made his acquaintance in October 1966 he was getting a little dispirited himself, for it was impossible to say when an improvement in Xuyen Moc's position would take place. Duc came from Go Cong in the Mekong Delta. He felt it was unsafe to bring his wife and children to Xuyen Moc and so he had seen very little of them for five years.

12. AN ISOLATED OUTPOST

One of the eight inch guns of the 1st/83rd US Artillery Regiment stationed at Nui Dat. These guns possess extraordinary precision over long ranges (see Chapter 15).

An APC of A Squadron, 3rd Cavalry Regiment, controlling ox cart traffic along Route 2 near Nui Dat. The APCs supported most of our operations.

Commencing the planning after the An Nhut reconnaissance, 12 February 1967 (see Chapter 14): from left, Colonel Warr, Major Carroll and the author.

The battalion lifting off from Luscombe Field, Nui Dat, late in the afternoon of 18 February 1967 to launch Operation Renmark (see Chapter 15). This was the only operation for which we carried steel helmets. The risk of Viet Cong mortar bombardment of Battalion Headquarters was appreciable.

12. AN ISOLATED OUTPOST

Duc had laid out the defences with some originality. Not content with simply a fortified compound which could not keep the Viet Cong out of the village at night, he had surrounded the compound with twenty-two defended posts which were scattered in an irregular manner around a perimeter some three hundred yards out from the compound. Each of these posts was sited so that it could receive supporting fire from the two posts on its flanks in the event of an attack, and each was manned by seven Popular Force soldiers. During the day time, this number was reduced to two to permit the defenders to go about their own business and to patrol the immediate environs of the village.

The village was made up of five hamlets, four of which were grouped together around the main road junction while the fifth, a Catholic New Life hamlet, stood by itself to the north-west, separated from the main village by five hundred yards. Each of these two settlement groups was surrounded by a ditch, rampart and barbed wire fences. Although the Catholic hamlet was defended by only twenty Popular Force soldiers, its potential for resistance was far greater than this would indicate for most of the villagers were trained to bear arms. Around the hamlets were minefields and on all the roads which led into the settled areas, barricades were placed one behind the other so that it was quite difficult to thread one's way through even by day when they were partly opened. Within the four central hamlets was a small airstrip of some three hundred yards in length. However, the possibility of sniper anti-aircraft fire from around the village had prevented aircraft from using the landing strip and it had fallen into disrepair.

I made my first visit to Xuyen Moc motivated more by general curiosity than by any particular knowledge of the outpost's needs. Until October, all we knew about the village and its garrison was summed up by a blue circle on our maps which indicated that the village was still Government controlled. I wanted to know how the post had held out, what its problems were, what its worth was, how it could be relieved and what intelligence assistance it could give us. Prior to Operation Crowsnest I had made some preliminary arrangements with the RAAF for a helicopter. Normally, the RAAF pilots liked to have radio contact with any landing zone which they had to use. However, we thought that it would be most unlikely for Xuyen Moc to have a spare radio available for this purpose, even had we been able to contact them before the visit. Without direct contact with the landing zone, one did not know whether any artillery was being fired which could endanger the helicopter, or even whether the landing zone was secure from Viet Cong interference.

However, when I had explained the significance of making contact with this beleaguered outpost, the pilots agreed to make an attempt to land, depending on our assessment of the local situation as we flew overhead. We hoped that at least we would know whether the post was still in Government hands or not on the day of the visit, but until we had landed we would have no idea of what sort of local situation we were flying into.

We took off from Tiger Five, the battalion helicopter pad, at 10 am on the morning of October 4th. Accompanying me were Bic, the interpreter, and Private Brown, my batman and bodyguard. We ascended over Nui Dat in tight spirals to a height of nearly four thousand feet, quite sufficient to cope with any anti-aircraft fire which may have met us when we were a long way out from the base. The green rows of rubber trees passed beneath as we flew over Long Tan and looked out on a flat expanse of jungle, still bright green in the wet season. Here and there were large clearings across which ran the unmistakable marks of ox carts. The early part of the Dat Do rice harvest was evidently on its way to the caches of D445 Battalion and the Fifth Viet Cong Division. We swung south to follow Route 23 so that we could see the state of the damage inflicted by the Viet Cong. I gave up trying to count the number of culverts which had been destroyed and the number of holes which had been dug across the road. As one flew on over mile after mile of jungle which defied visual penetration one came to feel that Xuyen Moc was the end of the earth—nothing could be further away from one's concept of civilisation!

After five miles we passed the staggered junction of both sections of Route 328 running away from Route 23. The red earth of the surface of the former was smooth for as far as the eye could see. Shortly afterwards the clearing in which Xuyen Moc lay came into view. The village looked perfectly peaceful. Small columns of smoke twisted upwards into the moist air from huts of bamboo and houses of brick. A few herds of cattle moved between the edge of the jungle and the outer barbed wire of the village defences and men could be seen at the road blocks guarding the approaches to the village. As we swung low over the centre of the village we could see a broad square of earth which formed the market place. Around the market place on three sides were lines of shops. On the fourth side was the district headquarters compound. Small figures began to run

12. AN ISOLATED OUTPOST

out of the compound as we came low overhead. While we made another circuit of the village they grouped in a field one hundred yards in front of the compound and set off a canister of purple smoke. We took this as a good indication of where they wanted us to land and made a final steep drop to land twenty yards away from the assembled group. No sooner had Brown, Bic and I jumped out of the helicopter than the aircraft had taken off again, not caring to risk enemy mortar fire from the jungle, a little over one mile away.

Once the noise of the helicopter had passed away sufficiently for speech to be heard, Bic set about locating the District Chief, who had just come through the group from the rear. Duc greeted me with a broad smile of welcome and a few words of English. He took me across the field and through the barricaded gateway of the compound. It was interesting to note that Duc's sentries paid him the respect of presenting arms as he passed by. Once inside the privacy of Duc's office I was able to introduce myself and meet his two very young, but equally keen-looking lieutenants, Pham Van Minh and Huynh Ba Trang.

We talked for over an hour while Duc told me the story of Xuyen Moc. It was evident that he had built up a very useful intelligence network and that he was prepared to trust me by telling me in great detail of the local Viet Cong activities. We then discussed his problems and how we might help with their solution. After a glass of flower tea, he took me for a walk around his defences, pausing on the way to show me the hole in the ceiling of his sleeping quarters made by an incoming mortar bomb. He had been in the command post at the time of the attack. The walls and ceiling were pitted with countless numbers of holes made by the flying shrapnel. The compound bore many similar signs of damage caused by Viet Cong attacks. However, it was remarkably clean, both outside in the courtyard and inside within the troops' quarters. The two field guns were protected by sandbagged walls of circular construction so that the guns could traverse in any direction, although this meant that the guns were without overhead cover and so their crews were in danger from mortar bombs. One emergency device which had been of use during the last heavy attack was a wooden arrow, ten feet long and pivoted to swing in the horizontal plane. Around the edge of this arrow was a row of flare pots so that the outline of the arrow could be displayed to someone flying overhead at night. When D445 Battalion had attacked the post, Duc had requested air support. Because he spoke little English himself and lacked an interpreter he could not speak easily to the forward air controller by radio, so the arrow had been used to indicate from which side the Viet Cong were attacking, enabling the pilots to take heavy toll of the incoming enemy.

The sound of the returning Iroquois aircraft terminated our inspection, and I took leave of Duc, promising to return as soon as I could. After the operations on Nui Thi Vai we were able to establish frequent contact with Duc. Colonel Warr paid several visits to Xuyen Moc and presented Brigadier Jackson with a detailed report on the state of the Government forces, the Viet Cong activities, the advantages which contact with the post had brought and the problems with which Duc was grappling. Tony White flew out to give medical treatment to the villagers and to the garrison, who had not seen a doctor for years. Xuyen Moc became one of my regular ports of call like Binh Ba, Binh Gia and Duc Thanh so we now had a good intelligence cover of northern and eastern Phuoc Tuy. Duc accompanied me on helicopter flights around Xuyen Moc and along Route 23, pointing out the locations of tax collection points and of local bases and tracks used by the Viet Cong.

By late 1966, the security of Xuyen Moc had become one of the most urgent tasks yet to be accomplished in Phuoc Tuy, and it became possible to consider plans for its relief and for reopening Route 23 under Government control. The person most directly responsible for the maintenance of the garrison at Xuyen Moc was the Province Chief, Colonel Dat, for the post represented one of the six districts of his province. We learned that he hoped to reopen Route 23 in early 1967, with the assistance of the Task Force, and if need be, of additional American forces. Consequently the long-term problems of Xuyen Moc appeared to be close to a solution, provided that the Government did not lose the bridgehead into enemy territory which this outpost represented before the relief operation could be mounted.

The September elections in Xuyen Moc showed that there was no danger of local support for the South Vietnamese Government being eroded by the economic pressure of the Viet Cong, for ninety-four per cent of those eligible turned out to vote. However, this result did not mean that the people regarded their personal problems as solved. In particular it did not mean that the tolerance of the people of their conditions in Xuyen Moc would endure until Government control had been re-established over Route 23. Consequently we were at pains to demonstrate to the

12. AN ISOLATED OUTPOST

people that concern was being felt about their welfare, that they were not forgotten in central Phuoc Tuy, and that the balance of military forces in Phuoc Tuy was swinging through a marked change.

We were assisted in maintaining contact with Xuyen Moc by an operation mounted by the Sixth Battalion in December, Operation Ingham. This operation was aimed at some of the main bases of D445 Battalion near the Song Rai and Route 328 and required a fire support base to be located at Xuyen Moc. The area through which the Sixth Battalion was to move was so far to the east of Nui Dat that the battalion could not be supported from the normal gun position, whereas a great part of the movement was within artillery range of Xuyen Moc. The Fifth Battalion had to provide a rifle company to protect the gun position at Xuyen Moc, and so the villagers had their first sight of a large force operating from their locality. The presence of these troops led to visits from the civil aid staff of Task Force Headquarters and to preparatory work for the eventual reopening of Route 23. At about this time the American senior adviser to Colonel Dat was able to make an advisory team available to assist Captain Duc, fulfilling one of Duc's most urgent requests and indicating clearly that Xuyen Moc's isolation was drawing to a close.

Contact continued to develop between the Task Force and Xuyen Moc during the early months of 1967 and planning proceeded between Colonel Dat, Brigadier Graham (who had relieved Brigadier Jackson when the latter's term of duty on Vietnam had expired in January) and the staff of the Second Field Force, the American headquarters which controlled all Allied activity within the Third Corps area. Mid-March was selected as the earliest time at which sufficient Vietnamese, American and Australian forces would be available to launch an operation to eject the Viet Cong from the area between central Phuoc Tuy and Xuyen Moc and to rebuild Route 23. Once the road had been rebuilt by American and Australian engineers, two Vietnamese Regional Forces companies were to be stationed along the road to protect the major bridges from sabotage.

Although this operation, Operation Portsea, required the Fifth Battalion to work in the neighbourhood of Dat Do for most of its duration, we did have the final satisfaction of guarding Route 23 after it had been rebuilt in mid-April for the passage of the first road traffic to Xuyen Moc. The isolation of Xuyen Moc had been broken and the tenacity of this garrison which had been able to defy encirclement for five years was finally rewarded.

13

A Re-evaluation of Strategy

After our return from Long Son island, the pace of our operations eased during late November and December. Several more American convoys were scheduled to use Route 15 during this period and so we had to return to the routine of road security duties in alternation with the Sixth Battalion after the return of the latter from Operation Ingham. We were also engaged in several cordon operations directed at Hoa Long for by this time the pressure of other commitments had relaxed sufficiently to enable us finally to clean the hard core of Viet Cong cadre out of the village. In between these battalion operations, each of the rifle companies carried out patrols and laid ambushes on tracks known to be used occasionally by Viet Cong for moving into central Phuoc Tuy. Although the battalion was still quite busy during November and December, pressure on the Battalion Headquarters staff was relaxed, permitting more attention to be given to the fundamental basis of our long-term strategy.

This break came at a convenient time, for after six months of operations against the Viet Cong we no longer had to treat them as a theoretical entity. Our earlier approach had had to be conservatively based because we did not know our enemy's weaknesses as clearly as his strengths. Now that we had established ourselves at Nui Dat and had enjoyed some success in breaking Viet Cong power in the central part of Phuoc Tuy we had a basis for ruthlessly scrutinising both our aim and our methods to see if we were acting to bring the war to a successful end in the shortest possible time with the least number of casualties. The Task Force commander, Brigadier Jackson, and later Brigadier Graham, had laid down a broad policy for operations which permitted the battalions an appreciable degree of initiative. In order to use this freedom to the greatest effect we carried on a continual debate concerning our operations.

The driving force behind this rethinking of our attitudes was Colonel Warr. He had been stimulating discussion of our methods ever since the battalion had been raised and scarcely a week passed in which he did not ask me what our aim in Phuoc Tuy was and then proceed to debate the matter for half an hour or so. After some months of this dialectic, in which all the officers of the Battalion Headquarters and the company commanders participated, we felt that we had established enough of a principle, based on both our education and our experience, to warrant its formulation in words and its wider distribution for further comment and effect. Colonel Warr asked me to prepare a paper analysing what we knew and deducing a course of future action for the battalion.

The most fundamental question seemed to be the determination of our aim. Was it to kill Viet Cong, to bring the main force to battle, to isolate the main force from the people, to assist in civil reconstruction, to restore Government control to villages or to cut the Viet Cong supply lines? As strategy can be most effectively applied only with knowledge of the opponent's aim, it was important to consider exactly what the Viet Cong were attempting to do in order to achieve a victory.

Quite clearly the fundamental element in the Viet Cong strategy was the people. They were fighting the war for control of the people and they could achieve this in limited war only by winning the support of a large group of the Vietnamese nation. The Viet Cong were not fighting for specific pieces of territory, for they held that no ground was vital if they were confronted by superior forces. The one essential element for the success of a guerilla war was the support of the peasants, for if that sea refused Ho's fish refuge and nourishment where else would succour be obtained?

The Viet Cong had commenced the war by assailing the minds of the peasants. The first Viet Cong forces were the village cadres which had lain dormant from 1954 to 1957. Beginning slowly and concentrating on increasing their own numbers with additions of high quality and dedication, the cadres set about undermining the position of the Government by attributing all the ills of peasant life to Diem and by promising remedies when the Viet Cong came to power. Once they had the committed support of a group of peasants the cadres were able to build their own military power, sufficient in some areas to take them over, village by village, from the Government. Where the Government was too strong to be ejected outright, its troops were harassed and fatigued by constant pinpricks. As Viet Cong support throughout some localities grew, so it became possible for them to form small standing forces composed of regular soldiers. The first of these, of company size, began to roam about the country in 1959, attacking small Government posts, ambushing convoys, and terrorising Government officials so that the Viet Cong seized control of the spaces outside the forts and compounds. Without being able to prevent the Government forces from moving about in medium concentrations, they took psychological control of the open countryside and jungles away from the Government.

The psychological supremacy established by the Viet Cong aided their recruitment and after two years the mobile companies were expanding themselves into battalions, capable of driving Government forces out of the settled areas. The process continued with growing success and, in 1964, main force regiments composed of three battalions of infantry and a support weapons battalion were raised. The men were mostly South Vietnamese, a good number of the officers were North Vietnamese and the weapons were Chinese, Russian or Czech. Yet the purpose of these regiments was not to win the support of the people, but to throw back the forces of the Government and by a process of continued expansion and amalgamation to inflict final crushing defeat on the Government Army. In order to achieve this aim, the main force soldiers had to keep apart from the people, based in deep jungle and mountains, emerging from a veil of tight secrecy to strike a decisive blow and then to disappear before a stronger blow could be struck back by the Government. Once the Government forces had been thrown back, the cadres came forward and began taking over the control of the people.

All of this process may be familiar, but it is important to examine the growth of the Viet Cong in its historical context in order to evaluate the relative importance of the cadres in the villages and the main force units. It emerges clearly that it is the cadres who are the active elements in achieving the aims of the Viet Cong. It is through these groups that the Viet Cong have built themselves up and it is they who control the efforts of the peasantry under Viet Cong influence. The main force units exist as a shield and as a sword in front of the cadres but without the cadres the main force achieves nothing more than the neutralisation of the Government military effort, and the way is left open for the Government cadres to extend the scope of their control.

After this consideration of the aims of the Viet Cong and their methods of achieving these aims, we can return to consideration of the Government aims. It is common sense that the aim of any government which hopes to endure in South Vietnam is broadly based popular support. This can only be enduring if the Government can provide security on a continuing basis so that civic action and the Revolutionary Development programme can proceed uninterrupted. Unless villages are protected and free from Viet Cong control, the Government teams can be assassinated, and the building materials, the food and the medical supplies will go to the Viet Cong instead of to the peasants and their families. Consequently, while the broad aim of forces on the Government side is to win and hold the support of the people, this is not a practical possibility until the local Viet Cong influences have been removed and the main force rendered impotent to interfere with the Government workers.

Therefore, while the most direct means of winning the war lies in eliminating the Viet Cong cadres from the villages, positive Government action to administer the population cannot be put into effect until the main force Viet Cong regiments in a particular locality have been neutralised and are kept from interfering with the restoration of Government control. Hence the first step in the conduct of operations in a province which has been the theatre of action for large main force units, has to be the removal of the main force threat from the populated areas.

Whilst these considerations do not go as far as specifically to require the destruction of Viet Cong main forces for the restoration of effective Government control, the notion of the necessity of the destruction of an enemy's armed forces for the attainment of victory is so deeply entrenched in the minds of many, including both participants in and commentators on the Vietnam war, that the proposition that the prime target of the war is the Viet Cong main force requires special examination.

In essence, military strategy usually boils down to a choice between direct and indirect methods. Direct methods imply the physical destruction of the enemy's means to wage war as a preliminary to the imposition of one's political will on the enemy, and are exemplified by the Franco-Prussian war and by the Western Front of the First World War. Indirect methods seek to attain the political objective of the war by avoidance of a frontal clash between opposing forces as exemplified by the tactics of Fabius Cunctator, Lawrence in Arabia, and Guderian in 1940. Indirect methods have had their most recent expression in the doctrines of Mao Tse Tung and their application has been seen in China, in Indo-China, and, until the formation of large main force units by the Viet Cong, in Vietnam.

One of the most articulate proponents of direct methods has been Carl von Clausewitz, in whose works the advocates of direct methods have found ample support by notions such as:

> 'The aim of all action in war is to disarm the enemy.'

> 'We have only one means in war—the battle.'

> 'The bloody solution of the crisis, the effort for the destruction of the enemy's forces, is the first born son of war.'

> 'Philanthropists may easily imagine that there is a skilful method of disarming and overcoming the enemy without great bloodshed, and that this is the proper tendency of the Art of War … That is an error which must be extirpated.'

However, a more careful reading of Clausewitz shows that he himself recognised a few limitations to these dicta, viz.:

> 'The object of a combat is not always the destruction of the enemy's forces … its object can often be attained as well without the combat taking place at all.'

And:

> 'The waste of our own military forces must, *ceteris paribus*, always be greater the more our aim is directed upon the destruction of the enemy's power. The danger lies in this—that the greater efficacy which we seek recoils on ourselves, and therefore has worse consequences in case we fail of success.'

It is interesting to compare with Clausewitz the doctrines of the Chinese strategist, Sun Tzu, who wrote *The Art of War* in the fourth century BC and to whom Mao Tse Tung owes much for the formulation of ideas which are often wrongly ascribed to Mao. Sun Tzu has expressed his ideas on the destruction of the enemy's forces thus:

'1. Generally in war the best policy is to take a state intact; to ruin it is inferior to this.

2. To capture the enemy's army is better than to destroy it; to take intact a battalion, a company or a five-man squad is better than to destroy them.

3. For to win one hundred victories in one hundred battles is not the acme of skill. To subdue the enemy without fighting is the acme of skill.'

These ideas of Sun Tzu are fundamental to the indirect method and they stand in clear opposition to those of Clausewitz. The relative success of indirect methods over direct methods has been amply demonstrated in the history of warfare, as described particularly by Liddell Hart in his *Strategy—the Indirect Approach*. However, in many parts of Vietnam such as along the Demilitarized Zone and in the Central Highlands, the strength and aggressiveness of the main force Viet Cong was such that little scope was left for indirect methods. In Phuoc Tuy at this time the situation was very different for the main force regiments had already been driven out of the central part of the province by direct offensive action. Provided that the main force units were kept isolated from the people they could maintain themselves in health and fighting efficiency only by assistance from other areas, especially North Vietnam. For the Viet Cong in Phuoc Tuy such local isolation would be a grim situation for they were at the end of a supply line from the north several hundred miles long, all of which was subject to interdiction and was under heavy stress to meet the existing demands which were made of it. The physical strain of living in remote jungles and mountains would be very likely to reduce these main force units to such a low level of effectiveness that they would cease to be anything more than nuisance value.

Another important factor to be considered in dealing with the main force units was the Viet Cong mentality. The men in the main force units had been indoctrinated with the idea that the formation of their units was the beginning of the end for the South Vietnamese Government. They had been successful for the first year of their operations. Following that they had been baulked by American and Australian forces for several months. Thus their morale must have been suffering after this apparent reversal of fortunes. No doubt they were able to rationalise their impotence for a short period, but they stood to lose many of their men to the Chieu Hoi programme if they were kept frustrated by inactivity, constantly on the move to escape our harassing artillery fire and air strikes. As their time

13. A RE-EVALUATION OF STRATEGY

became more fully occupied by defensive manoeuvring they would lose their grip over the vast tracts of country through which they had roamed at will. Their intelligence network would tend to deteriorate as people saw Communist fortunes sink, while the sources available to the Government would tend to improve with better control over the villages.

The question of casualties was also of the utmost importance. It was obvious that operations against main force Viet Cong would result in higher casualties than operations directed at the village cadres. In particular, it was always possible that the main force could concentrate stronger forces than our battalion for a short period on ground of their own choosing if we went pursuing them, and so inflict heavy casualties on us in a short encounter. On the other hand, operations directed at villages were unlikely to result in many casualties to our own troops for if the degree of surprise necessary to trap the Viet Cong cadres had been achieved, then these Viet Cong would not be in a position to put up a heavy fight.

When we analysed the results of our operations over the previous six months, these considerations were well borne out. In eight conventional operations in which we were fighting Viet Cong main and mobile force troops, we suffered six killed and thirty-one wounded while the Viet Cong lost thirty-three killed and two captured. In five cordon and search operations we suffered one death and none wounded for the loss to the Viet Cong of sixteen killed, forty-seven captured, and one hundred and twelve suspects taken.

Time was another vital factor. Each of our operations had to be scrutinised in terms of the result gained for every day of operational time spent by the battalion. Not only was there the sheer cost of our soldiers' time to be considered, but the war could not be permitted to drag on indefinitely, enabling the Viet Cong to propagandise that they were uncrushable and to sustain their own morale, thus making the war all the more difficult to win for the Allies. Analysis of our operational effectiveness in terms of Viet Cong removed from their system per day of operational time showed conclusive results. The numbers of Viet Cong removed from their forces could be computed conservatively by adding the numbers of Viet Cong killed, captured and those who surrendered under the Chieu Hoi policy in any one operation, or as a direct result of any particular operation. The conventional operations showed the following ratios for Viet Cong removed per day of operational time:

Hardihood	1.43
Sydney 1	0.09
Sydney 2(b)	0.33
Holsworthy 2	0.00
Darlinghurst	0.00
Toledo	0.43
Canberra	0.00
Queanbeyan	1.00

The cordon and search operations yielded these ratios:

Sydney 2(a)	3.00
Holsworthy 1	8.50
Bundaberg	10.50
Yass	2.50
Hayman	5.20

The fruitfulness of cordon operations at this time in Phuoc Tuy was obviously far superior to that of the conventional operations, but only because of the Task Force's earlier successes against Viet Cong main force units, such as the achievements of the Sixth Battalion at the battle of Long Tan, in which 245 Viet Cong were killed in a few hours. However, such successes could not be hoped for unless unusual circumstances prevailed, such as a Viet Cong attack on the base area. In this case, a choice of operational types would become less than academic for a direct threat to the security of Nui Dat could not be tolerated no matter what other operations were offering good prospects.

These arguments have considered only the two extreme alternatives of conventional operations and the cordon and search. Of course there are many types of operation which combine aspects of both extremes. These operations may be generally classified as interdiction in which the aim is to get between the main force and the villages to cut off those supplies and information which cannot be severed at the source. In a more conventional war such as the Burma Campaign in the Second World War, land interdiction is a very difficult method to use decisively because of the difficulties of penetrating into the rear areas of an enemy without suffering huge losses. In guerilla warfare the opposing forces can range over vast spaces because most of the countryside is defended by neither side, and so interdiction becomes an important and often a decisive tactic.

13. A RE-EVALUATION OF STRATEGY

In this situation of irregular warfare, the least regular of the opponents is distinctly more vulnerable to interdiction for his means of supply are, *ipso facto*, much the more tenuous and usually the more meagre. For example if a Vietnamese Government soldier lost his rifle in combat, it was much easier for him to receive a replacement than it would have been for a Viet Cong soldier in the same predicament. Also the psychological and political importance of contact with the people over whom the war was being fought rendered the Viet Cong even more vulnerable to interdiction. The Government forces were in the centres of population and could achieve direct and influential contact with the people, provided that they treated the people decently. The Viet Cong were out in the jungles and mountains and had either to travel from their bases to the centres of population or else they had to send reliable members into the villages to insert themselves into village society as discreetly as possible. But even their resident cadre personnel had to transmit reports and receive instructions and material supplies and so they could be rendered ineffective by close interdiction. Thus interdiction offered considerable potential as a means of combating the Viet Cong both in the villages and out in the main force units.

Our experience with interdiction had been limited up to the end of 1966 to one operation, Crowsnest, at Ngai Giao, where local supplies were captured before they had been collected by a visiting main force unit. While interdiction operations did not run the risks of heavy casualties in the same way as the conventional operations, it was obvious that they could tie down large numbers of troops for long periods of time in waiting for the Viet Cong to visit one particular place or to use one special set of trails. Consequently we were unable to reach any precise conclusions about the method of interdiction in the same way that we had been able to draw deductions from consideration of the cordon and search method and the conventional method. While it was clear that cordon operations were superior to conventional ones as a general rule for single battalion operations, each individual proposition for an interdiction operation had to be examined on its own merits in order to fit it into a table of priorities with other possible operations.

Having made these general considerations as to the effectiveness of various operational methods it was necessary to examine the possibilities of applying these conclusions to the coming few months of operations in Phuoc Tuy. In December 1966 the two main force regiments, 274 and 275, were still lurking deep in the jungles to the north-west and north-east of the province. It was quite out of the question to mount any significant operation against them from within our own resources. Not only were the Viet Cong too far from Nui Dat for a single battalion to venture, but the wild nature of the country made it easy for the Viet Cong to evade any searchers in their base areas unless the searchers were sufficiently numerous to place a tight cordon around a base area several miles across before moving in to make contact with the Viet Cong. This type of operation called for battalions by the dozen, and so as far as our own initiative was concerned there was little which we could undertake against the main force regiments without American or South Vietnamese support.

There were still many villages with significant Viet Cong cadres within them, particularly around the east central region, on the edge of the rice production area and around the Long Hai hills in the south-east of the province. Close co-operation with the Vietnamese intelligence service revealed very detailed information concerning the numbers and identities of the Viet Cong cadres in each village. All that was lacking to enable the provincial authorities to pluck these cadres out of the villages were sufficient forces to cordon the villages skilfully and secretly. Several of these villages were small enough to be cordoned by a single battalion. The information concerning the Viet Cong enabled us to assign an order of priorities for clearing each of these villages, and so it was possible to begin the detailed planning and compilation of intelligence for several operations aimed at the village cadres.

We had discovered, chiefly from the captured diary of Nguyen Nam Hung, the deputy commander of 274 Regiment, the exact amounts of rice which the Viet Cong had taken for their main force units out of central Phuoc Tuy in late 1966. These quantities were sufficient to warrant a serious attempt to prevent the 1967 rice harvest from passing into the hands of the Viet Cong. The most important area was that around Dat Do, the rice bowl of the province. However, Hoa Long had also been used on occasions by Viet Cong agents, tax collectors and food gatherers as a source of supplies, and the former hamlets of Quang Giao and Xuan Son to the east of Binh Gia were still being used by small groups of Viet Cong food growers. The road system in Xuyen Moc district, especially Route 328, was carrying continual Viet Cong traffic between the coastal regions and the base areas in the north of the province. If this traffic was permitted to flow unhindered we could have been confronted with a large scale main force offensive as a result of their increased strength and confidence.

13. A RE-EVALUATION OF STRATEGY

Members of D Company beginning the defences at the Horseshoe, March 1967 (see Chapter 16). A Sioux helicopter of 161 Recce Flight is hovering below the rim of the crater.

Pte. Wales of D Company looking south from the crest of the Horseshoe over Dat Do towards the Long Hai hills on the horizon.

Building the fence around Dat Do, March 1967 (see Chapter 16).

Sergeant Chinh, our senior Vietnamese interpreter, at Binh Ba (see Chapter 14).

The handover. Colonel Warr presenting Colonel Smith, CO 7 RAR, with the 'tiger pig', 26 April 1967 (see Chapter 17).

These local considerations relating to the various types of operation indicated that special emphasis was required on the rice production area. Cordon operations for several of the villages which made up the rice bowl were necessary and the outflow of rice had to be stopped. These practical considerations fitted in well with the theory outlined above, and reinforced the conclusions that the war in Phuoc Tuy was going well for the Government and that prospects for 1967 looked bright.

The translation of these ideas into practical effect commenced early in 1967. Brigadier Jackson had completed his term of duty in Vietnam in January and was succeeded by Brigadier Graham. Naturally, Brigadier Jackson had not wished to commit his successor to a long programme of predetermined operations and so there was a great deal of long range planning to be done after Brigadier Graham had taken over the command of the Task Force. During January, as a result of discussions between Brigadier Graham, the senior staff of Task Force Headquarters and Colonel Warr, the operational programme of the Fifth Battalion for the remainder of its tour in Vietnam took shape. This shape was approximate to allow flexible responses to Viet Cong initiatives and to administrative limitations, but nonetheless the principles behind these operations were quite firmly fixed as we proceeded into a new phase of the war.

14

Against the Village Cadres

The first battalion operation for 1967 was a return to Binh Ba. Since October 1966 the security of the village had been in the hands of a Regional Forces company. Although often undermanned to a strength of forty or fifty men, this company had not been seriously challenged by the Viet Cong and it had constructed defences of sufficient strength to cause the Viet Cong severe casualties if they did attack the post. However, the post was only a small part of the village and it was easy for the Viet Cong to bypass it in order to obtain access to the people. The large size of the village coupled with the smallness of the garrison made it impossible for the Vietnamese troops to ambush all the approaches leading into the village every night. The Viet Cong discovered this and began, in November, to infiltrate a small group of cadre and tax collectors back into Binh Ba. They acted with caution, visiting the village on only one or two nights per month. By December they had found some sympathisers amongst the villagers, albeit mostly teenagers, and we were confronted with an attempt to regain the ground from which we had just ejected the Viet Cong.

This was only to be expected for Binh Ba had been one of the major Viet Cong prizes of the previous years and it represented a substantial source of revenue and prestige. In a way it was pleasing confirmation of the value which we had placed on Binh Ba ourselves. Moreover, the incidents of November and December demonstrated that the Viet Cong were still prepared to put their efforts into the villages even though their main force operations had been severely curtailed.

Reports of the new Viet Cong activity in Binh Ba came from some of the villagers themselves and from some of the Vietnamese troops. The soldiers had detected movement at night around their compound and along the airstrip. Small groups of Viet Cong had been making their reconnaissances of the defences and of the approaches to the village. On two occasions shots were fired into the compound just to indicate that the defenders were being constantly watched. Several of the soldiers had made friends in the village and occasional reports of Viet Cong visits began to come in to the Vietnamese company commander. He passed the information on to the two Australian warrant officers who were attached to the company as advisers, and the warrant officers told me the news when I visited Binh Ba every few days. The Viet Cong had not been bold enough to visit either of the Frenchmen nor to intimidate Father Joseph, so we could learn nothing additional from them.

When we received word that the Viet Cong were re-establishing a cadre in the village Colonel Warr began to make plans for another cordon of Binh Ba between Christmas and New Year. However, just before Christmas the Viet Cong withdrew from the village and so the operation was postponed until we received better indications for success. These came in early January with reports that several Viet Cong were back in the village. After conferring with Brigadier Graham, Colonel Warr fixed the date for the cordon as January 9th.

The first problem with mounting this operation was the insertion of the cordon, for the Viet Cong in Binh Ba were doubtless very alert and ready to flee at the least suggestion of another cordon. In particular they would be closely watching the behaviour and conversation of the Vietnamese troops in the village to glean any hint of an Australian operation directed at the village. Consequently the operation had to be mounted without the knowledge of the Vietnamese company, but with sufficient restriction of their movement about the time of our cordon so that we would not be ambushed by them in mistake for Viet Cong. Fortunately we were able to count on the assistance of Major Prescott at Duc Thanh. At Colonel Warr's request he arranged for Captain Be to confine the Binh Ba company to its compound while we were in the vicinity. No reason for this confinement was given to the Vietnamese troops and so they did not know whether the restriction of their movement was due to the presence of large Viet Cong forces, or to the proximity of an Australian operation.

14. AGAINST THE VILLAGE CADRES

Not wishing to risk an ambush by using the same route to Binh Ba as on Operation Holsworthy, Colonel Warr selected an approach which led out to the north-east of Nui Dat and swung into Binh Ba on a westerly tack. The general order of the move was much the same as before. The battalion was to leave Nui Dat around 10 am and to take most of the day in covering six miles through jungle to a harbour area close to the eastern edge of the Gallia Plantation. This harbour area was divided by a creek, the Suoi Da Bang, and while this creek was convenient for the replenishment of our water bottles and as a directional aid for our navigation it presented a rather inconvenient obstacle which made wet feet for the night inevitable.

The people of Binh Ba were to be interrogated at their own village this time, instead of being taken to Ba Ria, so that the whole operation could be completed within thirty-six hours. Special facilities for interrogation and processing of the people had to be planned and constructed within the first hour of our day in the village. In view of the increased security of the village it seemed reasonable to gather the people together on the green just in front of the market in the centre of the village. In handling large scale interrogations it was important to separate the men from the women and, after the interrogation, the innocent from the suspects, so several enclosures were necessary, viz.:

> two to hold the men and women who had not been interrogated,
> one for the interrogators to use,
> two to hold those men and women who were suspects, and
> two to hold those who were innocent until the whole village had been searched for weapons, caches, and persons attempting to hide.

These latter two enclosures were part of the first enclosures in which everyone was gathered.

We had discovered during some of the previous cordon operations that many of the villagers had not had time to have breakfast before they had been gathered out of their houses and so they had gone hungry for the first few hours of the day. For this operation, which was called Operation Caloundra, arrangements were made so that the people were not moved from their houses until they had breakfasted. A loudspeaker aircraft overhead was also to advise the people to have their breakfast as soon as the cordon was announced to them. So that the day would bring the villagers some assistance as well as some inconvenience, Task Force Headquarters arranged for distribution of food and clothing, medical and dental treatment, and for the showing of South Vietnamese Government films on improvement of living standards, especially health and hygiene, and on the work of the Government armed forces.

The huge operation order which Caloundra required was written by our new S3, Major Peter Cole. Major Cole had taken over from Major Carroll in December when they had exchanged jobs. Major Cole was well suited for this position being a graduate of Duntroon and the Australian Staff College and having had extensive experience as a company commander in New Guinea with the Pacific Islands Regiment.

The battalion wound out of the base through the wire defences in front of B Company. It was a beautiful morning. The sun was filtering through the dark green leaves of the rubber trees in bright slanting shafts. The day was still sufficiently young for the temperature to be mild and it was no effort to appreciate the soft brightness of the rich foliage we were filing through. During the first part of the approach we had to cross through the south-eastern corner of the La Son sector of the Gallia Plantation. This area was closed to the local inhabitants because of its proximity to our base so tension mounted when one of the flank scouts signalled that some Vietnamese were approaching us from the east. We went to ground and waited for clarification of their intentions. Fortunately the group was composed of women who had been out in the jungle gathering bananas from an overgrown plantation—probably one of those through which we had passed on Operation Hardihood. The women were rather surprised by the sudden appearance of Australians girded for war all around them. Through Chinh, my interpreter, I explained to the women that they had placed themselves in danger by entering an area which had been closed by Colonel Dat for they could have been mistaken for Viet Cong. The women had come from Hoa Long so they were escorted back to their village under observation from our supporting Sioux helicopter. We hoped that they were not in fact Viet Cong for it was possible that they could have sent a warning to Binh Ba once they had returned to their homes. However, there were many places to which we could have been heading from that point so we did not worry greatly about losing chances of achieving surprise through this encounter.

14. AGAINST THE VILLAGE CADRES

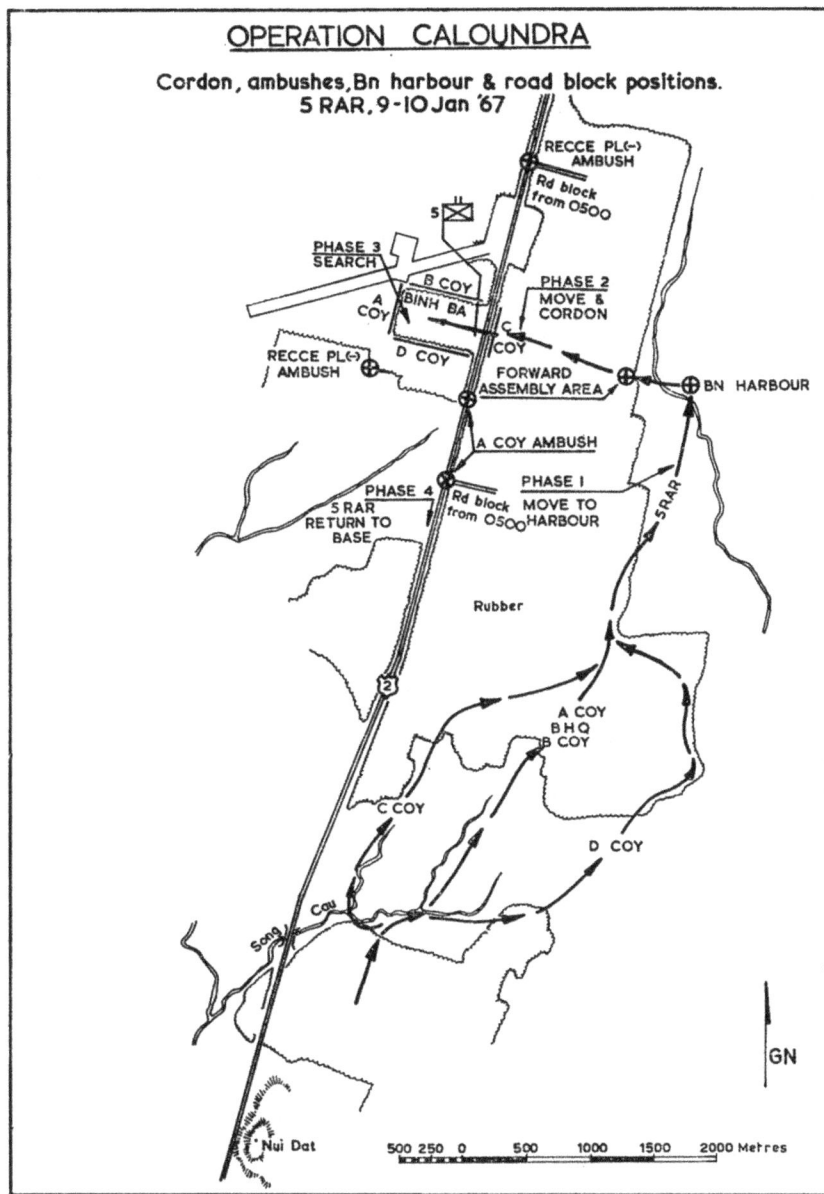

Fig. 19. The second cordoning of Binh Ba, Operation Caloundra, 9–10 January 1967.

The evening harbour was laid out in advance of our arrival by our new second-in-command, Major Ivor Hodgkinson. Major Maizey had left us in December to become the senior operations staff officer at Task Force Headquarters. Major Hodgkinson had recently commanded a company in the Borneo fighting and had been awarded an MBE for his skill and daring. Just as darkness was falling we began to move out of this harbour area to the edge of the rubber plantation so that we would have, we hoped, no night movement through the jungle which hid us from any Vietnamese plantation worker who may have been in the plantation in the late afternoon. However this intention was not achieved for a large part of the battalion. Movement out of the harbour area was slower than had been planned and darkness became complete while one half of the battalion was still on the eastern side of the Suoi Da Bang. The moon was not due to rise until midnight and so visibility was reduced to nothing. Fortunately we had only a few hundred yards to go to the edge of the plantation, but it took nearly two hours for the battalion to cover this distance.

The chief problem was the creek crossing. The creek was only a few feet deep but the banks were steep and slippery and the bottom was soft mud. The first few men through it stirred up the bottom making it harder to plough through and they made the banks into slippery slides which took some effort to clamber up. Thus the passage of the creek became slower and slower as man followed man. A long queue of men formed on the eastern side, waiting their turn to cross, while the intervals between men on the western side grew steadily larger until the point was reached where one man climbing out of the creek would stand on the bank, peering into the blackness with no idea of which direction the man in front had taken to follow the winding path through the jungle. Fortunately everyone's navigation was fairly proficient and all the companies met at their correct locations on the edge of the plantation.

The night was quite cold and we felt frozen after being accustomed to sleeping without need of a blanket in the hotter part of the year. To add to the discomfiture we were wet and mud covered from the waist down and we had to remain still for several hours until we began the final part of the approach to the cordon position a few hours before dawn. However, it was the only part of the operation during which we could get any sleep so many of us were soon aware of the cold only at infrequent intervals when it woke us up.

14. AGAINST THE VILLAGE CADRES

The final stage through the rubber trees was easy going except for an obstacle created by the village defences which the Viet Cong had destroyed. Several men fell into a ditch six feet deep and liberally strewn with barbed wire, but no great harm was suffered. A Company, who were in the lead, were charged by some pigs which caused great confusion in the darkness, but no one panicked and no shots were fired. The cordon went into position without further incident. It then remained to be seen whether this was due to complete surprise or whether the Viet Cong had already departed before the cordon was closed.

The dawn heralded the usual procedures of troops and Vietnamese police going around the houses while the loudspeaker aircraft told the villagers what was happening. The Assault Pioneer Platoon busied itself with the construction of the holding enclosures and the provincial interrogation team of twenty-eight men arrived. Unfortunately these interrogators took a long time to organise their system in this new location. They had become accustomed to operating in Ba Ria where they had a familiar set of enclosures and facilities for handling large numbers of people. They had to interrogate some fifteen hundred people during the one day so we became a little anxious at their delay, fearing that the results of twenty-four hours' effort by several hundred men might go for nought as the people could not be held in the enclosures overnight. However, all went well and the whole population was screened.

The results of the interrogation were heartening for several suspects were arrested, indicating that surprise had been achieved by our careful move. The Viet Cong circle in Binh Ba had been broken by a boy aged twelve who had admitted to carrying messages for the Viet Cong. He then identified the persons to whom he had brought messages and so a new cadre-in-embryo composed mostly of persons under twenty was dissolved and our determination to keep the Viet Cong out of Binh Ba was demonstrated. Although Binh Ba was visited on a few occasions after Operation Caloundra by Viet Cong, they had not come back into the village to make another attempt to establish a cadre before we finished our period of duty in Vietnam.

During January 1967 we participated in a series of Task Force operations directed at the Viet Cong in Hoa Long. In October 1966, both Australian battalions had joined forces to provide a complete cordon for a Vietnamese battalion, the 1st/43rd Rangers, to search the village and gather the people for interrogation by the provincial team in Ba Ria. This operation had yielded over thirty Viet Cong but this was by no means the whole of the Viet Cong population of Hoa Long. Agents were still coming into Hoa Long taking messages to and fro, taxation was taking place occasionally and villagers were still being forced by the Viet Cong to perform tasks such as transporting bags of rice at night.

Consequently a much more thorough cleaning out of Hoa Long had to be done as soon as time permitted. The major difficulty in a cordon and search operation at Hoa Long was the size of the village. Three thousand persons lived there and its perimeter called for three battalions if it were to be cordoned all at once. It was clearly beyond the resources of the Task Force to tackle the whole village at once and to comb it thoroughly so it had to be partitioned in some way and done piecemeal. The village was divided into four sectors by the two roads which crossed at right angles close to the village centre. These roads formed convenient boundary lines for it was possible to place a cordon along them in a matter of minutes by swiftly moving APCs. The outer perimeter of each sector could be cordoned by four infantry companies, so the operation could be carried out by the APC squadron and five companies of infantry if one company was provided for searching the sector to be cordoned. Thus each sector was approximately a battalion-sized operation and the whole village could be covered in two operations for each battalion.

Of course this method was not perfect for the Viet Cong in the second, third and fourth sectors to be searched would have guessed that their turn was coming. However the series of cordons was spread over several weeks so that the resident Viet Cong were placed in the dilemma of either continuing to live in Hoa Long and so risking arrest at any time or of leaving the village for good. Either of these outcomes suited our purpose. It was intended to keep returning to Hoa Long even after the whole village had been searched so that the Viet Cong would never feel secure there. We did not expect the Viet Cong to yield Hoa Long to the Government without a protracted fight which would continue for as long as the Viet Cong had resources within Phuoc Tuy.

The cordoning of the two sectors of the village which were allocated to the Fifth Battalion was uneventful. In both cases the cordon was positioned without incident and each day of interrogations yielded a few Viet Cong. After the first cordon we were very glad to receive a letter from a Vietnamese journalist who had watched the operation and who had talked to the villagers during the day of the search and interrogations. He pointed out a number of ways in which we could minimise the inconvenience which these operations imposed on the people. Two of his suggestions were particularly useful. These were to process quickly those prominent local persons whose loyalty to the Government was unquestioned so that their loyalty might be fostered, and to use some fencing material other than barbed wire for the enclosures. We had used the expanding coils of barbed wire, commonly known as concertina wire, because it was the only readily portable fencing material which we possessed which presented some discouragement to someone who wished to break out of the enclosure. Of course the appearance of putting well intentioned villagers en masse behind barbed wire was very bad and the journalist suggested that we did not need to go to the extent of barbed wire because the presence of a few armed soldiers was quite sufficient to deter any one from attempting an escape. If this was the case then all we required were simple one strand fences of white tape or something similarly inoffensive for purposes of handling the people during the interrogation process and for guiding them to the medical and dental officers' tents and the civil aid team.

These suggestions were incorporated into the second cordon and they produced excellent results. Other refinements which had been developed included Vietnamese music which was arranged by Bandmaster Bob Taylor for the battalion band, provision of awnings for shade, copious amounts of fruit drink which was very popular with the children, and a letter of apology for the inconvenience caused by the operation which was sent to each household on the day following the cordon. Arrangements were made for talks to be given to the assembled villagers collectively and to apprehended Viet Cong individually by some returnees, on why they had left the Viet Cong. A local Vietnamese official was also present to explain to the people the reasons for the cordon, search and interrogation.

After the cordon operations in Hoa Long, a barrier fence was placed around the village to prevent traffic between the village and the Viet Cong and to keep the Viet Cong influence away from the people. The fence was built of concertina barbed wire, six feet high and six feet wide and was thickened with aprons of stranded barbed wire. Three gaps were left in it for the people to enter their fields. These gaps were controlled by Vietnamese police by day and were closed and guarded by night. A Company controlled the operation and did much of the construction. They were aided by a company of returnees who worked with a will and infectious good humour. After part of the fence had been erected but not anchored, the commander of the returnees turned on a demonstration of

Viet Cong breaching techniques. Several of his men, armed with short lengths of stout bamboo rushed to the fence, placed their bamboo under it, lifted the bottom coil of the fence wire with it and slid under the gap, keeping the barbed wire off their bodies with the bamboo which they rolled rapidly in their palms. The purpose of the fence was explained to the people of Hoa Long and Captain Kim's men took over responsibility for patrolling it constantly.

During the last week in January, A Company laid a number of successful ambushes on the tracks which run close to the foot of the eastern slopes of the Dinh hills, linking central Phuoc Tuy with the Hat Dich base area in the north-west. On the afternoon of January 26th signs of ablutions and teeth cleaning carried out that morning were found by a creek, indicating that Viet Cong were near by. Major Carroll planned to move into his ambush position under cover of darkness at 7.30 pm. Just as the company was preparing to move from its harbour at 7.15 pm, fifteen Viet Cong walked into the company perimeter from the north-east. One Platoon opened fire, killing one Viet Cong and wounding several others. Five men were seen to fall. Artillery fire was brought down onto enemy movement heard outside the company perimeter shortly before midnight. On the following morning the dead Viet Cong was buried and the blood trails of the wounded were followed for three-quarters of a mile. With the dead man were found his Garrand M1 carbine and a pack containing letters identifying the Viet Cong as members of the Chau Duc District Company.

On the afternoon of January 27th A Company moved to a new ambush area to the south-west. Major Carroll and Lieutenant Hartley, commander of One Platoon, made a forward reconnaissance and discovered the tracks of three Viet Cong no more than twenty-four hours old. An ambush was planned for the area and the officers moved back to the company. Again, just as the company was in the exposed situation of preparing to move, a group of twenty-five Viet Cong moving cautiously from the south-west came onto the rear sentry of One Platoon. The sentry killed one of the Viet Cong and wounded another. The enemy reorganised and put in a flank attack on a front of one hundred yards. The other machine guns of One Platoon broke up this attack and the platoon countered with a hooking movement into the flank of the Viet Cong. They withdrew to the south, split into two parties and ran off through the thick vegetation.

14. AGAINST THE VILLAGE CADRES

At midday on January 28th, Major Carroll divided the company into three separate ambush groups in order to cover as wide an area as possible. Evidently the group of Viet Cong who had tried to get through the company and escape to the north on the previous day were becoming desperate. D Company of the Sixth Battalion was nearly a mile to the south and the Chau Duc company was alternately striking the two Australian companies.

Lieutenant Sheehan, who had become commander of Three Platoon in January, was making a reconnaissance in the early afternoon of the area which he was to ambush when suddenly six Viet Cong entered the opposite side of a clearing which he was crossing. Sheehan opened fire instantly, wounding one of the group who spun around, flinging his arms in the air. The group then ran off while artillery fire was called in onto their escape route. As a result of the contact Lieutenant Sheehan and his two escorts, Privates L. E. Gates and N. B. Hexter were wounded. The three casualties, the only ones suffered by A Company during five successive contacts with the Viet Cong in three days, were quickly evacuated by helicopter. Lieutenant Sheehan was wounded so seriously that he had to be returned to Australia.

At 2 pm on the following day, January 29th, ten Viet Cong were seen approaching cautiously by a sentry of One Platoon. He opened fire and the enemy immediately deployed into extended line and assaulted the section position. This attack was broken up by firing a Claymore mine into the enemy who then commenced to cover their withdrawal by fire and movement. While one group of Viet Cong moved, the others fired at One Platoon to prevent our men from pursuing. When the first group had withdrawn some fifty yards they covered the second group by firing at One Platoon while the former pulled back to a fire position well in rear of the covering group. While this was taking place Lieutenant Hartley had been organising another flank attack onto the withdrawing enemy. This attack broke up the Viet Cong tactics and they dispersed in full flight.

They ran straight into another ambush which had been set behind them by Two Platoon. Two Viet Cong were killed instantly and two others were wounded. The Viet Cong responded with an immediate counter ambush hook and threw grenades into the Two Platoon position. This determined action enabled them to recover the Browning automatic rifle from one of their men who had been killed. The Viet Cong then fled to the north leaving heavy blood trails. A Thompson sub machine gun was found with the two dead men. One of these was a man of some importance, probably a platoon commander, for several certificates of commendation for bravery were found in his wallet. Both of these men belonged to the C20 Chau Duc District Company. No further contact with the Viet Cong was made that night and A Company returned to Nui Dat by helicopter on the following afternoon.

In February the attention of the whole Task Force was focused on the vital rice production area of the Dat Do district. We had been collecting information on the Viet Cong cadres in the villages of this district for several weeks and had formed a plan to cordon the northern part of Dat Do village. However it was suspected that this intention may have become known by the Viet Cong and so the plan was altered to cover the next most suitable village, An Nhut, just to the west of Dat Do. An Nhut was a village of nearly one thousand inhabitants, most of whom were Government supporters. Several men from the village were members of the C25 Long Dat District Company, the local guerilla unit. Others had joined D445 Battalion and there were a number of resident cadre in the village. The village chief had been murdered by Viet Cong in November 1966. The village stood like an island in a flat sea of rice fields and so it was very easy to isolate. Route 23 ran through An Nhut dividing the village into northern and southern sectors, of which the latter was nearly twice the area of the former. The perimeter of An Nhut was nearly two miles long and so was just within the capacity of four rifle companies to encircle.

It was clearly difficult to position forces close to An Nhut so that their presence would not compromise the security of the operation. The battalion had to be positioned within easy reach of An Nhut during the day before the cordon, despite the open paddy fields for some miles around. The nearest jungle was at the foot of the Long Hai hills, one and a half miles to the south-west of An Nhut. However, the security offered by this vegetation was lessened by the presence of another village at its edge, Tam Phuoc, which was under an appreciable degree of Viet Cong influence. Although it was still possible to avoid Tam Phuoc by moving around the southern side of the village to come out onto the edge of the paddy fields a little further to the south-east, the distance from the edge of the jungle to An Nhut was too great for the whole battalion to use that line of approach during one night.

14. AGAINST THE VILLAGE CADRES

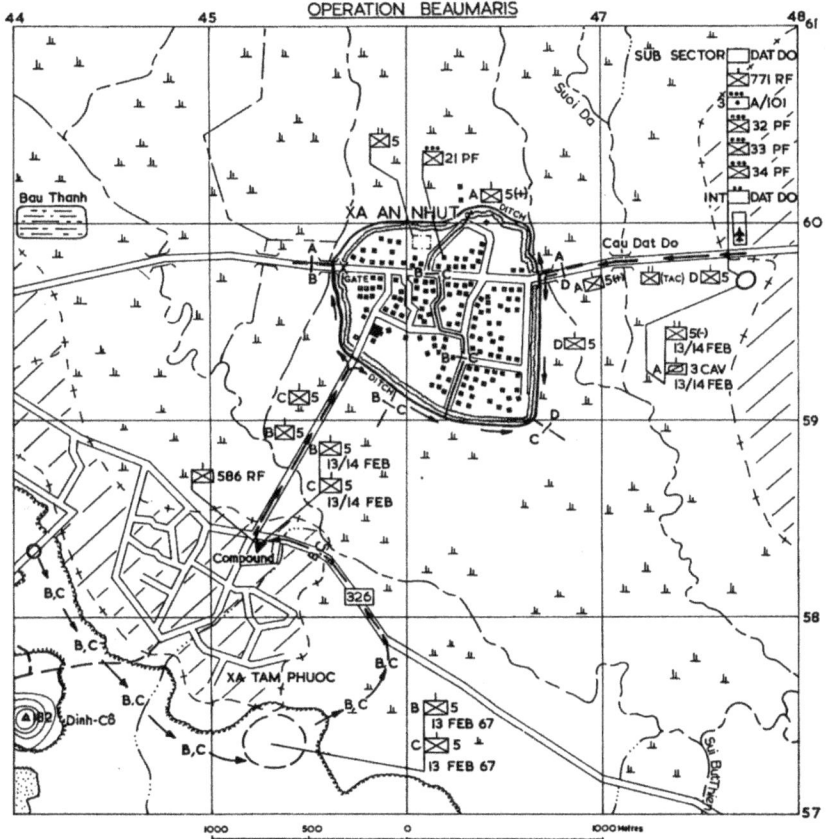

Fig. 20. The cordoning of An Nhut, Operation Beaumaris, 13–14 February 1967.

However another suitable harbour area close to An Nhut was available. On the western edge of Dat Do lay the district compound and airstrip. This area was fairly secure and it offered access to An Nhut, less than a thousand yards distant, without disturbing any of the population of Dat Do during the night approach. By harbouring two companies near Tam Phuoc and the other two at the Dat Do airstrip the battalion could concentrate around An Nhut effectively in the course of one night.

However the deployment of troops near Tam Phuoc to the south of An Nhut and at Dat Do to the east could have suggested a cordon of An Nhut to any Viet Cong in the neighbourhood. Colonel Warr decided to use a cover plan to explain the movements of the companies around Tam Phuoc and to rely on secrecy for getting the remainder of the battalion into Dat Do on the night before the cordon, so that the credibility of the cover plan for the first two companies would not be jeopardised. This cover plan was a thrust into the northern part of the Long Hai hills to clean out some of the C25 Company's bases. It was to be suggested to the local people by two means. The companies were to travel in APCs to the northern edge of Tam Phuoc and to proceed into the jungle immediately to the north of the hills. The direction of their ostensible goal was to be made more apparent by an artillery fire programme onto the northern part of the hills. This bombardment was to begin in the early afternoon of the day before the cordon, just as the companies were setting off into the jungle. Secrecy for the two companies and Battalion Headquarters at Dat Do was to be obtained by bringing these troops to the airstrip inside closed APCs just on last light. The troops were then to remain inside the vehicles until darkness had become complete. The presence of the APCs was not likely to arouse special attention for they had been operating independently to the south of Dat Do on several occasions and so the most likely explanation of their presence at Dat Do for the night was to save time for operations on the following morning by harbouring at Dat Do instead of Nui Dat, fifteen miles away by road.

The date for this operation, Operation Beaumaris, was selected as the night of February 13th–14th after consideration of moonlight data and the Task Force operational programme. Colonel Warr decided that a reconnaissance was necessary to see whether we would encounter any problems with local Vietnamese forces such as guards on the bridges on Route 23 who might open fire on the paddy fields at random during the night of our approach. It was impossible to conduct such a reconnaissance by night so we made it from a convoy of APCs on an afternoon drive through the villages of Long Dien, An Nhut, Dat Do, Tam Phuoc, and An Ngai to cloak our particular interest in An Nhut under the guise of a routine road patrol. We saw to our concern that the five bridges on Route 23 on either side of An Nhut were provided with sentry posts. We did not know whether or not they were manned every night and we thought it better not to make specific enquiries of the local Vietnamese troops, such as the Popular Forces platoon in An Nhut, for fear of compromising the operation. Instead small groups of men were sent to the bridges at last light on February 13th to occupy the post and to prevent any Vietnamese sentries who were manning them from firing during the night. Again this move threatened the secrecy of the operation, but we

14. AGAINST THE VILLAGE CADRES

hoped that our intentions would still remain hidden by occupying every bridge between Long Dien and Dat Do and by moving our men after curfew and under the cover of dusk.

Similar problems were presented by the Vietnamese Regional and Popular forces groups in Long Dien, Dat Do and Tam Phuoc. These difficulties were unobtrusively overcome by sending a liaison officer and a radio operator to each post during the morning of February 13th to request the local commander to keep all his men inside his compound at night and to refrain from firing any weapons in the interests of our operations in the Long Hai hills.

The preliminary moves of B and C Companies around the southern side of Tam Phuoc went well and they harboured inside the edge of the jungle to the south-east of Tam Phuoc late on the afternoon of February 13th, having swung their direction of movement from south to east in mid-afternoon. A and D Companies with Battalion Headquarters travelled to the Dat Do airstrip, leaving Nui Dat at 7 pm. We dismounted from the closed APCs after 8 pm and emerged from their confined stuffiness into the soft mild air of a Vietnamese night, unlit by moonlight. After posting sentries we lay on the ground behind the armoured vehicles and tried to obtain what few hours of sleep we could before the final phase of the move which was to begin at 2 am. However, neither Colonel Warr nor myself ever obtained much sleep on these cordon nights for we divided the part of the night when we were not moving into shifts between us to listen for any urgent calls on the battalion commander's radio.

The cordon was placed around An Nhut without a great deal of difficulty. One problem which presented itself was the possibility of encountering South Vietnamese mines and booby traps around the outside of the village. All villages seemed to have some of these devices and they were a serious hazard to our operations for no one had recorded their location and they could be avoided only by staying well back from the perimeter ditches and fences. An Nhut had been enclosed within two wire fences with a belt of mines laid between them. The American adviser at Long Dien, the district headquarters which controlled An Nhut, informed us that the mines had been taken out during the previous wet season and that the wire had been taken from the steel pickets which had supported the fence. However, until we had checked the ground with mine detectors we could not be sure that it was safe. A Company encountered part of the perimeter fence as they were feeling their way around the northern side of An Nhut at 3 am and Major Carroll ordered his men to swing out from the village to avoid further risk.

The cordon was closed at 4 am. Although it was still over two hours before dawn we took this additional precaution because we had learned that the Viet Cong in some of the villages had begun to make a habit of leaving their villages each morning around 4.30 am in order to avoid being caught by an Australian cordon. A company of Vietnamese troops, the 772 Regional Forces, came down from Long Dien shortly after 8 am to assist our troops with the search and clearance of the village. This part of the operation progressed smoothly until 9.15 am, when a loud explosion came from C Company, followed by an urgent appeal on the radio for the medical officer and for a Dust Off aircraft.

When C Company had reached their cordon position, a preliminary check had revealed no mines or booby traps in the area of the fence so the Company Headquarters had moved right up to it. The company commander had held a conference of his officers and senior NCOs close by the fence. At the conclusion of the conference, someone, while getting to his feet, must have set off a mine which had been perfectly concealed. The effect of the explosion was devastating and particularly tragic for it killed three of the company's officers and wounded another five men. The officers killed were Major Bourne, the company commander, Captain Milligan, the second-in-command, and Captain Williams, the artillery forward observation officer attached from the New Zealand 161 Battery. In one blow the Company Headquarters had been wiped out. Major Bourne had just taken over command of the company from Major Miller who was about to lead the battalion advance party back to Australia. Major Bourne, a Malayan veteran and a graduate of the Staff College had been on the staff of the Task Force Headquarters for several months. He was killed on his first operation with the battalion. Captain Milligan had just joined up with the company after spending the previous day and night in the Tam Phuoc compound, guarding the safety of our troops from that direction. The suddenness and severity of this blow distracted our thinking for the remainder of the operation. The specific cause of the explosion was impossible to determine for the mine had blown itself to tiny pieces, but probably it had been part of the old mine field.

The remainder of the day proceeded smoothly. Loudspeakers announced the reasons for the village search and interrogation to the people. They were told to have breakfast and to carry their lunches with them as they

14. AGAINST THE VILLAGE CADRES

came to the central enclosures of white tape. Once they were gathered together, the local District Chief explained the procedures of the day, and some former Viet Cong who had surrendered under the Chieu Hoi programme addressed them, stressing the emptiness of Viet Cong policy and the hopelessness of the Viet Cong prospects in the war. The band played to the people, they were offered soft drinks and given colourful brochures explaining Government policy. The elderly, the mothers and the expectant mothers were interrogated first. After interrogation the people moved through the dental and medical treatment tents to the civil aid point where they were given food and clothing. The serious intention of these proceedings was masked under the mantle of a Sunday-school picnic as small children ran around the band whose tunes wafted pleasantly on the warm air through the marquees and across the sunny field which contained everyone. As our medical officer remarked, on these occasions the Government must have seemed like the Cheshire Cat to the villagers, arriving and giving a bountiful grin for a day, only to disappear leaving nothing but the grin at the end of the afternoon. We felt that when the situation permitted the permanent stationing of elementary welfare personnel in these villages, the platform of the Viet Cong would finally disintegrate.

Proceedings around midday livened when a man who had been hiding in the roof of a house broke out of the cordon and set off at a furious pace across the paddy fields. In order to avoid firing at him several of our men set off after him across the dry mud of the paddies which was being baked by a scorching sun. The chase went on for over half a mile until our men eventually ran the suspect down and overcame a prisoner who may one day be a live supporter of the Government rather than a corpse now.

The interrogation team of thirty Vietnamese worked hard, interrogating 1,111 adults and catching four female cadre members, two male cadre members, fourteen suspects whose apprehension had been desired for some time, two deserters from the Army, one draft dodger, five Viet Cong sympathisers who had aided the Viet Cong with supplies, and ten persons who were to be interrogated further. This operation closed our series of village cordons as the direction of Task Force operations swung to interdiction. During six weeks we had captured nearly forty Viet Cong in six days of operations for the loss of three of our own lives. These forty village workers would be difficult for the Viet Cong to replace and the people of Phuoc Tuy were witnessing that Viet Cong in the populated areas were becoming easy prey for the Government.

15

In the Long Hai Hills

One of the most important villages of the south central rice-producing area of Phuoc Tuy was Phuoc Hai. It lay on a broad stretch of yellow dunes and faced onto the South China Sea. Fishing was the chief occupation of the eight thousand inhabitants, and their daily catch was so large that Phuoc Hai was an important source of fish for the Saigon market as well as for Phuoc Tuy. Fish was important to the Viet Cong as well as to the Government and so the village had attracted a large amount of Viet Cong attention. Phuoc Hai was on the western edge of a vast, almost uninhabited stretch of country which ran for forty miles along the coast to Ham Tan and another thirty miles to the first large town of Phan Thiet. The hinterland to this coastal region was the May Tao mountains and the whole area had been a guerilla base since the Japanese occupation. Hence control of Phuoc Hai was very desirable for the Viet Cong, and they had infiltrated a large cadre into the village and had recruited guerillas and regular soldiers from its youth.

After the cordon of An Nhut our attention turned to Phuoc Hai. We knew who many of the village cadre members were and a cordon looked to offer good prospects. Unfortunately the village was too large to be cordoned by one battalion so a Task Force operation, Operation Ulmarra, was proposed to take place between February 24th and 26th. The usual difficulties of establishing the cordon without betraying our intentions before the operation presented themselves. One battalion could be flown into the cordon by helicopter at dawn on the morning of the cordon, but the other would have to make a long approach march and appear to be engaged in some other pursuit, for it was vital to the success of the cordon to have a large part of it in position before dawn and this could be done only on foot. The nearest area of jungle from which the battalion could emerge during the hours of darkness before the cordon was to be closed was at the foot of the Long Hai hills, one and a half miles to the south-west of Phuoc Hai.

These hills had been in our thoughts for several months for they were known to contain several bases and caches used by both D445 Battalion and the C25 Company. The American 173rd Airborne Brigade had swept rapidly through the hills in June 1966 after Operation Hardihood. They had suffered a high casualty rate and had discovered many bases which they had not had time to destroy. Two smaller operations in the hills had been conducted by Vietnamese troops, aimed at rooting out the headquarters of the Viet Cong Long Dat district which controlled all Viet Cong activity within the Long Dien and Dat Do districts. They had been successful as far as they had gone, capturing the district secretary, his typewriter and records, several other less important Viet Cong, weapons, ammunition and equipment. They had also located several Viet Cong bases, some of which they had destroyed. Consequently there was a need for a larger sweep through the hills to destroy all of the bases and to capture any supplies which the Viet Cong had taken into the hills recently.

Such a sweep seemed to be a good prelude to the cordon of Phuoc Hai. A battalion could work its way through the hills from north to south and concentrate in the jungle at the south-eastern corner on the evening before the cordon was to be placed around Phuoc Hai. The Fifth Battalion was assigned to this role while the Sixth Battalion was to complete the north-eastern part of the cordon by helicopter at dawn on February 25th. We were to commence the move through the Long Hai hills on February 18th so we had six days to cover the area.

Our intelligence collection and appreciation had commenced several months previously and so our files on the area were thick. A preliminary survey of information regarding Viet Cong installations in the hills had been made by our Intelligence Section during January, when a quiet period permitted the compilation of a great deal of intelligence data for several contingency plans. Consequently the final collection and consideration of information was not a lengthy process.

15. IN THE LONG HAI HILLS

The Viet Cong who lived in the hills had been forced back from the outer fringe of jungle into the deeper parts through the operations of 1966 and harassing artillery fire. The most significant occupant of the hills was the C25 Company which was recruited by the Long Dat District Committee from the several villages which surrounded the hills. The company had dug up most of the main roads around the hills,[1] Route 23 to the north, Route 326 which ran for five miles along the north-eastern edge of the hills and Route 44 which ran along the western side of the hills, on the coast, leading to Long Hai then swinging around the Long Hai Point to run north-eastwards for five miles to Phuoc Hai. Route 23 had been repaired but the other two roads were still cut on the eastern side of the hills. The company had raided the Government outposts of Popular Forces troops which existed in most of the villages around the hills and it had murdered and terrorised local officials. Until late 1966 armed members of C25 Company could often be seen in villages by day. After this time they appeared as guerillas only at night. D445 Battalion had used the sanctuary of the hills on several occasions in 1966, although it did not keep significant elements permanently based in the hills.

In December activity in the hills flared up as the C25 Company and D445 Battalion made raids on the Government posts in Tam Phuoc, Phuoc Hai, Dat Do and on two small posts on the arm of Route 44 which connected Dat Do and Phuoc Hai, Hoi My and Phuoc Loi.[2] The Sixth Battalion had responded to these raids with a thrust into the hills, and since then enemy activity out of the hills had been slight. However during Tet, the Lunar New Year in early February, the Viet Cong advertised their presence by flying large Viet Cong flags, one at Long My, on Route 326, two miles to the north-west of Phuoc Hai, and another on the summit of Nui Chau Vien, the highest point of the southern part of the hills. This latter flag had been illuminated at night by a spotlight.

The approaches to the hills presented several problems, the worst of which was the possibility of mines and booby traps. The road cuts on Routes 326 and 44 required particularly careful negotiation for they were such obvious places to surround with mines. Once off the roads we had to continue to take great care for the whole area of the hills was known to contain many mines and booby traps.

---

1   See Fig. 1 (p. 4) and Fig. 22 (p. 259).
2   See Fig. 1 (p. 4) and Fig. 22 (p. 259).

Thirty-four base camps had been located by the previous operations and by special reconnaissance patrols. Most of these were concentrated on the lower slopes on the eastern side of the hills. In fact the western side contained very few installations so it was thought more important to concentrate our attention on the eastern side of the hills and on the crest line. This area was some five miles long from north-west and south-east and three miles wide. The hills were steep and rose to eleven hundred feet. A deep valley running north and south cut off a small part of the hills in the north-west from the main mass.

The base camps on the eastern side presented a suitable concentration for a heavy airstrike just before we were to enter the hills and so the Americans had organised a B52 raid onto them, to commence at 6 am on February 18th, ninety minutes before our first troops were to arrive to the east of the hills. Many of the bases consisted of tunnels and bunkers so we hoped that their tops would be blown in by the heavy bombs, leaving only minor demolition to be carried out by the men on the ground.

The frequency of airstrikes and harassing artillery fire onto the hills made it unlikely that we would strike any large numbers of Viet Cong, although some were undoubtedly present in order to guard their bases, to liaise with the villages and to conduct observation of all movement in the area from the hilltops. We expected any Viet Cong who were in the hills when we arrived to go into a counter sweep operation by splitting up into small groups and taking evasive action.

Everything necessary for the operation was prepared and the orders were given on the afternoon of February 16th. In the early hours of the following morning the Government post at Phuoc Hai was attacked by two companies of Viet Cong. They failed to get into the post but they did not leave off the attack until just after dawn. A relieving force of Government troops from the Regional Forces company at Hoi My set out for Phuoc Hai at first light. By this time we had all become familiar with the often used Viet Cong technique of attacking a post without attempting to overrun it in order to draw out a relieving force which could then be ambushed and cut to pieces outside of any fortifications. The commander of the relieving company was careful to take the precaution of moving to Phuoc Hai by an indirect route, well to the east of the road connecting the two villages, Route 44.

This caution paid handsome dividends for the company struck the flank of a two company Viet Cong ambush which was covering the road. Although the Viet Cong were superior in numbers they were caught in a bad position and the Government company was able to hold the Viet Cong off without suffering many casualties. However, assistance was necessary and it was the turn of the Sixth Battalion to supply the troops which Brigadier Graham wished to send. Two companies, A and B, were flown by helicopter into a landing zone behind the Viet Cong to cut off their withdrawal. Unfortunately these companies landed right alongside the rear base of the Viet Cong and they came under fire as soon as they stepped out of the aircraft. By this stage it was known that the Viet Cong were the D445 Battalion. A Company mounted an attack to thrust the Viet Cong out of their defences but the enemy held their ground so firmly that to have pressed the attack further would have cost many casualties. B Company also became involved in heavy fighting which went on for six hours. Viet Cong snipers were concealed over a wide area and harassed the attackers continually, concentrating on the company commanders, who were recognisable from their actions in controlling operations, and the several radio antennas which went with the Company Headquarters.

Another Australian force in the APCs of A Squadron, Third Cavalry, pressed in from the west, to relieve the Government company. One of the APCs was destroyed by recoilless rifle fire. It was recovered on the following day covered with Viet Cong slogans written in blood. One battalion was too small to place a tight cordon around the area held by D445 Battalion and so the Viet Cong escaped after dark through swamps to the northeast taking their dead and wounded with them. The force which A and B Companies of the Sixth Battalion had encountered had been protecting the withdrawal of the Battalion Headquarters and the heavy weapons including mortars which had fired onto Phuoc Hai. Probably they had been ordered to stand firm at all costs until nightfall when they could follow the part of the battalion which had already withdrawn.

American Chinook heavy helicopters had lifted 101 Battery and our A Company from Nui Dat to a forward fire base at Dat Do from which the Viet Cong were shelled continuously. Caught as they were between A and B Companies of the Sixth Battalion on the east and the APCs on the west with artillery and airstrikes descending on them, the Viet Cong had a thin time of things. This defeat was of special significance. We had known that the Viet Cong had been making reconnaissances of the area to the south of Dat Do for some weeks. An attack which they were going to make before the Lunar New Year had been frustrated by a sweep which the Sixth Battalion had carried out. However D445 Battalion had announced to the people of the Dat Do district that they were coming to establish themselves permanently in the area and that the Australians were not going to move them out. Thus the villagers had seen that the Viet Cong were unable to carry their intentions into practical effect and that they were taking a severe beating on every occasion when they attempted large scale operations.

Once the Sixth Battalion had gone out from Nui Dat, we had to remain in the base in order to secure it so the operation into the Long Hai hills, Operation Renmark, was postponed. It was possible to bring the Sixth Battalion back to Nui Dat on the afternoon of February 18th, and we received notification that Operation Renmark would commence at 4 pm. The B52 strike had taken place as planned and it was important to follow it up as soon as possible. Furthermore our time in the hills was limited by the need to be in position for the cordon of Phuoc Hai on February 24th.

After doing calculations of helicopter loadings, Colonel Warr saw that the latest time at which the battalion could depart from Nui Dat and deploy as a whole in the hills was 3.30 pm. After further discussion with Brigadier Graham, the first helicopter lift was arranged for this time. Battalion Headquarters, C and D Companies flew into a landing zone adjacent to the planned initial location of the headquarters on Route 326, half-way between Tam Phuoc and Long My. B Company travelled out by APC and A Company which had been guarding the forward fire base of 101 Battery on the Dat Do airstrip joined us on the following morning.

B, C and D Companies set off into the hills while A Company protected the headquarters and the fire base of 103 Field Battery. At 11.45 on the morning of February 19th B Company sighted two Viet Cong at short range, half-way up the eastern face of the northern hill. The company deployed as the Viet Cong hurled a grenade at the forward members of Four Platoon and opened fire with small arms. Four Platoon under Lieutenant Carruthers returned the fire and swept forward. The Viet Cong withdrew, probably to the south. Four Platoon heard two more Viet Cong shouting to their left and another engaged the platoon with fire from the right so probably the platoon had contacted a squad of enemy. Carruthers found that the Viet Cong had been using a small camp on the hillside containing three two-man weapon pits protected by overhead cover, a kitchen and a meeting place. Several documents were found in the camp. After a thorough search the camp was blown up.

In the meantime I had been sent aloft in the supporting Sioux helicopter to attempt to spot the fleeing Viet Cong and direct B Company onto them. Unfortunately the Viet Cong had fled into a particularly thick part of the jungle and I was unable to see anything beneath the foliage.

D Company met with considerable success in discovering enemy installations. They were searching the southernmost of three sectors which covered the northern half of the hills, and so they were the closest in the first phase of the operation to the concentration of Viet Cong camps. Their first find was a sugar bag full of documents and a platoon defensive position, some two months old. The documents were chiefly propaganda to be distributed amongst the local villages. After finding some tracks of Viet Cong, D Company followed them to a company-sized defensive position which had been dug for a long time but which had been used by small groups recently. They proceeded to demolish the base with explosives. Shortly after 3 pm, the Reconnaissance Platoon, which was searching with D Company, contacted four Viet Cong.

The Reconnaissance Platoon was a platoon which had been specially formed to replace the Anti-Tank Platoon. Colonel Warr began this experiment in November after our operational experience indicated that we had a need for a special team which could carry out reconnaissance to a distance of a few miles ahead of the battalion. The platoon was composed of selected volunteers and was commanded by Second Lieutenant Deak. It had been trained in a special course which we had run at Vung Tau in November and December. The platoon was organised to operate as a number of small teams, each equipped with radio. Space precludes description of the large number of individual reconnaissances and ambushes which the platoon undertook. Suffice it to say that the platoon was kept extremely busy, being lucky to have one night a month in base at Nui Dat. The platoon was very successful in its operations, killing many Viet Cong in swift encounters in the jungle and producing a great deal of intelligence information to assist my work.

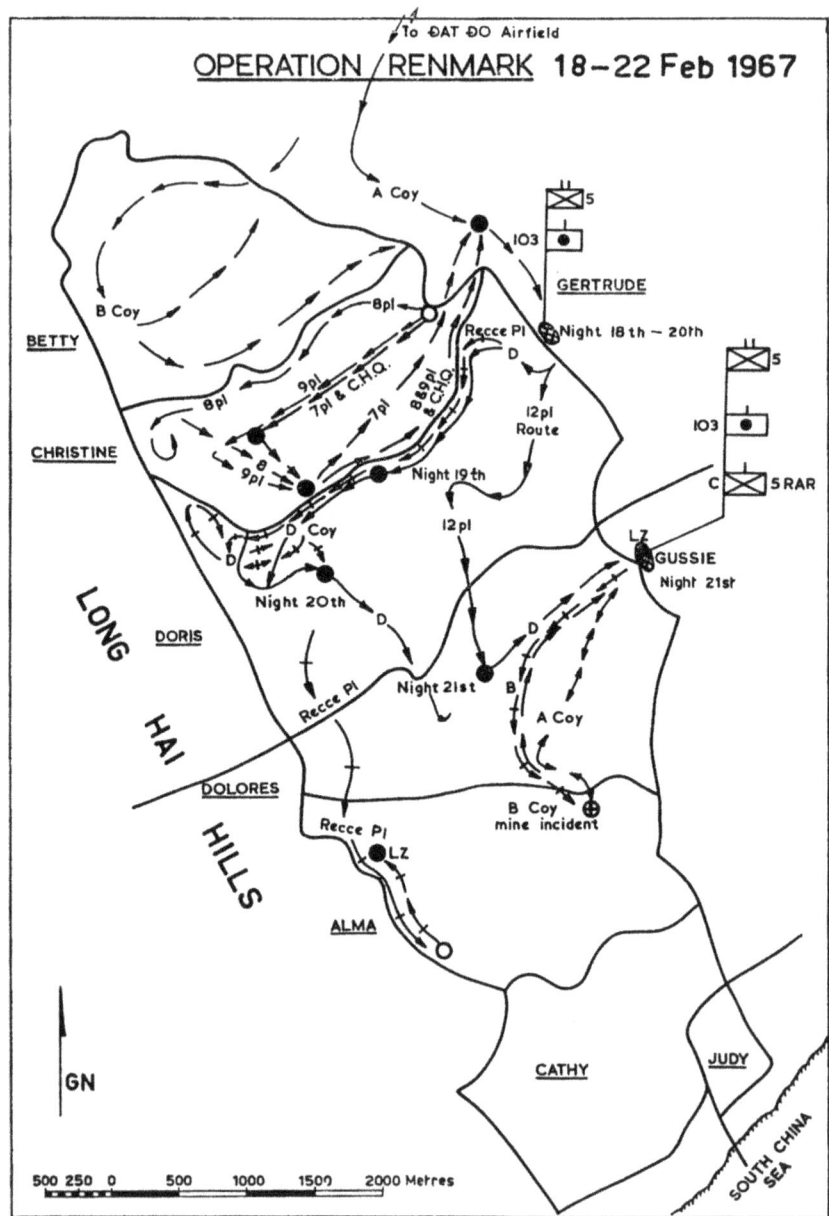

Fig. 21. The search of the Viet Cong base areas in the Long Hai hills, Operation Renmark, 18–22 February 1967.

15. IN THE LONG HAI HILLS

The Viet Cong contacted by the Reconnaissance Platoon included a woman who was armed with a Garrand M1 rifle. After a quick fire fight the Viet Cong fled to the south-east. Deak called in artillery fire onto their withdrawal route. When the platoon cleared through the area where the Viet Cong had been located they found the body of the woman and her weapon.

During the night A Company reported lights moving on the northern face of the southernmost of the hills, Hon Vung. These lights were close to a reported enemy base and artillery was fired at them. They were quickly extinguished.

D Company continued to have success on the following day, finding the following installations:

- a squad sized base camp,
- a company base with 46 pits, all provided with overhead cover and containing some .30 calibre ammunition,
- a company base with fifty pits and a well which appeared to be three months old,
- 22 graves, one to two months old, and
- 3 rice bins each capable of holding five tons of rice, two underground and one above ground, all empty.

The camps and rice bins were all destroyed. Near one of the camps an unexploded five-hundred-pound bomb was found. This was given a wide berth as we did not have the necessary skill for dealing safely with such a complicated destructive mechanism.

On the following day, February 21st, D Company found another company-sized camp, equipped with crawl trenches between the main weapon pits and guarded by panji pits which had sharp spikes in the bottom to trap an unwary attacker. Air and artillery bombardment had destroyed the camp. Three more camps, all destroyed by bombardment, were discovered nearby. One of these camps was equipped with many large bunkers and appeared to have been a headquarters. It may have been the headquarters of the Long Dat District Committee for some time. Another of the camps was capable of holding two companies. The most significant find by D Company however was a series of foot tracks, made by a group of approximately one hundred men within the previous week. The tracks were undeniably Viet Cong for they had been made by the familiar Ho Chi Minh sandals. The tracks headed to the south-east and could have been made by the Viet Cong who attacked Phuoc Hai or by a group who were fleeing from us.

B and C Companies had completed their first search areas by the morning of February 21st and the operation moved into its second phase. This phase was to cover a search of the southern half of the hills. D Company were to move to an area immediately to the south of their first area, C Company were to relieve A Company of headquarters defence and the latter were to search the central southern area, immediately south of D Company, and B Company were to move to the southernmost sector. Battalion Headquarters and the guns were to move forward to a new position, a little over a mile to the south-east.

C Company moved directly to the new headquarters area in mid-morning of February 21st, and began to secure it for occupation. Shortly after their arrival several shots came from some nearby scrub. It appeared as if some Viet Cong were firing at the Sioux helicopter which was overhead. The Viet Cong fled at the approach of our troops leaving five empty .30 calibre cases in their firing position. After midday a convoy of the guns, B Company, Battalion Headquarters and A Company moved in APCs from the old headquarters area to the new.

Jack Carruthers looked cheerily defiant of the world, his huge, bushy red moustache none the worse for the dust which covered him and his platoon as they rode on the outside of the leading APCs. He made a few lighthearted remarks to me about the steepness of the hill which B Company would shortly be clambering up in the broiling afternoon heat as I went by his halted vehicle at the new headquarters site. After depositing my kit I had a chance for a few words with Bruce McQualter. I had just received in the mail a photograph of him which had been taken during our leave in Hong Kong in December. It was a bad time to give it to him as few things stayed clean on forward operations. He was about to give it back to me when he quipped that I would be sure to lose it amongst all my papers and maps. He ran off exuberantly and climbed into his Company Headquarters vehicle. At 1.41 pm he called up on the radio to announce that his company was on its way with the APCs to the southern sector.

15. IN THE LONG HAI HILLS

At 2.07 pm we were alarmed by a loud explosion from the direction in which B Company had gone. The commander of the APCs announced over the command net that his leading vehicle had been blown onto its side by a mine. The convoy had been working its way through the jungle, parallel to a track running to the south-east, taking care to keep off the track because of the danger of mines. After crossing a creek the leading vehicle came to a long clearing running across its path and linking with the track whose direction the convoy was following. The growth on the far side of the clearing was extremely dense and so the first APC swung right to move along the clearing to the track, intending to cross the track at that point and move through the jungle on the far side. The vehicle travelled slowly and silently in low gear up to the junction with the track, slowing down to a halt before crossing the track, so that the commander could see if the track was clear.

Just as the forward part of the APC reached the intersection a tremendous explosion went off, blowing the twelve ton vehicle into the air and hurling it some ten feet away to land on its side. A circular hole two feet across was blown right through the forward part of the hull. The blast wave inside the vehicle blew the rear door off, which landed on one of the men who had been hurled from the top of the vehicle, killing him. Several of those inside the vehicle were blown out the back door by the blast, and it was very fortunate for them that the door had been blown off first. Most of these men escaped with bruises and shock. Another man who had been on the top of the APC, where it was often safer to ride when mines might be encountered, was thrown to the ground in the same place where the vehicle landed, crushing him.

The APCs immediately swung into counter ambush procedure with alternate vehicles slewing to left and right, giving all-round observation and fields of fire for the .50 calibre machine guns. Four Platoon had been riding on the leading vehicles and most of the leading section of the platoon had been either killed or injured by the blast. The cause of the detonation of the mine was never identified. The only evidence remaining was a crater at the junction of the track and the clearing six feet across and four feet deep, and a home made contact switch designed to be set off by pressure. The switch was a simple split bamboo cane with a wedge inserted near the start of the split and the two split ends bound in copper to each of which were attached copper wires covered with turquoise insulation. The wedge and the natural resilience of the bamboo kept the two contacts apart unless a pressure of a few pounds was applied to the copper bound ends. Such a device was ideal to bury a few inches beneath the surface of a track and in conjunction with an electric detonator could set off an explosion of any size.

It was evident that the mine had been set off when the APC was directly over the charge. This could have been done by a pressure switch on the mine itself or by a man hiding in the undergrowth at the side of the track holding the pressure switch in his hand. However, careful examination of the surrounding jungle revealed no trace of Viet Cong occupation and no hide of any type. Nor was any movement seen after the detonation of the mine. Hence it is unlikely that the mine was command detonated by human agency. On the other hand, had the switch which was found been part of the mine itself it is inconceivable that so flimsy a device could have survived the blast. Either it had been an alternate trigger on the main track or it had been left lying in the bushes by the Viet Cong who had set the main mine.

The force of the blast of the mine suggested that it was far larger than any conventional anti-tank mine. Probably it was an unexploded five-hundred-pound bomb such as the one discovered by D Company. Occasionally these bombs failed to detonate on landing and the Viet Cong were presented with a weapon of enormous destructive power which they kept for use against armoured vehicles. The absence of any fresh tracks in the area of the explosion suggested that this mine had been placed in position some months previously.

B Company had been travelling on the APCs in the order Four Platoon, Company Headquarters, Five Platoon, and Six Platoon. As soon as the APCs had gone into their counter ambush procedure Major McQualter dismounted from his vehicle and quickly sized up the situation. The most vital need was to get medical attention to those injured by the explosion. Up to this point, three of B Company and two APC crew men had been killed and nine others had been injured. Major McQualter summoned the company medic, Corporal Nichols, and the stretcher bearers from Five and Six Platoons.

Most of the members of Four Platoon had quickly dismounted and taken up fire positions on the ground alongside and in front of the vehicles which faced out towards either edge of the clearing. Lieutenant Carruthers and Sergeant Wass were standing at the rear of the second APC, commencing to organise assistance to the injured and estimation of the damage done. Major McQualter came forward with the two stretcher bearers from Five and Six Platoons, Corporal Nichols, Corporal Bouse, the company stretcher bearer NCO, and his two radio operators, Private Tape and Private Anthony. He was followed by the acting CSM, Staff Sergeant Benson, who besides being Drum Major of the battalion, was also a highly trained medic.

Just as the group approached the rear of the second APC where Carruthers and Wass were standing a second explosion from the midst of the approaching group rent the air. Someone had trodden on the pressure switch of a deadly 'jumping Jack' mine. The mine had bounded four feet into the air before exploding with colossal force and hurling large chunks of shrapnel into those nearby. This second explosion occurred at 2.11 pm. So much had happened in the space of four minutes. All of those in the vicinity of the mine were struck by the flying steel. The most seriously injured were Major McQualter and Lieutenant Carruthers. Sergeant Wass was also extremely badly wounded. Staff Benson received extensive wounds and all of the medics, stretcher bearers and radio operators were both wounded and dazed by the blast.

The survivors of the blast had to then cope with the psychological problem of not knowing where to put their feet next for fear of setting off more deadly explosions. It was obvious that the company was in a Viet Cong mine ambush. The convoy was halted by a large anti-vehicle charge in an area seeded with anti-personnel mines which would be set off by the troops dismounting from their vehicles to avoid any anti-tank rockets which might be fired at the stationary targets.

Just at this moment, Captain Tony White arrived on the scene. As soon as Colonel Warr had heard the blast he summoned the Sioux helicopter which had been at Battalion Headquarters and sent Tony off to B Company. In the meantime, the commander of the APCs had called Battalion Headquarters to announce the first group of casualties and request a Dust Off aircraft. Peter Isaacs notified Task Force Headquarters and within minutes an Iroquois was overhead, awaiting the preparation of a landing zone at the point of the explosions. Tony had to cope with an atmosphere of deep shock and fear when he arrived. Some men had responded to the crisis extremely well. Corporals Nichols and Bouse, although wounded themselves, began treating the other casualties which had grown to thirty-one in number. Other men had to be handled firmly to shake them out of a dazed condition so they could begin to get on top of the situation by commencing to search for mines and to clear a landing zone for the Iroquois Dust Off helicopters.

Another severe problem for Tony was to ascertain who was to be treated first out of the large group of casualties, several of whom were in danger of imminent death. Fortunately the 36th US Evacuation Hospital at Vung Tau was only five minutes away by Iroquois and the worst cases were on operating tables within twenty-five minutes of being wounded. Major McQualter was still just conscious when Tony arrived and urged him to treat the Four Platoon casualties first. Shortly afterwards Bruce lost consciousness. Several aircraft were needed to carry out all the casualties and the last were evacuated at 3.30 pm. All this time Captain White had been moving about amongst the casualties, a fearful scene of carnage, without regard to his own personal safety which was menaced by several other mines which were being discovered.

Colonel Warr ordered B Company, now commanded by Lieutenant Pott of Six Platoon, and the APCs to remain stationary until a relieving force of A Company and a team of sappers had arrived. Major Carroll was ordered to move through to B Company with the greatest caution and to assume command of the group for the night. After a tense three-hour approach, during which several clusters of 'jumping Jack' mines were discovered, A Company reached the remnant of B Company and Major Carroll organised a combined harbour for the night.

While this drama had been taking place the Task Force Headquarters had been busy in commencing reaction to another threat. The headquarters of 275 Regiment had moved southwards from its earlier location and was now provocatively close to the boundary of the Task Force area of responsibility, ten miles to the east of Nui Dat. The movements of the commander of the Fifth Viet Cong Division also indicated an interest in operations close to Nui Dat, while 274 Regiment, which had been dormant since December, was in a position to participate in a divisional assault on the Task Force base. Consequently, with reluctance, Brigadier Graham had decided on the afternoon of February 21st that we would have to return to Nui Dat. Captain Godwin of the Task Force operations staff flew out to the new Battalion Headquarters and discussed the move with Colonel Warr. After some calculating, the time for the airlift back to Nui Dat was fixed at 10 am. B and D Companies were to go by helicopter while the remainder of the battalion was to move by road in trucks and

15. IN THE LONG HAI HILLS

APCs. Everyone regretted the need for this decision after we had taken such a heavy blow. It was important for the morale of the battalion to carry the operation through to a successful conclusion, rather than to be pulled out just when we had taken a beating. However, the security of Nui Dat was the *sine qua non* of our operations in Vietnam and so it had to take first place.

Just before 9 pm, Major Carroll reported some lights up on the northern slope of Hon Vung which overlooked the area in which the explosions had taken place. Artillery fire was directed onto the hillside by Captain Tony Wales, the New Zealand forward observation officer with A Company. It seemed as if some men were in a cave whose entrance passage had a bend several feet from the cave mouth. Around this bend was the main chamber which was lit. A blanket over the entrance to this chamber was blowing aside from time to time, and the red glare of a fire inside the cave was being reflected onto the wall of the entrance passage. It was this flickering red glow which A Company had seen and it took some little while to work out what was causing it. The artillery fire was very accurate, and Major Burge, who had taken over command of 103 Battery in November, laid on an extensive fire plan. The success of the artillery was illustrated to all of us at the foot of the hills when the hillside was illuminated by a secondary explosion set off by one of the shells. It must have struck a trip flare, indicating that the target was a well defended Viet Cong base. Further shelling produced a chain of small secondary explosions as caches of small arms ammunition were detonated. The weight of the artillery fire was increased by the eight inch guns from Nui Dat, which shifted their fire up and down the slope with fine precision. The target looked such a promising one that an air strike was arranged for the following morning.

During the first part of the morning of February 22nd, the companies began to concentrate at the Battalion Headquarters location. A Company found an anti-tank mine on the track which they followed out of the danger area. The mine was successfully defused. The APC which had been blown up by the first mine was a complete write off, so its frame was stripped of anything useful to us or to the Viet Cong and it was then burnt with petrol. At 9.35 am the air strike onto the Hon Vung caves began. A mixture of high explosive and napalm descended onto the rocks, the napalm trickling down into the caves and burning where the blast of the high explosive could not reach.

The battalion reassembled at Nui Dat by 1 pm and prepared special precautions for an attack on the base. We then began a series of company patrols through the area surrounding Nui Dat which lasted until the next major operation, preventing us from going back into the Long Hai hills to settle the score with whoever remained in the southern part. The only troops to return to the hills were a patrol of the Provincial Reconnaissance Unit, a specialised team of Vietnamese, trained in long range reconnaissance, advanced field craft and sabotage. This patrol was commanded by Captain John Leggett, an Australian who was attached to the provincial headquarters. It was a courageous feat for twenty lightly armed men to enter this Viet Cong base and their audacity was repaid by the result. They found two Viet Cong guarding the caves on the steep hillside, one of whom they killed while the other fled. In the caves they found three Claymore mines, two other anti-personnel mines, ten Chinese Communist grenades, one thousand rounds of Soviet 7.92 mm. rifle ammunition, one thousand rounds of .30 calibre pistol ammunition, and one 60 mm. mortar bomb. The area had been devastated by the airstrike and the artillery. The .50 calibre machine guns of the APCs which had fired directly into the mouth of the illuminated cave on the night of February 21st had been particularly accurate.

However, Operation Renmark continued in the minds of many, for two of the casualties, Major McQualter and Lieutenant Carruthers, were fighting for their lives in hospital. Despite severe head and body injuries, each man held onto life with great tenacity. Lieutenant Carruthers died on February 24th and Major McQualter died at 5 am on March 5th. After the losses at An Nhut these further casualties were a great blow. Altogether we had lost seven killed and twenty-two wounded in the Long Hai hills. The personal impact of the loss of these close friends and comrades made itself deeply felt. The losses also went a long way towards obliterating the notion of immortality which tends to influence the thinking of optimistic soldiers after some time in battle.

16

Interdiction in the East—the Horseshoe and the Fence

During the latter part of 1966 and in the early months of 1967, much thought had been given to the permanent denial of the Phuoc Tuy rice harvest to the Viet Cong. In order to complete the strategy of defeating the Viet Cong through control of the population rather than through control of the jungle, it was necessary to accompany the operations against the village cadres with a large scale interdiction programme. This was to be aimed not at the denial of the resources of single villages to the Viet Cong, but the denial of the resources of the whole central district of the province. From Nui Dat we could keep the northern access routes closed to the Viet Cong, and patrols between Nui Dat and the Dinh hills were able to close the western approaches to the movement of large amounts of supplies. However the eastern approaches into central Phuoc Tuy were still wide open, and it was through these routes that the Viet Cong were best served, because they led to the largest Viet Cong bases in the province. Consequently a plan had to be developed to close the area to the north and east of the Dat Do district to significant Viet Cong movement.

The minimum length of the boundary of the area to be protected from the Viet Cong was close to twelve miles. To have patrolled this distance from Nui Dat would have involved much wasteful movement to and fro, patrols would be operating outside artillery range unless a special fire base was established, and the numbers of troops required to patrol such a distance in order to seal it off by patrol action would have tied the whole Task Force down to an extent where it could no longer undertake any major initiatives. Certainly patrolling was indispensable so that we knew exactly what was happening in the area but it was not the only means of preventing access. A barrier fence and minefield would present a formidable obstacle, provided that it was patrolled daily to check for breaches or attempted breaches. The patrolling commitment required for the maintenance of the fence and minefield would be far less than the activity needed to close the area off entirely by a moving fence of men. Only large main force Viet Cong units had the capacity to breach such major obstacles. Unless they were prepared to fight a daylight battle for the fence, they could make only occasional breaches which could be sealed the following day. It was unlikely that the Viet Cong would think that the risks involved in such breaching operations would be worth the gains which they produced.

However, even these patrolling requirements made necessary the establishment of a small additional base, somewhere close to the midpoint of the line of interdiction. The stretch of country from Nui Dat, through Long Tan, around to the east of Dat Do, and to the east of the villages on Route 44 between Dat Do and the sea, was the area through which Viet Cong movement into central Phuoc Tuy could take place. Just to the north-east of Dat Do, approximately half-way between Nui Dat and the coast rose the steep slopes of what had once been a small volcano. A crater rim, roughly circular in plan except that the southern sector had been blown out, rose to a height of two hundred feet above the surrounding plain. The crater was six hundred yards across and the defences of a complete rifle company, its administrative installations, and a gun position for artillery of any size could all be sited within it. The fields of fire for defenders on the lip of the crater were limitless while an attacking force would have to assault up a slope of two hundred feet on a gradient of nearly two in one. Thus an excellent defensive position was available for a small force at a convenient point for controlling the eastern approaches and for preventing Viet Cong movement into Dat Do from Long Tan. Furthermore the hill was well placed for launching operations to the east, particularly towards Xuyen Moc.

Brigadier Graham's plans for interdicting to the east were completed in February 1967. They called for one rifle company and a troop of field artillery to be established permanently in the crater of what came to be called the Horseshoe Hill, because of its shape. The country between Nui Dat and the Horseshoe was to be controlled by patrolling from both bases and a barrier fence and minefield was to be built from the Horseshoe to the coast, covering seven miles in its course. At the same time a massive thrust

16. INTERDICTION IN THE EAST — THE HORSESHOE AND THE FENCE

was to be made out to Xuyen Moc to clear the country from the coast to over fifteen miles inland of Viet Cong and their bases, caches and other installations. Substantial American assistance had been made available in the form of a brigade from the Ninth US Infantry Division. A squadron of the Eleventh Armoured Cavalry Regiment and a Vietnamese regiment had also been allotted to the operation, Operation Portsea.

The fence to be constructed was to consist of two parallel belts of barbed wire, six feet high and six feet wide, separated by one hundred yards. A dense minefield was to be laid between the two fences. Several gaps were to be left in the fence so that local farmers could work by day on land outside the fence. These gaps were to be manned by Vietnamese police and to be closed at night. People who went out through the fence in the morning were to be checked back in at night so that no one could disappear to the Viet Cong by day without the police knowing. Similarly, any Viet Cong who tried to enter the district from outside by day would be discovered because he would not have been recorded as one who had gone out through the fence earlier that day. Any person who attempted to pass through the fence at night would have to cut his way through the wire and cross a belt of mines without treading on one or setting off a trip wire. While such a feat may have been possible for a single individual acting with stealth it would have been close to impossible for a long convoy of ox carts carrying rice, and even if they did get through the obstacle, their time of passage would be known and a pursuit by helicopters and APCs would quickly catch such lumbering quarry.

The Fifth Battalion's part in these operations was to provide the company to build and man the Horseshoe base, to build the fence and to secure the Nui Dat base while the Sixth Battalion were out with the Americans on Operation Portsea. The company which had to vacate its base at Nui Dat and start afresh at the same primitive level at which we had begun after Operation Hardihood was D Company. This company had occupied a base position high on the slopes of Nui Dat itself, a mile away from the rest of the battalion in the rubber plantation to the north. Task Force Headquarters wanted Nui Dat for another unit and so D Company were chosen to go to the Horseshoe. The company took these gloomy tidings philosophically, aware that they would have less than seven weeks out in their new area before their return to Australia.

So that D Company were able to construct their new defences as rapidly as possible, B Company under their new commander, Major Ron Hamlyn, were ordered to precede the arrival of D Company at the Horseshoe, to secure it and clear it of any mines and booby traps, before maintaining a screen of patrols in front of D Company to the north and east for three days. B Company flew out to the Horseshoe by helicopter at 7 am on March 6th. D Company followed at 10 am by APC and the Horseshoe was occupied without incident.

The commencement date of these operations had been timed to fit in with the plans of the larger American forces participating in Operation Portsea, but it was also influenced by a captured Viet Cong document which revealed that the province committee had ordered the collection of the 1966–67 rice tax in March 1967. Collection from the villages was to be completed by March 10th, from the district caches to the provincial headquarters by March 20th, and from the provincial caches to the main force bases by March 30th. Focal points of Viet Cong activity in the Long Dat district were to be the villages of Hoi My and Phuoc Loi. Continual attacks were to be launched on the Government outposts in both villages in order to regain control over their people, as a part of a 'Regional Expansion' plan. The reconstruction of the cadres in these villages was also to be commenced and an enquiry made into the shortage of youths for replacement of losses. Special supply missions had been assigned to district and village quartermasters. The items most needed were shovels, Claymore mines, 60 mm. and 81 mm. mortar bombs and 105 mm. shells for the manufacture of mines, small arms ammunition, medicines and rice. These stores requirements pointed towards a build-up for operations in the coming monsoon in May. Thus March was a very appropriate time to commence the severance of connection between the main force bases and central Phuoc Tuy.

The curiosity of the Viet Cong was quickly aroused by the great activity at the Horseshoe. On the first night of our occupation they sent in a force of some twenty-five men to see what we were attempting. Fortunately an ambush had been laid on their approach route some thousand yards north of the Horseshoe. Ten of them were seen at 8.20 pm on a road twenty yards from the sentry manning the left machine gun of Four Platoon. At the same time a group of three or four Viet Cong moved in onto the right machine gun of the platoon. The sentry opened fire, killing two of them and wounding a third. Others came forward and dragged away the wounded man who was heard moaning. Immediately the group on

16. INTERDICTION IN THE EAST — THE HORSESHOE AND THE FENCE

the road went to ground. Another group of ten Viet Cong crossed in front of the platoon, moving along a creek line. The Viet Cong continued to probe the defences of the platoon until 2.30 am. On the following morning the two bodies and the scuff marks made by the man who was dragged away were found. The platoon also intercepted a man who rode into the area of the previous night's action on a bicycle. He was carrying a sketch plan of a nearby village, a list of drugs and had a photograph of Ho Chi Minh in his wallet. He was sent to Task Force Headquarters as a suspect. A further search of the area revealed one .45 calibre sub machine gun, five hand grenades and some equipment and documents. Possibly the man apprehended had been sent in to collect the weapons lost by the Viet Cong.

On the following morning, Five Platoon came upon a Viet Cong camp. It was quite small, containing only four two-man weapon pits with overhead cover. However, there was a suspicious area of soft ground within the camp which looked as if it could have been a camouflaged command post. When members of the platoon dug down through the soft earth they found a large cache of rice, containing some five tons which they destroyed because it was loose and dirty, making recovery uneconomical.

B Company returned to Nui Dat on March 9th. By this time D Company had dug themselves into ground which was composed of loose stones and very difficult to work. Bulldozers cleared the undergrowth off the forward slopes of the hill so that no cover was available to Viet Cong who might creep up on the camp. As the days went by the pits were developed into bunkers and wire fences were built in profusion around the hill at several levels on the forward slopes. The flow of materials, concertina wire, pickets, timber baulks, galvanised iron, artillery ammunition and rations went smoothly and within two weeks, D Company had established a base which they could have held against a regiment of Viet Cong.

Once the Horseshoe had become well established, work on the fence could proceed, based on the Horseshoe as a secure anchor. C Company, commanded by Major Ron Shambrook, were the first to construct part of the long barrier. Their work began on March 16th and they continued until relieved by A Company on March 25th. Our rifle companies were concerned solely with the construction of the two belts of wire. The specialised task of mine laying was to be carried out by the engineers after the fence had been completed. The course of the fence lay around the eastern side of Dat Do, swinging around the south-east corner of the village to run parallel to Route 44, five hundred yards to its east to the next village Phuoc Loi, one mile south of Dat Do. The fence was then to skirt the eastern side of Phuoc Loi and run through to the coast, meeting the sea just to the east of Phuoc Hai. The fence was sited so that it could be patrolled easily by Government troops on the inner side and so that it was covered by machine guns from the Horseshoe and the Government posts at Phuoc Loi and Hoi My. However, the initial stage of the plan called for construction only as far as the river south of Phuoc Loi, the Song Ba Dap. This river, flowing eastwards to the sea, presented a fair obstacle to bulk transport of rice so the most vital part of the fence was that between the Horseshoe and the Song Ba Dap.

During these nine days C Company built nearly three miles of the fence. One of the problems which they encountered was the presence of some wells directly in the path of the fence. After detailed discussion with local officials in which the final course of the fence and the locations of the gaps were decided, it was agreed that the wells could not remain without unduly lengthening the fence. The loss of a well was a serious matter to a Vietnamese peasant so the well-boring equipment of our engineers was put to use to make new wells inside the fence and closer to the houses of the villagers than the old wells.

Special precautions had to be taken each night to guard against the Viet Cong stealing fence materials, booby trapping the fence which had already been erected, or laying mines and booby traps in the area through which they thought the fence was going to run. Each of the platoons of C Company protected the area close to the fence while the Reconnaissance Platoon laid ambushes on likely approaches further out from the fence. On the night of March 18th, the platoon was ambushing some tracks one mile to the south-east of Dat Do. At 8.30 pm four Viet Cong ran down the track at a steady jog in front of the platoon. Our men opened fire, killing two and wounding the other two. Lieutenant Deak then heard orders being given a short distance away to the east. It was fortunate that he had laid a diamond shaped ambush with all-round defence rather than a linear ambush along the track, for other Viet Cong launched an attack onto his flank. However they were caught in the fire of one of his machine guns and the attack was broken up. During the attack the Viet Cong had fired a Browning automatic rifle, wounding Private Twaites in the left leg with such devastating effect that the leg had to be amputated below the knee later that night. Deak withdrew the platoon to a new location and Twaites was evacuated by the perilous means of a night Dust Off. The Viet

Cong encountered must have been a part of a larger force for voices were heard to the north-east and south-east of the platoon, indicating the presence of some twenty enemy. It was most fortunate that Deak had had the foresight to withdraw, for shortly afterwards the Viet Cong began to bombard the old ambush position with mortars from a base plate position a mile to the south. Evidently the enemy encountered in the ambush had been but one arm of several probes which the Viet Cong were making to examine the whole situation between Dat Do and Phuoc Hai.

While the Fifth Battalion were busy with the Horseshoe and the fence, Task Force preparations for Operation Portsea had been approaching completion. After an initial postponement of three days, the operation was planed to commence on March 21st. During March 20th, several American artillery batteries stationed themselves out at the Horseshoe so that they could provide fire support for the rapid advance which was planned for the following day. Over one hundred APCs were to flood out over the plain to the east and north-east to the Song Rai. This force, together with the Sixth Battalion, was poised at Nui Dat ready for movement at dawn on March 21st.

As these preparations were being made, 275 Regiment was preparing an attack on the small Government post of Lo Gom, several hundred yards to the north of Phuoc Hai. Lo Gom was one of the smallest outposts in Phuoc Tuy, defended by thirty-eight Popular Force soldiers who were peasants by day and sentries at night. The post had no artillery, it was exposed and could be attacked from all sides. It was ideally situated for the Viet Cong to deal a heavy psychological blow to the image of Government strength which was growing out of the Horseshoe and the fence. However, these characteristics made Lo Gom just as ideal for revealing the growth of morale amongst the Government troops and the growing impotence of the main force Viet Cong.

The second battalion of 275 Regiment accompanied by another battalion, possibly D445, made a defensive camp near the west bank of the Song Rai in the thick jungle between Route 23 and the coast during the night of March 19th. They lay up during the daylight hours of the 20th, emerged at dusk, and headed south-west for Lo Gom. They covered the seven miles in five hours and began to form up for an attack on the post at 2 am. Fire began to pour into the outpost at 3.20 am. The sentries sounded the alarm and the thirty-eight defenders rushed to their posts, pulling on equipment as they ran through the darkness. Fortunately the post was surrounded by belts of barbed wire fencing and minefields which had recently been installed under the supervision of our sappers. At the same time the important bunkers of the post had been rebuilt and greatly strengthened.

The weight of the Viet Cong attack fell first onto these defences. They attempted to breach the minefields and the wire by firing towards the post rockets which grazed the ground, setting off the mines in their path and blowing gaps in the wire. Further rockets were fired at the command post bunker. Had these defences not been rebuilt they would have given way, allowing the Viet Cong attack waves to pour over the defenders, overwhelming the post within minutes. Instead, although the defences were severely damaged, the Viet Cong were unable to achieve a quick success. The defenders were able to shoot down all those who penetrated to the inner fortifications while time was gained for the artillery at Dat Do, the Horseshoe, and Nui Dat to place a ring of bombardment around the post on the Viet Cong forming-up positions.

The battle raged for over three hours as the thousand men of the two battalions tried to overcome the thirty-eight. Even at dawn the Viet Cong were still attacking until an airstrike sent them fleeing into the jungle. Caught within the wire surrounding the post were the bodies of thirty-six Viet Cong, while one man clutching six rifles was still within the minefield, trying to find a way out. The casualties to the defenders had been one killed and ten wounded. Even if the Viet Cong had not removed many of their dead, 275 Regiment had failed dismally. Two of the defenders whom they had failed to kill were women, the wives of soldiers, one of whom was shortly to give birth.

A sweep through the area used by the attackers yielded two wounded prisoners and the following equipment flung away by the retreating troops: one Chinese flamethrower, one 40 mm. recoilless rifle, seventeen Soviet automatic rifles, one American carbine, eight Chinese rifles, three Chinese light machine guns, two thousand rounds of small arms ammunition and six hundred Chinese hand grenades. Attempts were made to persuade the man in the minefield to surrender and lay down his weapons so that he could be guided out. However, he persisted in shooting at anyone who exposed themselves to him, and after six hours of this procedure he was finally shot so that normal life around the post could continue.

16. INTERDICTION IN THE EAST — THE HORSESHOE AND THE FENCE

The two prisoners talked readily, as was the usual case with captured Viet Cong. They related the events leading up to the attack and described the withdrawal route. Two destroyers which had been cruising off the Phuoc Tuy coast in support of Operation Portsea then pounded the withdrawal routes with five-inch guns. Brigadier Graham was not anxious to engage in a hot pursuit of the Viet Cong on foot in case the real object of the attack had been the usual scheme to draw a relieving force into a bloody ambush.

During the morning of March 21st the APCs of the US Eleventh Armoured Cavalry swept out to the Song Rai to cut off any withdrawal to the north. About mid-afternoon to the east of the Song Rai they discovered one hundred and twenty Viet Cong packs, carefully concealed and laid out. The Viet Cong who owned these packs had evidently taken them off to participate in some vigorous action before returning to collect their equipment. Several of the packs belonged to North Vietnamese soldiers. In one of them, belonging to a North Vietnamese company commander, were found documents which revealed that the packs belonged to 275 Regiment. One of the documents was a map which showed a three battalion attack on Xuyen Moc. The map indicated the directions and strength of the attack but did not reveal the intended date. The area in which the packs were found coincided with the rear area allocated to this company for the attack on Xuyen Moc. Hence it seemed likely that the cavalry had caught the attack in the preparatory stage.

The map was swiftly interpreted at Task Force Headquarters and warning sent to Xuyen Moc. Two airstrikes were made on the forming-up areas for the battalions participating in the assault. The cavalry then swept around to the north-east and harboured inside Xuyen Moc for the night, daring the Viet Cong to follow through with their plans. No attack took place and what was left of 275 Regiment withdrew rapidly over fifty miles to the north-east.

The Sixth Battalion went out to sweep through the area through which the attackers of Lo Gom had withdrawn. Our A Company went with them on March 22nd, landing near the west bank of the Song Rai and sweeping back through the country which the Viet Cong had used to reach Lo Gom. The Sixth Battalion found copious evidence of the success of the naval shelling, and a light aircraft on reconnaissance discovered over one hundred graves in the area.

A Company's sweep took them until late on March 24th. Originally A Company had been intended to relieve C Company of their arduous task on the 23rd, but C Company were unable to cease work on the fence until March 25th. They then had one night in base at Nui Dat before flying out to the Song Rai to protect the forward fire support and engineer base for Operation Portsea. A large engineer effort was being put into rebuilding the bridges and culverts along Route 23 so that the road to Xuyen Moc could be reopened and the isolation of the post ended. C Company remained for three days at the fire support base, where Major Shambrook had an extremely difficult job co-ordinating the protection requirements of the gunners, sappers and cavalry who were all based there. B Company relieved A Company at the fence on March 29th, by which time it had reached to the eastern side of Phuoc Loi.

A Company returned to the base for a few hours and then set off to the west of Nui Dat to guard the north-western approaches to the Task Force base. On the evening of March 29th Three Platoon under Lieutenant Ben Morris were ambushing some fresh Viet Cong tracks. Half an hour after darkness had become complete the platoon heard voices of approaching Viet Cong. The enemy were allowed to come right up to the ambush position before they were blasted by a Claymore mine and automatic fire. The Viet Cong withdrew to the protection of a creek bed into which the platoon lobbed hand grenades. Out of eight Viet Cong counted two bodies were found in front of the ambush in the morning. Three blood trails left by wounded Viet Cong were followed for a short way and scuff marks made by bodies being dragged were found. The two dead men must have been important couriers for they were carrying 13,955 piastres (approx. AU$130), Communist psychological warfare publications in both English and Vietnamese, private letters to persons in Hoa Long, Long Phuoc and Ba Ria, and a notice of a meeting of the Chau Duc committee on April 8th. The group had been one of several from the Chau Duc District Company, C20, which A Company had ambushed in the previous few months.

On April 3rd Three Platoon had a further success with an ambush. They were lying in wait on a trail three miles to the west of Nui Dat. In the early evening, a few minutes after 7 pm three Viet Cong came down the trail from the north. The leading enemy scout must have noticed some traces of recent activity around the point at which the northern Claymore had been concealed. He stopped and began to make a careful examination. That was the last mistake he ever made for the Claymore was detonated just as he was about to discover what it was. He was killed instantly. His two friends took to their heels and ran into an artillery barrage which was brought down onto their withdrawal route. The platoon recovered the body and the man's weapon, a Garrand M1.

B Company's first few days on the fence, south of Dat Do, passed quietly. On the night of April 4th the company was in ambush on the south-west approaches to Dat Do. Just after dark two Viet Cong coming from the Long Hai hills walked into the position of Six Platoon. They were engaged with machine gun fire. One was killed and the other ran off, badly wounded. This incident was an interesting study in the slowness of the passage of information amongst village level Viet Cong for although B Company had moved into their evening location at 5.30 pm through open paddy fields in full sight of the villagers of Dat Do, no warning had been passed to the two Viet Cong who walked directly onto B Company's position.

Two days later B Company encountered further difficulties. At 11.30 am on April 6th a mine was detonated by a work party on the northern side of Phuoc Loi, killing Private R. E. Lloyd and wounding two others. All were members of Four Platoon. In Major Hamlyn's opinion, the mine had been planted by the Viet Cong, for it was directly in line with the path to be taken by the fence. However it was impossible to say how long the mine had been in the ground. It was another US 'jumping Jack'. At 7.25 pm that evening, Four Platoon opened fire on a Viet Cong scout who tried to creep up onto their position. The man escaped into thick bushes to the north. At 11.10 am on April 7th B Company was shaken by another explosion. Taking great care after the previous explosion, the company had been working behind a team of sappers who were searching the ground with mine detectors. Four Platoon had just received a new commander, Lieutenant Kerry Rinkin. Rinkin had been commissioned as a national service officer and he had transferred to the regular army. He was a very active leader and tried to set a vigorous example to his men in all their activities. On this morning he stood on one of the raised paddy bunds near the fence and explained to his platoon the area which had been cleared of mines by the sappers so that his men knew where they could work in safety. One of the boundaries of the cleared area was the bund on which Rinkin was standing. Immediately after this explanation, he stepped back off the bund into the uncleared area, perhaps because he lost his balance for a moment, and had the extreme misfortune to step onto another mine which had been planted in line with the fence and with the mine which had been detonated on the previous day. Rinkin was very seriously wounded and died shortly afterwards.

B Company withdrew for the night to the south-west edge of Dat Do. Four Platoon, now under the command of Lieutenant Lou O'Dea who had been transferred from Five Platoon, took up a position of all-round defence to harbour for the night. One Section was across the southern flank, Two Section faced to the north-west and Three Section covered the north-eastern approach. At 11.05 pm the machine gun sentry of Two Section thought he saw three Viet Cong move quickly towards him from the south-west. He fired a burst of automatic fire at what he saw and the whole platoon tumbled into their pits and stood to. One of the men in One Section looked to the west and saw a large number of rifle flashes outside the perimeter, advancing towards him. During the following exchange of fire one of the members of Two Section was hit as he was moving towards his pit.

Lieutenant O'Dea went forward and called the platoon medic to treat the wounded man. At first the wound did not appear to be serious but further examination revealed a serious laceration and a deep wound in the chest. A Dust Off aircraft was requested. Lieutenant O'Dea ordered the firing of artillery illumination shells over his area so that his men could examine the ground in front of them. The helicopter was brought into a landing zone twenty yards east of the platoon. Initial attempts to guide the aircraft in by torches failed so a small beacon fire of grass was lit to solve the problem. After the departure of the helicopter, O'Dea reorganised One and Two Sections into four man weapon pits so that control over the perimeter could be tightened. A fifty per cent stand-to was ordered and O'Dea then checked his men and saw that all was in order. B Company were withdrawn from the fence on the following morning and replaced by A Company.

This new team completed the assigned length of the fence by the early afternoon of April 11th and commenced to move into position for the Fifth Battalion's final operation—the clearing and patrolling of the road to Xuyen Moc. The engineers had completed their bridging and road repair operations and the resumption of normal unrestricted civilian traffic was scheduled to commence on April 12th after a break of several years. The battalion flew out in the early morning of the 12th and took up a series of company positions along the road between Dat Do and the Song Rai bridge. Patrols fanned out to sweep the jungle to a distance of several hundred yards out from the road. The road and its environs were checked with mine detectors to guard against any Viet Cong activity which had taken place during the previous night. No trouble of any kind was encountered and the road was open from 11.09 am. A ceremony conducted at Xuyen Moc by Colonel Dat and Captain Duc released a flood of traffic as civilians took advantage of the Government trucks provided to carry them into Dat Do and Ba Ria. We felt that our last operation had closed on a significant note with the restoration of full communications between the provincial headquarters and all of its subordinate districts. It was particularly satisfying to know that for the people of Xuyen Moc the tide of the war had begun to flow strongly in the direction of their own wishes.

17

The Final Balance

The arrival on April 20th of our relief, the Seventh Battalion, was a most welcome sight. These men had travelled to Vietnam on board HMAS *Sydney* and were airlifted off the flight deck of the carrier to Nui Dat by large Chinook helicopters. On the same day, our D Company went aboard the *Sydney* and set off for a nine-day cruise to ease the temporary overcrowding at Nui Dat during the handover period, returning to Vung Tau to take aboard the main body of the battalion on April 30th. The Seventh Battalion had a settling-in period of six days, after which they were to take over our operational responsibility. During the six days settling-in period their men began to accompany our patrols and to get to know the environs of the base. Great hilarity reigned within the Fifth Battalion as preparations for the journey home were made. The Seventh Battalion had adopted the pig as their emblem. The first thing they noticed on walking up the hill into the battalion defences from the airstrip was a large sign above the road displaying a rather tattered looking tiger greeting a fresh and immaculate pig. On the evening before the handing over of our operational responsibilities Colonel Warr gave Colonel Smith, the commanding officer of the Seventh Battalion, a piglet which had been adorned with tiger stripes by a local artist.

On the afternoon of April 26th our final patrol of the base area came back to be cheered in by the battalion and played up the hill by the battalion band. Our active role in the war was over. These patrols had gone out every day since our arrival at Nui Dat. They were unspectacular tasks but the Viet Cong had been made to realise that they could not come within attacking distance of Nui Dat without discovery. These patrols represented a considerable commitment in terms of effort. While we were out on operations the area surrounding the base was patrolled by the Sixth Battalion and our rear defences and administrative troops. As soon as the men returned from an operation they had to begin patrols around the base to allow the Sixth Battalion to go out. One company could handle the base area patrols. Another had to be on thirty minutes standby continually to act as the Task Force reserve. A third company often had to act as the protective force for the guns supporting the Sixth Battalion, so that only one company was left spare. This meant that the troops were working hard every day, including Sundays. In addition nearly every man did a two hour shift as a machine gun piquet, or manned a radio or a command post every night. On forward operations some people were on duty for four hour shifts at night, while those who were lying in ambush had to remain constantly alert, hardly moving a muscle for up to twenty-two hours at a stretch. Consequently the end of a year of operational duty was a major event in our lives.

Our thinking became less preoccupied by the demands of the future and we were able to look back on the activities of the year and weigh the effectiveness of what we had attempted. The most significant factor in the course of the year had been the increase in Government control which had been brought to Phuoc Tuy as a result of the commitment of the First Australian Task Force to the province.[1] The numbers of people and hamlets to which Government authority had been restored is shown in the table below:

SITUATION BEFORE MAY 1966		SITUATION AFTER APRIL 1967	
Population	Hamlets	Population	Hamlets
1. Under Government Control			
24,775	24	98,408	105
2. Isolated but anti-Viet Cong			
6,599	8	–	–
3. Under Strong Viet Cong Influence			
63,126	68	–	–
4. Under Complete Viet Cong Control			
8,498	12	4,594	7

---

1 See Fig. 1 (p. 4) and Fig. 22 (p. 259).

It is very difficult to divide all of the hamlets into four categories such as those above because of the considerable variety of the degree of Viet Cong influence from one hamlet to another. Hamlets have been included as under strong Viet Cong influence where infrastructures were well established and wielding a strong influence in local village affairs, where acts of Viet Cong terrorism were frequent, where Viet Cong soldiers were usually in the hamlets, and where the people paid regular taxation to the Viet Cong. Many of the hamlets classified as under Government control are still visited from time to time by Viet Cong and occasional acts of terrorism are possible, but the Viet Cong do not play a direct role in internal village affairs, their infrastructures have been rooted out or are inactive, and they no longer are subject to Viet Cong taxation and conscription.

Thus it can be seen that Government control has been re-established over ninety-six per cent of the population of Phuoc Tuy. It should not be imagined that this implies that the task in Phuoc Tuy is nearly over, for the security of these villages must be maintained until the complete collapse of both the Viet Cong and the North Vietnamese forces in South Vietnam and until the Vietnamese people have developed the machinery to administer the affairs of a populous state which has great potential for advancement in the second half of the twentieth century.

The second factor to be examined is the purely military balance of power within Phuoc Tuy. The Task Force established itself in central Phuoc Tuy and maintained its security despite the presence of considerably superior numbers of main force Viet Cong. The military initiative has been taken away from the Viet Cong and they have learned that to attempt any major operations is to invite heavy casualties for no permanent gain. The area of influence of the main force units has been decreased although by no means completely eradicated. The main force regiments have suffered appreciable casualties, notably those caused by the Sixth Battalion at Long Tan in August 1966, and east of Dat Do in February and March 1967. The district companies have been seriously weakened by small scale patrolling and ambushes set by platoons and companies, and the standard of the village guerillas who are still operating has been reduced to a very low level. However, both 274 and 275 Regiments and the D445 Battalion still exist and they must be credited with the capacity to inflict serious casualties on smaller Allied forces should the Viet Cong catch these Allied forces in an ambush or a surprise attack. These main force units are likely to continue in existence for a long time. Although they are being kept away from the people and are being denied the initiative, their corporate morale has not yet declined to the point at which they no longer see any point in attempting to inflict a military defeat on Government forces.

A third factor is the damage done to the bases, the food supply and the administrative installations of the Viet Cong. Hundreds of bunkers, trenches and tunnels were destroyed, several hundred tons of rice were captured and means to deny permanently the rice harvest of Phuoc Tuy to the Viet Cong have been put into effect. Large quantities of ammunition, medical supplies, weapons and documents were taken from the Viet Cong and the replacement of these items will consume a large proportion of their efforts. Furthermore, the Viet Cong know that they are taking an appreciable risk every time they concentrate large quantities of supplies in one area and thus their problems of storage and distribution of supplies are accentuated.

Each of these reverses for the Viet Cong has an added significance, for in this type of war, propaganda and psychological considerations are of extraordinary importance. For twenty years Communist leaders have been lecturing the people of Phuoc Tuy, instilling the idea of Viet Cong invincibility, of their superiority over the Government in all matters and of the inevitability of a Viet Cong victory. During 1966 and 1967 the people of Phuoc Tuy have witnessed the ejection of the Viet Cong as a military power in the populated areas of the province, they have received medical attention, food, public buildings and education from the Government instead of providing food, money, men and women for the Viet Cong levies, and they have heard from the growing numbers of men who have returned from the Viet Cong that their claim of inevitable victory appears to be an inversion of the truth. Thus the people have come to realise that the Viet Cong are unable to live up to their promises in the short term sense and so their credibility on long-term policies has been greatly reduced and disillusionment is setting in. On the other hand, the popularity of the Government which the Viet Cong have denounced so vehemently is benefiting from a back lash against the falseness of Communist propaganda and from a degree of surprise that this evil Government is concerned with the welfare of the individual. These forces have not reached their full power for they are just gathering momentum, but with adept Government handling it may be seen eventually that the Viet Cong are their own worst enemies.

17. THE FINAL BALANCE

This year in Vietnam had also reinforced many lessons concerning the nature of counter-insurgency warfare. We were convinced that the solution to the Vietnam crisis lay in the villages rather than in the jungles, but until such time as the Viet Cong main forces have disintegrated and the North Vietnamese desist in their efforts to make the South subject to them and to a system which the majority of South Vietnamese dislike there will be a need for the jungles to be patrolled and fought through. But these actions will not win the war for either side—they will simply help to prevent their winner from losing. In conventional terms the results of a policy of concentration on the villages are far from spectacular. It is interesting to place the battalion's body count statistics against those quoted in the table above. We killed seventy Viet Cong for a loss of twenty-three of our men. If one views the war in terms of dead bodies counted then these results do not justify the employment of eight hundred Australians at war for twelve months and an uninformed observer might jump to the conclusion that the war was at a stalemate. On the other hand, if one accepts that the goal of the war is the support of the people, these body count comparisons are the wrong statistics to consider. The important figures in this war are the numbers of people who support the Government, the degree of Government control and the speed with which the support of more South Vietnamese is won.

Apart from these strategic considerations, the year in Vietnam was of deep personal significance. We had met the Viet Cong and found them to be a widely varying force in terms of their proficiency. Their worst were rabble, their best were good fighters and cadre leaders by any standards. We pitied their miserable existence and the way in which their commanders were prepared to squander the lives of their men for very small military gains. We were revolted by their atrocities and amazed by their tactical ineptitudes such as the frequency with which they used lights for guiding their movement at night. They are a unique enemy, cunning in tactic but repetitive in strategy. They form part of an ideological crusade, but they are often pathetically ignorant of the doctrine on whose altar their lives are sacrificed. After we had come to know them it was difficult to maintain a personal dislike against the Viet Cong for considering the forces to which they had been subjected, they were understandable. This did not make the goal of their masters any more tolerable, but we were much happier to capture a Viet Cong than to kill him.

The villagers were impressive for their ability to endure adversity with stoicism while tending to hypochondria in small things. Many years of hardship had sharpened their sense of self-preservation and they were hard-headed when it came to questions of their own interest, but this competitive self-interest gave the civil aid programme more influence and showed us that the differences between Vietnamese and Australians were not irreconcilable. With firm leadership they showed dedication, endurance and courage to a remarkable degree as the defence of Lo Gom showed. One of the longest lived of our memories of the Vietnamese will be their sense of humour, for they could laugh at most things and their ability to make jokes with a fine point enlivened many a tedious situation.

The feeling of comradeship, of mutual dependence, which grew up within the battalion was a most powerful thing to feel. Without wishing to glorify war I know of no other environment which can make eight hundred men live together in a spirit of real comradeship, remote from their homes, separated from wives and families, under constant physical and mental stress. When a friend was killed we knew very clearly the extent of our dependence on each other. The most trying time for the battalion came in February, March and April when fatigue and bereavement fell heavily on us. Throughout this time the morale of the battalion held up well. Had we not been a happy battalion right from the start and remained so, then this time might have presented some severe problems. That it did not is sufficient tribute to leadership.

Shortly before we left for Australia, some of us were invited to a farewell function given by the Vietnamese in Ba Ria. We had come to know these people well during the course of the year. We had learned to rely on them for assistance with intelligence, with translation, with population control and with civil aid. They had relied on us for protection, for tactical proficiency and for the ability to deal with the Viet Cong when they took the initiative. We had exasperated each other on many occasions and then bridged our differences. We had developed a relationship which turned on the proficiency with which any task in hand was dealt with rather than on the niceties of diplomacy. The room in which the gathering took place was brilliantly adorned with flowers. One wall was covered with the bright red blossoms of the flame tree. Sprigs of oleander and of a small pink flower with the shape of a heart were arranged in front of the branches of scarlet. Each of these flowers has a special significance in Vietnam. The flame blossom means farewell, the oleander represents good luck and the third flower signifies 'in friendship from all my heart'. As I looked around at these people the year seemed to me to have ended on an appropriate note.

17. THE FINAL BALANCE

Fig. 22. Phuoc Tuy province, May 1967.

Appendix A

Fifth Battalion Roll of Honour Vietnam 1966–67

Pte. E. W. Noack	24 May 1966
Pte. J. R. Sweetnam	9 Jun 1966
Cpl. B. F. Coupe	10 Jun 1966
Pte. L. T. Farren	10 Jun 1966
Pte. R. J. Lubke	2 Jly 1966
L/Cpl. M. Tomas	8 Jly 1966
Pte. R. J. Kennedy	15 Aug 1966
Pte. G. F. Warburton	1 Oct 1966
Cpl. N. J. Womal, MID	17 Oct 1966
Pte. G. H. D'Antoine	18 Oct 1966
Pte. B. P. Watson	10 Nov 1966
Pte. E. H. Nilsen	14 Nov 1966
Pte. N. A. Pracy	14 Nov 1966
Pte. P. C. Sullivan	27 Dec 1966
Maj. D. M. Bourne	14 Feb 1967
Capt. R. B. Milligan	14 Feb 1967
Pte. D. M. Clark	21 Feb 1967
Pte. M. D. Poole	21 Feb 1967
Pte. R. W. Sandow	21 Feb 1967
Pte. J. C. Webster	21 Feb 1967

L/Cpl. G. B. Green   21 Feb 1967
Lt. J. Carruthers, MID   wounded 21 Feb 1967
                                  died 24 Feb 1967
Maj. M. B. McQualter, MID   wounded 21 Feb 1967
                                  died 5 Mar 1967
Pte. R. E. Lloyd   6 Apl 1967
2/Lt. K. P. Rinkin   7 Apl 1967

Appendix B

Citation accompanying the award of the Distinguished Service Order to Lieutenant Colonel J. A. Warr

Lieutenant Colonel Warr was commissioned into the Australian Army in 1947, after graduation from the Royal Military College, Duntroon. Since that time he has either served with the Royal Australian Regiment or held staff appointments in Australia or abroad. When the Fifth Battalion, The Royal Australian Regiment, was formed Lieutenant Colonel Warr was Second in Command until September 1 1965, when he was appointed Commanding Officer and the unit was warned for movement overseas. As Commanding Officer he was responsible for the training and welding together of both regular soldiers and national servicemen into an efficient combat unit in a short period of time. During a year's service in Vietnam the Fifth Battalion, The Royal Australian Regiment, was in almost continual contact with the enemy whilst executing offensive patrol tasks, search and destroy missions, and cordon and search operations. The techniques for these latter operations were developed so successfully by Lieutenant Colonel Warr that they have been accepted as standard procedures in the First Australian Task Force. Lieutenant Colonel Warr was responsible for the planning and execution in detail which is so necessary for successful operations by a battalion group in air mobile operations. His thorough preparation and orders, his sound tactical knowledge, his calmness and leadership under fire was largely responsible for the accomplishments of the Fifth Battalion, The Royal Australian Regiment, in Vietnam.

Citation accompanying the award of the Military Cross to Second Lieutenant M. G. J. Deak

On October 17 1966, during Operation Queanbeyan in Phuoc Tuy Province, South Vietnam, Battalion Headquarters of Fifth Battalion Royal Australian Regiment was held up by Viet Cong in a natural ambush position on a steep mountain track. The Anti Tank Platoon commanded by Second Lieutenant Deak was directed to clear the area. The enemy was located in natural fire positions on both sides of a deep re-entrant with a gradient of one in two. One section of the platoon covered by the remainder swept up the re-entrant but the Section Commander was mortally wounded and the remainder pinned down by fire.

Second Lieutenant Deak re-deployed the remainder of his platoon and under fire directed additional covering fire onto the objective from another company 800 metres away. He then successfully directed the fire of armed helicopters onto the enemy positions and then led his platoon back into the re-entrant and cleared the enemy position without loss.

At all times during the three and one quarter hours engagement, Second Lieutenant Deak showed complete disregard for his own safety even when it became apparent that the enemy were concentrating their fire on leaders. The calm and competent manner of Second Lieutenant Deak was a major factor in steadying his platoon under fire in a difficult situation. The success in clearing the Viet Cong ambush position was due in the main to the fine example of leadership and courage set by Second Lieutenant Deak.

Citation accompanying the award of the Military Cross to Second Lieutenant J. D. McAloney

On 18 October 1966, during Operation Queanbeyan in Phuoc Tuy Province, South Vietnam, Second Lieutenant John Douglas McAloney commanding the Assault Pioneer Platoon of Fifth Battalion The Royal Australian Regiment was given the difficult task of clearing booby traps from a rocky, thickly jungled, cave riddled spur. The area was the scene of a bitter engagement between other elements of Fifth Battalion, The Royal Australian Regiment and the Viet Cong on the preceding day during which the enemy had withdrawn deeper into the protection of the booby trapped caves. The clearance of the booby traps was to precede a detailed search of the caves. After positioning covering groups, Second Lieutenant McAloney, alone, entered the first cave entrance to commence delousing the booby traps. At this time, a Viet Cong sniper fired from another concealed cave entrance mortally wounding one of the Assault Pioneer sentries. With complete disregard for his own safety, Second Lieutenant McAloney moved from the shelter of the cave out to the wounded man and dragged him to a more secure area. After arranging for the evacuation of the casualty, Second Lieutenant McAloney, alone, again approached the suspect cave and personally tossed gas grenades into both the front entrance and possible exits. As the gas and subsequent firing of M79 grenades into the cave still failed to dislodge the occupants, preparations were made to employ flame throwers. Firstly Second Lieutenant McAloney again moved out alone under covering fire to recover the weapon of the wounded man. This was lying in the line of fire for the proposed flame attack. Whilst doing this he was wounded in the right temple but persevered and retrieved the weapon. He then gathered a flame thrower team of two men and personally led them in a frontal flame assault on the caves area, burning out each entrance in turn. The personal courage and leadership shown by this officer throughout the three and one half hour period of the action was of the highest order. His determination to close with and destroy an experienced and concealed enemy, in extremely difficult terrain was an inspiration to all ranks.

Citation accompanying the award of the Military Cross to Second Lieutenant D. C. Rainer

On 21 October 1966, Second Lieutenant Rainer was in command of 10 Platoon D Company on a routine search and destroy patrol in the Nui Thi Vai hills of Phuoc Tuy Province South Vietnam.

His platoon was searching a foot track, when the forward elements came upon a small rice cache and then a suspected enemy sentry post. Shortly afterwards, he saw a complex of three huts, set in an extremely rocky and steep re-entrant. He deployed a section in a wide sweep to the right and led two sections astride the main track. All members had to move carefully through bamboo panjis which surrounded the area. He could hear voices and the smell of food and fires. At this stage he had no idea of what was in the village, however he crawled forward with his two sections, to within 15 feet of the largest hut.

The right hand fire support section opened fire. Immediately, approximately ten to twelve enemy fled out of the large hut. They ran into the fire of the assault section and when the firing ceased, the platoon had killed ten enemy. Approximately four enemy fled away from the fire and escaped to the east. No casualties were sustained in his own platoon.

The success of the contact highlighted the degree of professional proficiency that Rainer had attained with his platoon. His platoon strength was only slightly larger than the number of the enemy, however, quite fearlessly, he deployed his men in what proved to be a perfect ambush.

Rainer had again displayed outstanding qualities of leadership and thoroughness in his duties as a platoon commander. Because of these qualities he was able to deploy his platoon so they could achieve such a successful contact.[1]

---

1   2/Lt. Rainer had been awarded a Mention-in-Despatches for an action on 15 September 1966.

APPENDIX B

Citation accompanying the award of the Military Medal to Private C. J. Cogswell

On October 8 1966, during Operation Canberra in Phuo Tuy Province South Vietnam, B Company Fifth Battalion The Royal Australian Regiment was directed to clear the Nui Thi Vai Hill which was a large rocky, steep, densely covered feature. The area was known to be heavily booby trapped by the Viet Cong. Private Cogswell and another soldier as forward scouts located a booby trap, deloused it and a few minutes later heard voices of enemy close by. Private Cogswell advised his platoon commander by hand signal and covered by the other scout moved forward to investigate. Initially he sighted fifteen Viet Cong and later thirty Viet Cong. Private Cogswell and the other scout remained in a position of observation for approximately fifty minutes; at times the enemy came within five yards of their position but the scouts were not seen. Based on the information passed back by Private Cogswell and the other scout and other information it was concluded that the Viet Cong could be up to battalion strength and B Company was ordered to withdraw four hundred metres to allow artillery and air strikes to be made on enemy positions. Both scouts then skilfully extracted themselves without disclosing their presence to the Viet Cong and so alerting them. Artillery and air strikes were then made on the enemy base which was later successfully destroyed.

The skill, courage and determination displayed by Private Cogswell was of very high order and enabled the area to be cleared without casualties to his platoon or company.

Citation accompanying the award of the Military Medal to Private P. Fraser

On October 17 1966, during Operation Queanbeyan in Phuoc Tuy Province South Vietnam, the Anti Tank Platoon of Fifth Battalion The Royal Australian Regiment was directed to clear a Viet Cong ambush. During the clearing a section commander was mortally wounded by a sniper and fell in an exposed position. Heavy enemy fire prevented movement of any members of the section. Private Fraser, the stretcher bearer attached to the Anti Tank Platoon was told by the platoon commander not to go forward to the casualty until the area had been cleared. Private Fraser however crawled forward under fire, reached the casualty and dressed the wound. Whilst Private Fraser was with the casualty a sniper concentrated his fire on Private Fraser and with the fire falling only inches from him, Private Fraser continued to assist the casualty.

The Platoon Commander then arranged for covering fire to be given by the remainder of the platoon at which time Private Fraser turned his back on the enemy fire to shield the casualty from fire and assisted a carrying party to evacuate the casualty.

During the extraction of the casualty Private Fraser showed complete disregard for his own safety in an effort to give maximum attention to the care of the casualty.

APPENDIX B

Citation accompanying the award of a Mention-in-Despatches (Posthumously) to Corporal N. J. Womal

On October 17 1966, during Operation Queanbeyan in Phuoc Tuy Province in South Vietnam, the Anti Tank Platoon of Fifth Battalion, The Royal Australian Regiment was directed to clear a Viet Cong ambush located in a deep re-entrant on the side of a steep mountain. Corporal Womal, a section commander in the platoon was ordered to clear with his section across the re-entrant under covering fire from the remainder of the platoon. When the section reached the middle of the re-entrant, Corporal Womal was mortally wounded by a sniper who had obviously concentrated on him because he was controlling his section by voice and hand signals. From the position where he fell, Corporal Womal continued to control the covering fire of his section machine gun. In spite of a large volume of accurate enemy fire from several different positions which prevented Corporal Womal's section from moving, Corporal Womal propped himself on one elbow in an exposed position to indicate by voice to his platoon commander the exact location of the enemy and continued to direct the section machine gun fire onto the enemy. Corporal Womal died shortly after being evacuated from the re-entrant.

The courage and leadership displayed by Corporal Womal under fire was of very high order and an inspiration to all members of his platoon. His efforts in directing fire and controlling his section even when wounded contributed directly to the successful extrication of his section without further casualties and the location of the enemy positions which were subsequently effectively dislodged.

Appendix C

5 RAR Nominal Roll, 1966–67

This nominal roll has been included in the reprint of *Vietnam Task* with the consent of the author to recognise all who served in the battalion on active service in Vietnam in 1966–67. The roll has been created from records held by the Department of Veterans' Affairs, Defence Archives and the 5 RAR Association. Officers are listed at the end of the roll in rank order.

Disclaimer: Whilst every endeavour has been made to ensure completeness and accuracy, it is inevitable that some omissions or errors have been made. These are totally inadvertent and regretted; however, no responsibility for this is accepted by the 5 RAR Association. If any person is aware of omissions or errors, they are invited to pass details to the Secretary 5 RAR Association (secretary@5rar.asn.au). As the manuscript is electronically based and printed on demand, periodic amendments may be made to the nominal roll prior to subsequent printing.

Legend for symbols:
† **Killed in Action**
# **Died of Wounds**
* Wounded in Action
^ Battle Casualty

VIETNAM TASK

Regt No	Rank	Name
61609	CPL	Ackerley J
5713759	PTE	Adams RP
61183	CPL	Aitken BR
3787072	PTE	Aitken DB
17636	CPL	Albrecht TA
2412212	PTE	Aldcroft B
214961	LCPL	Alexander BJ
5713604	PTE	Alexander MR
2781610	PTE	Alexander RI *
37912	CPL	Allen EA
2782097	PTE	Allen JD
2781430	PTE	Anderson RJ
3786746	PTE	Anderson TPP
29504	SGT	Anderson WS
42763	LCPL	Annells DR
2781290	PTE	Anthoney RL *
215582	CPL	Anthony G
5713741	PTE	Antonio RW
5410806	SGT	Armitage RG
43007	LCPL	Armstrong RB
4410810	LCPL	Arnold DS
3787073	PTE	Arnold RL
55047	PTE	Arnold WF
214225	SGT	Arnould L
4717642	PTE	Arthur GL
3786771	PTE	Asbury WH
5713606	PTE	Ashton GE
2781647	PTE	Assange WV
214868	LCPL	Avis BI
4717449	PTE	Axelby M
2782098	CPL	Babbage DW
2781472	PTE	Bahnsen TJ
2782860	PTE	Bailey HW
212535	CPL	Bailey LD
214207	CPL	Baird HA
214199	CPL	Baker FR ^
3786658	PTE	Baker RB

Regt No	Rank	Name
38080	LCPL	Ball GG
33668	WO1	Balzary PJ
215765	LCPL	Bamblett BJ
213486	SGT	Banks RC
3786772	LCPL	Barker BJ
4717870	PTE	Barrett DL
43667	LCPL	Bartel LP
216801	CPL	Bartley GJ
212987	LCPL	Bartley RJ
215277	PTE	Barton KL
213604	SGT	Bartos JC
2782963	PTE	Basman RJ
6708539	PTE	Batchelor GF
14820	WO2	Bates JH
1731247	PTE	Battle PC
17781	PTE	Baulch RC
3786704	PTE	Bayre RJL
5713607	PTE	Beauglehole RW
214362	LCPL	Bellamy RG
2781297	PTE	Bellingham MF
3411726	PTE	BenhamGJ
6708275	PTE	Benn DL
2781298	PTE	Benson DL
242743	SSGT	Benson KR *
212941	PTE	Berg RA
2781299	PTE	Bernotas AS *
3786705	PTE	Best RA
3787077	PTE	Bilston JE
2781301	PTE	Binney WW
3786660	PTE	Birtles RC
38703	PTE	Bishop DJ *
3786683	PTE	Blackwell DJ
2781439	LCPL	Blanch PW
5713611	PTE	Bockisch L *
3786776	PTE	Bolitho RJ
2781305	PTE	Borger KJ
3786777	PTE	Borlase GR

APPENDIX C

Regt No	Rank	Name
6708223	PTE	Bott RR
1200256	PTE	Botterell JS
3786608	PTE	Bourke DF
3411582	CPL	Bouse JA *
38785	PTE	Bowman DJ
3786910	PTE	Box RE *
216282	CPL	Boyd PI
18303	LCPL	Boyle RJ
3411678	PTE	Bradley B
3786980	PTE	Brand TA
216519	PTE	Brandt RJ
3786624	PTE	Brannan WE
2781307	CPL	Brazier PT *
53116	SGT	Brendish GA
216037	PTE	Brett SJ *
216643	PTE	Brien RG
3786679	PTE	Briggs RC
1200344	PTE	Brock MW
6708240	PTE	Brooks IS
214469	PTE	Broomfield GD
2412450	PTE	Brophy EF
37500	SSGT	Brown AY
1411206	PTE	Brown NW
212644	SGT	Brown RJ
212671	SGT	Brown RR
18165	PTE	Brown TD
3787085	PTE	Bruce CH
3786864	PTE	Bruin GJ
1731056	PTE	Brunckhorst MB
3786720	LCPL	Bryan DA
215784	PTE	Bryant NR *
18289	PTE	Buckle FR
3787600	PTE	Budd J
2781441	LCPL	Budden BF
3787086	PTE	Buhagiar JS
3786875	PTE	Bullen RJ
54596	SGT	Bunting PJ

Regt No	Rank	Name
53157	CPL	Bunting RA
3787258	PTE	Burdeu JC
42292	LCPL	Burge BR
18305	LCPL	Burns WJ
3787423	PTE	Burton MR
2782453	PTE	Butcher KJ
15309	CPL	Butler JT
210875	SGT	Cahill FB
18419	PTE	Calder JH
2411548	CPL	Caldwell RJ
29690	SGT	Calvert RW
2783366	LCPL	Cameron BI
216446	LCPL	Campbell DM
2783189	PTE	Capp PC
1411137	PTE	Cappler JE
4410794	PTE	Carlyon LN
1731354	PTE	Carney WD
3786806	PTE	Carroll PW
3787217	PTE	Carter KA
32273	CPL	Carter RD
42391	SGT	Carter RH
2781537	PTE	Carter RJ
1411214	LCPL	Carthew RG
14942	SGT	Case NJ
2781313	PTE	Case TE
2782655	PTE	Cassidy GJ
2781538	PTE	Cavanagh KJ
2781314	PTE	Cavanagh WR
2412233	PTE	Cavill RN
2781542	LCPL	Celler DP
3786996	LCPL	Cervinski P
215646	LCPL	Chambers JR *
215776	PTE	Chapman RP
5713802	PTE	Checkley JR
215509	LCPL	Cheeseman TWG *
3787266	PTE	Chester JN
6708241	PTE	Chick DB

273

VIETNAM TASK

Regt No	Rank	Name
214418	CPL	Christen R
2781316	PTE	Christian T
16544	LCPL	Church DF
215490	PTE	Clare NG
5713804	**PTE**	**Clark DM †**
2782847	PTE	Clark FR *
3787091	PTE	Clarke A
4717606	PTE	Clarke EW
43442	PTE	Clarke FH
3786902	PTE	Clarke FJ ^
22608	WO2	Clarke JP
2781590	LCPL	Claydon MJ *
4717621	PTE	Clayton IJ
214476	SGT	Cleary VP
38905	PTE	Clewer RW
2781799	PTE	Coffey JP
2781318	PTE	Coffey RC
43755	PTE	Cogswell CJ *
3787176	PTE	Colbert PK
3786751	PTE	Cole JW
215557	LCPL	Coles WL
53744	SGT	Collins DL
4717477	PTE	Collins GW
5713623	PTE	Collins PG
1731575	PTE	Connell PJ
16495	CPL	Connor JB
37860	PTE	Connor NR
2781545	LCPL	Connors GB
38068	CPL	Conole KC
215524	PTE	Cook H
2781546	PTE	Coombes RS
1200480	PTE	Cooper RC
2781591	PTE	Coote SW
3786680	PTE	Coret GCP
2782560	PTE	Cork BJ
15358	**CPL**	**Coupe BF †**
61392	PTE	Cowen CW

Regt No	Rank	Name
3786981	PTE	Cox WP
5411528	PTE	Craib MG
54920	CPL	Craib PW *
2782049	PTE	Craig P
2781651	PTE	Craig PJ
1200327	PTE	Crain RW
215359	CPL	Crane N
4717478	PTE	Cranwell IJ
1200362	PTE	Criss RJ *
2781324	PTE	Cross JLD
6410173	PTE	Cross MG
54829	PTE	Crotty KG
2782823	PTE	Crowther JB
3787966	PTE	Cruikshank BJ
18163	CPL	Crummer AR
3786982	LCPL	Cullen TB
5713628	CPL	Cullen TK
3786753	PTE	Cummins BF
215109	PTE	Cunningham BG
23814	SSGT	Cunningham WN
18746	PTE	Curtis JNL
1200193	PTE	Czekaj (Crystal) W *
216202	LCPL	Dale BH
2781327	PTE	Dale RA
2781592	PTE	Daley ET
2781612	PTE	Dallimore JH
3411761	PTE	Daly KF
54865	**PTE**	**D'Antoine GH †**
4411066	PTE	Dart RM
18170	LCPL	Davern TJ
311483	CPL	Davis GS
1731268	PTE	Davis JR
3787598	PTE	Davis KG
15353	LCPL	Davis KR
3410574	SGT	Davis SJ
42873	PTE	Dawson MB

APPENDIX C

Regt No	Rank	Name
216045	PTE	Dawson PE
2781333	PTE	Deacon RM
36688	PTE	Delbridge CF
43343	PTE	Delsar BR
215048	CPL	Dempsey MJ
2412396	PTE	Denning J
2781549	PTE	Devine PK
2781336	PTE	Devlin KJ
4410743	PTE	Dewick GS
2781478	PTE	Dibden CR
3786918	PTE	Dinoto C
3787471	PTE	Docherty RF *
1731274	PTE	Doeblien BB
215337	LCPL	Doherty JR
3411846	CPL	Donovan D
3411395	CPL	Donovan FA
2781552	LCPL	Dorrough H
311437	SGT	Douglas J
2781593	PTE	Douglass JW
3789136	PTE	Doyle JA
2781554	PTE	Drayton KL
28837	SGT	Drennan WT
5713633	PTE	Drew KJ
54332	CPL	Drimatis N
2781654	PTE	Dring FR
216855	PTE	Dudley CE
3786995	PTE	Duell PR
6708281	PTE	Duffey JP
38668	PTE	Duffy TJ *
214935	CPL	Dunbar WR
216233	CPL	Dunn NI
213028	CPL	Dunn RT
216066	PTE	Dunne GN
215615	PTE	Dunne TJ
2781343	CPL	Durrant RJ
2781344	PTE	Dwyer MN *
4718353	PTE	East WH

Regt No	Rank	Name
3786998	PTE	Eaves RT
4410903	PTE	Eccles BT
2781345	PTE	Edgar RJ
2781777	PTE	Edmonds KH
43554	CPL	Edmonds RJ
61729	PTE	Edson PJ
37952	PTE	Edward JT
5713634	PTE	Edwards RS
3411652	PTE	Edwards WH *
3787107	PTE	Egan JK
2783620	PTE	Elder BA
1411148	PTE	Engel MG
2781558	PTE	English DV
215181	PTE	English SR
5713637	LCPL	Erkelens HC
212984	CPL	Evans AG
38797	CPL	Evans E
61618	CPL	Evans HC
3786920	PTE	Evans MF
3786972	PTE	Everard BG
43887	PTE	Everett JE
2781594	PTE	Eyles AT
214383	SGT	Faddy PL
216377	CPL	Fahy E
3786783	PTE	Falzon PE
2782107	PTE	Farrell RC
3786921	**PTE**	**Farren LT †**
3786755	PTE	Fenech A
4717623	LCPL	Fennell GM
2782064	PTE	Ferguson RS *
2781351	PTE	Ferrier RJ
3786629	PTE	Fielding RH
43391	PTE	Filmer BJ
1200792	LCPL	Finlayson GP
3787112	PTE	Finney N
5713639	LCPL	Fisher DB
216578	LCPL	Fitton B

275

VIETNAM TASK

Regt No	Rank	Name
216633	PTE	Fitzgerald JG
5411558	PTE	Fitzgerald JJ
3787094	PTE	Flanders GG
3786922	PTE	Fletcher RC
5571	WO1	Foale LT
6708570	PTE	Folder WJ
1730803	PTE	Foran IW *
213452	SGT	Ford DC *
215043	PTE	Foreman JS
4410831	PTE	Foster DC
4717646	PTE	Foster GW
2783635	PTE	Fox NW
216121	CPL	Frances CL
37576	CPL	Francis RN
4717624	LCPL	Fraser P
29019	SSGT	Fridolf MJ
5411149	CPL	Frugtniet HL
16590	SGT	Fryer GA
16193	PTE	Fuller JE
3786681	PTE	Gadd EF
3787040	PTE	Gambold BW
3786784	PTE	Garbutt KE
61092	SSGT	Gardiner TG
4717494	PTE	Garland RD
3787118	PTE	Gates LE *
214198	PTE	Gay TJ
42717	PTE	Gaynes VJ
2781357	PTE	Gee BA *
4411024	PTE	Geisler JP
18387	PTE	Genninges WE
18446	PTE	Gentry-Pike CD
61570	PTE	George DL *
37079	SGT	Gibson JA
61580	LCPL	Gilbank HC
14900	CPL	Gilbert GG
2782481	PTE	Gilbert KF
5713647	PTE	Gilders WH

Regt No	Rank	Name
216230	PTE	Gilmore GC
1411135	LCPL	Godfrey PC
55179	PTE	Godfrey RJ
51811	WO2	Goldspink NH
43301	PTE	Gontar G
3786891	CPL	Goodman DS *
4717496	PTE	Gordon DJ
5713648	LCPL	Gosney WD
4410849	PTE	Gott T ^
14456	SGT	Graham NC
1731298	PTE	Graham RG
4717625	PTE	Gray DB
2782127	**LCPL**	**Green GB †**
215902	PTE	Green JF
4411019	CFN	Greig RG
216922	CPL	Grelck JV
3787065	PTE	Griffin BT
2781620	PTE	Griffiths GD
2781484	PTE	Griffiths TM
3787120	PTE	Grigonis FA
43781	PTE	Growden G
43572	LCPL	Haldane MJ
214758	CPL	Hall JC
214506	CPL	Hall KJ
5713656	PTE	Hall KP
2782728	PTE	Hall MJ
54389	SGT	Halliday J
215683	CPL	Hamilton AD
37835	LCPL	Hancy RS *
61571	LCPL	Hansch LD
5714101	PTE	Happ PD
43387	CPL	Harbourd RG
4717652	PTE	Harding DG
4717626	PTE	Harding LJ
2781622	PTE	Harding RK
2782207	PTE	Hardman C
2781656	PTE	Harries DW

APPENDIX C

Regt No	Rank	Name
1411186	PTE	Harrington JH
3787202	PTE	Harris JS
3411472	LCPL	Harris MJ
64349	CPL	Harris NJ
4410641	PTE	Harris ST
38198	PTE	Harris TJ
215812	LCPL	Harrison EWD *
3411600	CPL	Harrison KC
1731118	PTE	Harrison MT
38939	PTE	Harstad BA
213929	PTE	Harvey G
214232	CPL	Harvey WC
16188	SGT	Hassall BAJ
1731304	PTE	Hasted GN
54856	PTE	Hawkins RC *
4410757	PTE	Hay TW
2412438	PTE	Haynes KG
54877	LCPL	Hayward FC
2781624	PTE	Head SJ
213897	CPL	Heldon CR
3786684	PTE	Heley DF
215732	PTE	Hellyer JA
3788593	PTE	Henderson RJ
2783991	PTE	Hennessey PJ
243164	SGT	Henrys ME
18353	PTE	Heron BD
38744	PTE	Hevey LJ
3787128	PTE	Hexter NB *
2412246	LCPL	Heyhoe JK
2412179	PTE	Heys DW
3411470	PTE	Hibberson LL
2412167	CPL	Hill AL
4410717	PTE	Hille DC
5411552	PTE	Hilliard CT
2781366	LCPL	Hillier AD
2781367	PTE	Hillier DE *
215366	CPL	Hilton RA

Regt No	Rank	Name
212969	SGT	Hindmarsh R
15705	CPL	Hoare FW *
3787252	LCPL	Hodges KJ
6708288	PTE	Hodges PE
1200522	CPL	Hodges TK
1411166	LCPL	Hogan JF
2781658	PTE	Hogbin JC
1411153	LCPL	Holden LA
3787131	PTE	Holland BI
214799	PTE	Hollands WG
3787132	PTE	Holliday DA
14619	SGT	Holliday RJ
35950	SGT	Holtman JF
216653	CPL	Hopson RK
3787043	PTE	Hore RD
43197	PTE	Hoskin BK
214737	LCPL	Hoy CJ
3411167	LCPL	Hubbard B
1731451	PTE	Hughes DR
22684	WO2	Hughson BM
5713665	PTE	Hunt WJ
2781496	PTE	Hunter MR
52844	SGT	Hunting RR
38739	PTE	Hurford AJ
2781497	PTE	Hurley JA
214444	SGT	Hush JR
3786985	PTE	Hyatt LK *
3787000	PTE	Hynson RF
6708287	PTE	Illman CM
17811	PTE	Inall AL
29039	PTE	Inch VR
61558	PTE	Ingleby RW
214618	LCPL	Ingleton RJ
3787133	PTE	Iredale MP
215355	PTE	Irwin DB
5713666	PTE	Ives BT
3786830	PTE	Ives KJ

VIETNAM TASK

Regt No	Rank	Name
213832	PTE	James TR
2782216	PTE	Jansz PJ
215258	PTE	Jarrett WJ
213206	LCPL	Jenkins W
14839	SGT	Johns RJ
4410985	PTE	Johnson BJ
6708286	PTE	Johnson CA
1411070	PTE	Johnson DG
2782785	PTE	Johnson PL
5411582	PTE	Jones HD *
3787137	PTE	Jones KA
4717387	PTE	Jones PL
3786760	PTE	Jordan KT
3787248	PTE	Joseph GN
6708251	PTE	Kane GE
3786929	PTE	Karlich I
2781501	PTE	Kay JJ
43268	CPL	Kearney RS
2782056	PTE	Keen EJ
215056	PTE	Keen RM
6708230	PTE	Kellett DS
216090	CPL	Kelly JA
213458	CPL	Kelly TJ
214138	CPL	Kenane RCT
215619	CPL	Kennedy DL
216304	CPL	Kennedy JJ
16196	**PTE**	**Kennedy RJ †**
216531	LCPL	Kennedy VJ
4717627	PTE	Kenyon JR
214231	PTE	Kerr LD
214302	PTE	Keys RS
18757	CPL	Kibby JA
38929	PTE	Kindred RE
3787063	PTE	King EM
61514	CPL	King M
6708310	PTE	King ND
3787141	PTE	Kitchin LM

Regt No	Rank	Name
43217	LCPL	Klose JD
2781504	PTE	Kneller AT
3411359	CPL	Knight PJ
37171	CPL	Koblitz H
4717612	PTE	Kuchenmeister CC
2781505	PTE	Kustreba I
2781447	PTE	La Forest PJ
214239	PTE	Ladmore JF
1200879	CPL	Lamb DF
4717390	PTE	Lang AC
58808	PTE	Lapko P
16389	CPL	Laverty BJ
2412380	LCPL	Le Breton MJ
5411097	CPL	Leach ID
37675	CPL	Leadbeater WK
6771	SGT	Leaman JB
2782234	PTE	Lear SH
3411686	PTE	Leask EJ
38000	SGT	Lea-Smith JA
43974	PTE	Leckie RJ
2782141	PTE	Ledger BJ
54912	PTE	Lee CN
43348	PTE	Lehmann GN
37344	PTE	Lengnick RC
1200661	LCPL	Lennon R
2782057	LCPL	Lesslie GJ
3786894	PTE	Lestrange RJ
342917	CPL	Levey GR
216078	PTE	Levick GT
61614	PTE	Lewis LV
42992	CPL	Lillebo WA
215591	LCPL	Lindsay A
5411414	PTE	Lister RG
2784015	**PTE**	**Lloyd RE †**
36775	CPL	Lodge IW
43676	LCPL	Logan JM
214650	SGT	London BK

APPENDIX C

Regt No	Rank	Name
38878	PTE	Long PE *
54792	PTE	Longley TJ
215861	LCPL	Longobardi RC
3787281	PTE	Lowe G
42720	**PTE**	**Lubcke RJ †**
18462	LCPL	Lucht CR
214548	CPL	Luck GD
4717628	PTE	Lynch TM *
216095	PTE	Lyons MC
4717737	PTE	Maalste H
2781637	PTE	MacDougall RN
3411705	LCPL	Mack CA
2412184	CPL	Mackay IR *
38391	LCPL	Mackay RJ
3787045	PTE	Mackay VJ
3787020	PTE	Mackie RJ
215260	CPL	MacKinlay RL
4717398	PTE	MacMillan DW
212700	SGT	Madden EJ
18622	CPL	Magee DC
54786	LCPL	Magowan LR
3411701	PTE	Maher PR
2781599	PTE	Maisey RG
213826	PTE	Malam DG
216057	PTE	Maloney PW
5713890	PTE	Mann DR
1200734	LCPL	Maraldo NP
3786792	PTE	Marie RK
2781601	PTE	Maroulis WN
54790	LCPL	Marshall RJ
4717630	PTE	Marshall WJ
54231	CPL	Marshall WP
4410799	PTE	Martin GJ
215945	LCPL	Mashford RL
216542	LCPL	Mason BE
3787155	LCPL	Masterson KJ
213262	SGT	Mavin KH

Regt No	Rank	Name
43254	CPL	Mavromatis MJ
54333	PTE	May RN
3786850	PTE	Maynard KJ
61626	PTE	Mayne PS
215508	LCPL	McAlister JP *
212633	SGT	McAllister JB
2781375	PTE	McBride MH
1411194	LCPL	McCall GG
3787064	PTE	McColl DW
3787001	PTE	McCombe DJ
214229	CPL	McCray GL *
215728	PTE	McCue TJ
38389	PTE	McCune DA
3411448	PTE	McDonald PJ
43201	PTE	McDonald TK
4717396	CPL	McDougall IA ^
215705	PTE	McEvoy L
28648	WO2	McGregor D
18243	CPL	McIntyre WK
1410929	CPL	McKenzie EL
3787216	PTE	McKenzie KJ
213559	CPL	McKenzie RN
1200142	CPL	McKeon BA
5713685	PTE	McLaren J
215372	PTE	McLean A
14429	PTE	McLean AC
3787068	PTE	McLean DR
1200589	PTE	McMillan R
3787044	PTE	McMonigle IA
215607	PTE	McNeill K
3411264	CPL	McNulty AB
4717629	PTE	McQuade TG
5713686	PTE	McShane BJ
29058	SSGT	Mealing MJ *
3786932	PTE	Melki MA
5713690	PTE	Mellowship DG
2781384	LCPL	Meredith GD

Regt No	Rank	Name
2781606	PTE	Meredith RW
2782082	PTE	Merrion KS
6708356	PTE	Midson KA
215505	PTE	Milham RJ
37281	CPL	Miller DJ
4410736	PTE	Miller LW
215008	PTE	Miller MD
13444	LCPL	Mills A
3787003	PTE	Mills CM
4410959	PTE	Mills DC
1200726	PTE	Mison BW
4717649	PTE	Mitchell B
37026	WO2	Mitchell TR
3786793	PTE	Mitrevics VP
6708260	PTE	Moles GD
38037	CPL	Monaghan TP
14829	PTE	Moore BP
36456	CPL	Moore RG *
215479	PTE	Moran CG
3411697	PTE	Moran KJ
3411813	PTE	Morison LJ
1411066	PTE	Moroney DM
1731406	PTE	Morrow KM
3786812	PTE	Morrow ML
53902	SGT	Mossman RWF
2781391	PTE	Muir SJ
37015	CPL	Mulby JT
2412426	PTE	Mundine RL
2781449	PTE	Murphy JV
2781393	PTE	Murphy WJ
216429	PTE	Murrant P
215069	LCPL	Musson PJ
4411008	PTE	Mynhart JC
4717402	LCPL	Naismith RH
2782494	PTE	Nation PG
1411129	LCPL	Naumann RW
216422	CPL	Nesbitt GM

Regt No	Rank	Name
1410904	PTE	Newstead GH
1200228	PTE	Newstead GW
6708511	PTE	Nichols PJ
215625	CPL	Nichols RFA *
3787048	PTE	Nieuwenhout A *
1200083	**PTE**	**Nilsen EH †**
311511	PTE	Nisbet PE
43687	PTE	Nitschke AW
4410713	PTE	Nitschke MR
4717546	**PTE**	**Noack EW †**
36777	SGT	Noack RJ
2412386	PTE	Nolan DG
36180	CPL	Nolan GN
2781395	PTE	Noonan M
4717759	PTE	Norman GR
4717760	PTE	Nottage GT
3786823	PTE	Nyhuis JG *
3787157	PTE	O'Brien AJ
3787385	PTE	O'Brien BJ
2781397	PTE	O'Callaghan JP
17910	LCPL	O'Connor LM
38402	PTE	O'Dell P
4717548	PTE	O'Donnell BL
4717550	PTE	Oldroyd DL
216072	PTE	Olson AA
16979	CPL	Orchard RL *
3787161	PTE	Ordner NG
212602	SGT	O'Reilly E
16038	CPL	O'Rourke CE
2782160	PTE	O'Shea PJ
2781509	CPL	Osmond BJ
2412330	PTE	O'Sullivan DM
214602	CPL	O'Sullivan LV *
14338	SSGT	Owens G
3786989	PTE	Page WJ
3787162	PTE	Paice RG
4717399	PTE	Painter J

APPENDIX C

Regt No	Rank	Name
3786797	PTE	Pantalone L
37517	PTE	Parker LJ
2781452	PTE	Parkes WJ
4717404	PTE	Patching RA
3787115	PTE	Patterson JP
2781665	PTE	PaynePT *
215838	LCPL	Peacock FR
2781453	PTE	Pearson WG *
3786642	PTE	Peate NC
61616	PTE	Peck NJ
215310	PTE	Peddell RL
3786938	PTE	Peirce PC
1200137	PTE	Pemberton BM
2412461	PTE	Peninton JW
54818	PTE	Penman DJ
213612	SGT	Perrin GR
16177	CPL	Perry RJ
2412385	PTE	Perry SJ *
18839	PTE	Peters NG
3411549	CPL	Phillip Z
3787165	PTE	Phillips GL
2782718	PTE	Phillips LC
3787069	PTE	Phillips PR
215733	PTE	Philp DA *
216333	CPL	Pike RA
2781569	PTE	Pilgrim DM
18447	PTE	Pinch LR
216938	PTE	Plant JR
215819	PTE	Poirrier RF
61475	CPL	Poke DR
342916	**PTE**	**Poole MD †**
3787521	PTE	Porter RH
4717561	PTE	Power WJ
3786885	PTE	Poyser CL
216044	**PTE**	**Pracy NA #**
18433	PTE	Presbury RG
213872	CPL	Quinn SR *

Regt No	Rank	Name
4717633	PTE	Raffan PJ
38115	CPL	Raine PC
3787013	LCPL	Ransome AJ
29006	PTE	Reading LL
215298	PTE	Redding AN
3786969	PTE	Reeves AF
16958	PTE	Reeves AW
38235	LCPL	Reid AB
17767	PTE	Reid GE
38087	LCPL	Reid NJ
44038	PTE	Reinertsen CG
215334	PTE	Reister J
2781457	PTE	Reynolds JR
54678	PTE	Rhodes ML
18131	PTE	Rice RK
4717563	PTE	Richards DP
21941	PTE	Ridgewell NJ
4717565	PTE	Ridgway MW
2781458	PTE	Riik DG *
2412265	PTE	Riley DE
5713710	PTE	Roach CR *
5713712	PTE	Roberts PH
214129	PTE	Robertson BA
2781459	PTE	Robertson FA
215254	PTE	Robertson RJ
37928	CPL	Robertson WI
38097	PTE	Robinson GH
38400	PTE	Robinson MA
3786639	PTE	Robinson PJ
27177	WO2	Roby PH
29481	SSGT	Rogers JM
216538	PTE	Rogers NA
15562	CPL	Rogers RW
4717569	PTE	Rogers RW
212682	PTE	Rose DJ
4717410	PTE	Rosewarne PT
215156	CPL	Ross CJ

VIETNAM TASK

Regt No	Rank	Name
14184	CPL	Ross RM
5713717	CPL	Rummer GD
4410746	PTE	Russell RC
215868	CPL	Ruttle BD
3786861	LCPL	Ryan KD
4717571	PTE	Sandford RT
4717413	PTE	Sando TK
43496	**PTE**	**Sandow RW †**
214235	LCPL	Sands J
3787178	PTE	Sarteschi GM
5713719	PTE	Saunders MJ
43698	PTE	Sayer (Marshall) JE
2781409	PTE	Scafidi JA
2412308	PTE	Scales JF
216572	LCPL	Scaysbrook KW
216962	PTE	Schaeffer RJ
215802	PTE	Scheuermann KW *
3787051	PTE	Schmidt FU
1200310	PTE	Schmidtchen DB *
215469	CPL	Schofield R
3787070	PTE	Schultz AR
18200	PTE	Schultz BJ
2781976	PTE	Scott G
3411693	PTE	Scott RG
61604	LCPL	Searl RA
2781461	PTE	Searle JH
212970	SSGT	Seats MA
3787006	PTE	Seiffert DM
3787301	PTE	Selleck NT
3786727	PTE	Shannon BM
4410871	PTE	Shannon DG
3787182	PTE	Sharp DW
4717575	PTE	Sharp PC
215907	PTE	Sharpe WS
2412082	CPL	Shaw DR
14514	SGT	Shawcross CB
215648	CPL	Sheringham RJ
1410796	PTE	Sherrington MG
16948	PTE	Sherwin-White IR
3787186	PTE	Shields RL
3788644	PTE	Shimmin WJ
216068	PTE	Shoebridge RP *
3787022	PTE	Shore SL
1410924	PTE	Sibson LJ
2412384	LCPL	Sielicki T
16331	CPL	Silk VE
34925	LCPL	Simpson DA
3411431	PTE	Simpson LJ
215194	SGT	Sims NR
2781513	PTE	Sinclair R
27089	CPL	Sinclair WW
3787187	PTE	Siwes HG
55069	LCPL	Slater R
2781410	PTE	Slattery PA
2412335	PTE	Smails B *
215794	PTE	Smale L
212897	SGT	Small NM
2783826	PTE	Smallwood TN
215023	LCPL	Smee KJ
18211	LCPL	Smerdon NJ
42252	CPL	Smith BL
53652	CPL	Smith GA
213849	CPL	Smith GG
43394	PTE	Smith IR
5411611	CPL	Smith KE
34578	WO2	Smith KO
3786617	PTE	Smith NR
3786647	PTE	Smith RGV
1200617	LCPL	Snoxell BJ
3787531	PTE	Sobey GK
18221	SIG	Soden WD
2411742	SSGT	Solomon RG
16317	LCPL	Sorrensen JA

APPENDIX C

Regt No	Rank	Name
216036	CPL	Sperring RL
4717579	PTE	Stanford P
13552	CPL	Stanley PF
61470	CPL	Steele WR
4717580	PTE	Stein PE *
17708	CPL	Stevens IJ
3786648	PTE	Stevens TJ
2781514	PTE	Stevens WA
1410999	PTE	Stewart JC
28878	WO2	Stewart JR
4717653	PTE	Stewart JW
1410968	PTE	Stringer ME
215154	PTE	Stuart RJ
214565	PTE	Stubbs JB
38388	PTE	Suckling (Hunter) AG *
17707	CPL	Sugistaff J
3787008	PTE	Suiter RE
3786696	**PTE**	**Sullivan PC †**
311548	PTE	Sullivan TB
215007	CPL	Sully RJ
4717582	PTE	Summers IR
2781515	PTE	Sutton CJ *
215958	**PTE**	**Sweetnam JR †**
43605	PTE	Tape DB *
3786962	PTE	Taylor D
342627	WO2	Taylor RL
4717587	PTE	Templeton A
3411057	PTE	Thacker AC
311401	LCPL	Thomas RH
1200335	PTE	Thompson NG *
4410921	PTE	Thomson IM
42754	PTE	Tierney JJ
2781516	PTE	Tiliks A
3786888	PTE	Toman TJ
5713739	**LCPL**	**Tomas M †**
3787309	PTE	Tommasi TM

Regt No	Rank	Name
3786951	PTE	Tonkin BN
216576	CFN	Toohill JT
2781518	PTE	Towner GL
3786619	PTE	Townsend GM
214823	LCPL	Trappel AE
3787036	PTE	Treloar DA
214098	SSGT	Trenear RA
2781421	PTE	Tuchin EA
243258	PTE	Tuck PL
216659	PTE	Tudor BR
37814	CPL	Tueno TJ
3786943	PTE	Turner B
2782115	PTE	Turner RW *
4717650	PTE	Turner T
38296	PTE	Twaits AB *
310236	WO2	Twigg RJ
3786730	PTE	Twyford NF
4717593	PTE	Tyrrell DN
19973	CPL	Urquhart LJ
4411017	PTE	Verrall PG
1200675	PTE	Vickery CC
215553	PTE	Vidler N
2781423	PTE	Vizzone DM
3786847	PTE	Vyner CJ
2412087	CPL	Wade SP
4717637	PTE	Wahl MW
4717638	PTE	Walden AR
2782852	PTE	Wales KC
2781522	PTE	Walker AR
214870	CFN	Walker JH
43601	PTE	Wall CL
2781523	PTE	Walter RN *
3786978	**PTE**	**Warburton GF †**
54560	CPL	Wardle CW
4717639	PTE	Warren KR
61163	SGT	Wass KJ *
43360	CPL	Waters GA

283

VIETNAM TASK

Regt No	Rank	Name
36501	SGT	Waters GE
5713748	**PTE**	**Watson BP †**
3787195	PTE	Watt B
43684	LCPL	Webb R *
5713751	**PTE**	**Webster JC †**
6410140	CPL	Webster RB
215060	PTE	Weekes GM
4717427	PTE	Wegener DW
2411550	SGT	Welch AJ
216130	PTE	Wells A
216663	PTE	Welsh P
5713752	PTE	Wemm RC
214639	PTE	Wennekes CS
38201	CPL	West ED
37763	SGT	Westerman AH
54758	PTE	Western D
3786732	LCPL	Whelan T
16506	LCPL	White EW
1731194	PTE	White KC
18454	PTE	White KM
3786815	PTE	White MR
5713753	PTE	Whitfield AT
42848	PTE	Wieringa JE
215394	LCPL	Wilcox GT
2781564	PTE	Wiles AJ
216821	PTE	Wilkie RJ
54318	SGT	Willcott BE
36267	WO2	Williams ER
3411685	PTE	Williams F *
2781533	PTE	Williams JE
4717599	LCPL	Williams JV
216545	PTE	Williams LR
4410639	CPL	Williams RE
37924	PTE	Williamson RN
214861	LCPL	Wills GR
3786770	PTE	Wilson BW
43567	PTE	Wilson GC

Regt No	Rank	Name
216505	PTE	Wilson SAM
1411127	PTE	Winkel WC *
4717641	PTE	Winterfield RA *
29124	SSGT	Witheridge T
3786804	PTE	Wolk U *
216896	PTE	Wollner DD
16978	PTE	Wollstein SD
15170	**CPL**	**Womal NJ †**
213619	CPL	Wood BC
2782134	LCPL	Wood PS
2783900	PTE	Wood RF
342873	CFN	Wood SJ
216565	PTE	Woolley PE
54562	LCPL	Woolley RG
1411218	PTE	Wooster SJ
24011	WO2	Wormald RC
16706	LCPL	Wrathmall FJ
3411687	PTE	Wright KR
3787200	PTE	Wright RC
2782681	PTE	Wylie BA
18354	CPL	Ziemski RA

APPENDIX C

Officers

Regt No	Rank	Name
3487	LTCOL	Warr JA
23916	**MAJ**	**Bourne DM †**
52680	MAJ	Carroll OM
240195	MAJ	Cassidy AP
235052	MAJ	Cole PG
25478	MAJ	Granter NEW
335104	MAJ	Greenhalgh PN
235127	MAJ	Hamlyn RD
57026	MAJ	Hodgkinson IRJ
235023	MAJ	Maizey SJ
235136	**MAJ**	**McQualter MB #**
27234	MAJ	Miller JF
18142	MAJ	Shambrook RT
17089	CAPT	Bade RW
14967	CAPT	Boxall RE
311478	CAPT	Isaacs PJ
53456	CAPT	Le Dan BG *
2146596	CAPT	Mallinson KG
29635	**CAPT**	**Milligan RB †**
382847	CAPT	Molloy WJ
335113	CAPT	O'Neill RJ
47031	CAPT	Pfitzner EF
214040	CAPT	Supple RW
147181	CAPT	Taske JE
38506	CAPT	Thompson RG
216799	CAPT	White HAD
235194	CAPT	Willcox DA
36911	**LT**	**Carruthers J #**
17105	LT	Hartley JC **
235287	LT	Morris EB
55071	LT	Negus GN

Regt No	Rank	Name
43585	LT	Rowe DJF
213471	LT	Sheehan TJ *
47046	LT	Wainwright GR *
38164	2LT	Cook JE
17864	2LT	Davis RJ
216701	2LT	Deak (von Berg) MGJ
1731087	2LT	Deane-Butcher JH *
214607	2LT	Gunning RR
54845	2LT	Lovell DG
38050	2LT	McAloney JD *
5713701	2LT	Neesham HT
43310	2LT	Nelson JP
55077	2LT	O'Dea L
1731021	2LT	O'Hanlon TH
1730857	2LT	Pott AE
54624	2LT	Rainer DC
217479	**2LT**	**Rinkin KP †**
5713714	2LT	Roe MJ
37277	2LT	Ross GH
4718066	2LT	Travers MH
54577	Chap	Bennett EJ
216363	Chap	Williams JF
2950004	Everyman	Bentley JW

About the Author

Robert O'Neill AO was born in Melbourne, Victoria, in 1936 and served in the Australian Regular Army from 1955 to 1968. He graduated from the Royal Military College Duntroon in 1958. He then studied for the degree of Bachelor of Engineering at the University of Melbourne in 1959–60 and was elected Rhodes Scholar for Victoria in 1961. He graduated as Master of Arts and Doctor of Philosophy from Oxford University in 1965.

Posted to Vietnam in 1966, he served as second-in-command of B Company 5 RAR from January to August 1966 and then as battalion intelligence officer from August 1966 to May 1967. He was mentioned in despatches in 1967. He transferred to the academic staff at RMC Duntroon in 1968 and then joined the Department of International Relations at The Australian National University in 1969, becoming head of the Strategic and Defence Studies Centre, ANU, from 1971 to 1982. He was the official historian of Australia's role in the Korean War from 1970 to 1982.

Professor O'Neill moved to the United Kingdom in 1982, where he became director of the International Institute for Strategic Studies, London, from 1982 to 1987, and then Chichele Professor of the History of War and fellow of All Souls College, Oxford, from 1987 to 2001. He served as chairman of the Council of the International Institute for Strategic Studies, 1996 to 2001, trustee of the Imperial War Museum, London, 1990 to 2001, and chairman of the IWM Board of Trustees, 1998 to 2001. He was a member of the Commonwealth War Graves Commission, 1991 to 2001. He also served as chairman of the board, Menzies Centre for Australian Studies, London, 1990 to 1995.

Intelligence officer Captain Bob O'Neill briefing soldiers in 5 RAR's open-air theatre, 'The Mayfair'.

He retired to Australia in late 2001. He served as inaugural chairman of the council, Australian Strategic Policy Institute, from 2000 to 2005 and as a board member of the Lowy Institute, Sydney, from 2003 to 2012.

Professor O'Neill was appointed an honorary Doctor of Letters, ANU, Canberra, in 2001; an honorary fellow, Australian Institute for International Affairs, in 2008; and a jubilee fellow, Academy of the Social Sciences in Australia, in 2018. He was appointed an Officer of the Order of Australia (AO) in 1988.

ABOUT THE AUTHOR

Other Publications by the Author

- *The German Army and the Nazi Party, 1933–39.* London: Cassell (1966).
- *General Giap: Politician and Strategist.* London: Cassell (1969).
- *The Strategic Nuclear Balance: An Australian Perspective.* Editor. Canberra: ANU (1975).
- *The Defence of Australia: Fundamental New Aspects.* Editor. Canberra: ANU (1977).
- *The Strategic Environment in the 1980s.* Editor. Canberra: ANU (1980).
- *Australia in the Korean War 1950–53 – Volume 1: Strategy and Diplomacy.* Canberra: Australian War Memorial and the Australian Govt. Pub. Service (1981).
- *New Directions in Strategic Thinking.* Edited with David Horner. Sydney: Allen & Unwin (1981).
- *Australian Defence Policy for the 1980s.* Edited with David Horner. St Lucia: University of Queensland Press (1982).
- *Australia in the Korean War 1950–1953 – Volume 2: Combat Operations.* Canberra: Australian War Memorial and the Australian Govt. Pub. Service (1985).
- *Vietnam Vanguard: The 5th Battalion's Approach to Counter-Insurgency, 1966.* Edited with Ron Boxall. Canberra: ANU Press (2020).

Index

A Company, 5 RAR, 37, 38, 41, 43, 51, 55, 64, 149, 163–5, 213–16, 236–7, 243, 248–51
An Nhut (village), 216, 219–20
Anthony, Pte. R., 235
Askew, 2/Lt. R., 156

B Company, 5 RAR, 36–8, 41–2, 44, 55, 57–8, 63, 73, 77, 96, 127–8, 165–6, 176, 177, 228, 232–6, 242–3, 250
Bade, Capt. R., 63, 80
Ba Ria (town), 12; attacked by VC, 18; interrogation centre, 73
Barron, 2/Lt., 111
Be, Capt. Nguyen Van, 105, 108, 114, 115, 206
Benson, S/Sgt., 235
Bic, Sgt., Vietnamese interpreter, 126, 187
Bien Hoa, American base, 117
Binh Ba (village), 16, 72, 81–2, 86
Bourne, Maj. D. M., 220, 261
Bouse, Cpl., 235
Boxall, Capt. R., 63, 80, 108
Brown, Pte. T., 187
Burge, Maj. M. E. P., 237

C Company, 5 RAR, 24, 36, 47, 55, 57, 64, 99, 114, 125, 136, 165, 220, 244, 248–9
Calvert, Sgt., 157
Campbell, Lt. B., 165

Canungra Jungle Training Centre, 22–3
Carroll, Maj. O. M., 21, 25–6, 43, 77–8, 98, 108, 112, 150, 152, 177, 208, 214, 220, 236–7
Carruthers, Lt. J., 66, 228, 232–5, 238, 262
Cassidy, Maj. A. P., 20, 177
Chieu Hoi (Open Arms) programme, 104, 107, 196, 197, 221
Chinh, Sgt., Vietnamese interpreter, 208
Civil Affairs Unit, 1 ATF, 81, 105
Clarke, Pte. D. M., 261
Cogswell, Pte. C. J., 267
Cole, Maj. P., 158, 208
Coupe, Cpl. B. F., 261

D Company, 5 RAR, 36, 45, 52, 55, 64, 65–6, 86, 90, 99, 110–13, 165, 229, 231–2, 242–3
Daly, Lt. Gen. Sir Thomas, 99
D'Antoine, Pte. G. H., 161–2, 261
Dat, Col. Le Duc, 14, 17–18, 73, 86, 91, 114, 188, 251
Dat Do (town), 13, 200, 217–19
Davies, Lt. W., 139
Deak, 2/Lt. M., 152, 157, 166, 229, 244–5, 264
Dinh hills, 11, 13, 17, 29, 54
Duc, Capt., 185, 187–8, 251
Duc My (village), 58, 60–4, 85
Duc Thanh (district), 14, 18, 72, 108

Elections (South Vietnam), 103, 104

Farren, Pte. L. T., 261
Fifth Battalion, RAR, formation of, 19; officers, 20–1; training, 22–4; move to Vietnam, 24–7; battalion HQ, 148–60, 175, 177
First Battalion, RAR, forms core of Fifth Battalion, 19; prepares for Vietnam, 19; aids 5 RAR advance party, 24; at Binh Ba, 31
Foale, WO I. L., 151
Francis (Dinh-quôc-Thuy), Father, 105–6
Fraser, Pte. P., 157, 166, 268

Gair, Maj. N., 160, 175
Gallia Plantation, 70–1, 92, 207, 208
Gates, Pte. L. E., 215
Godwin, Capt. B., 236
Graham, Brig. S., 189, 203, 227, 236, 240, 247
Granter, Maj. N. E. W., 20, 24
Green, L/Cpl. G. B., 262
Greenhalgh, Maj. P. N., 21, 112, 124
Guderian, Gen. H., 195

Hamlyn, Maj. R., 242, 249
Hannigan, Maj. R., 177
Hartley, Lt. J., 56, 214–15
Hassall, Sgt. S., 38
Hat Dich (VC base), 9, 16, 51, 54
Hexter, Pte. N. B., 215
Hoa Long (village), 13, 14, 17, 30, 31, 200, 208–9, 211–13
Hodgkinson, Maj. I. R., 210
Holsworthy (Australia), 19
Horseshoe Hill, fence to coast from, 240; fortified, 242–3
Hughes, Sir Wilfrid Kent, 172
Hughson, WO II, 151
Hung, Nguyen Nam, 51, 165, 200
Huong Sa (hamlet), 108
Huynh Ba Trang, Lt., 187

Interrogation system, 77–8, 207
Isaacs, Capt. P. J., 21, 31, 35, 98, 235

Jackson, Brig. O. D., 86, 107, 144–5, 175, 188, 191, 203
Joseph, Father, 72, 80

Kennedy, Pte. R. J., 261
Kim, Capt., 171–3, 214
King, WO II, 105

Ledan, Capt. B., 21, 35, 124, 148, 150, 152, 156
Leggett, Capt. J., 238
Liddell Hart, Capt. Sir Basil, 196
Lloyd, Pte. R. E., 249, 262
Long Cat (village), 17, 142–3
Long Dien (town), 12, 218, 219, 220
Long Hai (village), 177, 225
Long Hai hills, 11, 17, 29, 216, 223–38
Long Phuoc (village), 17, 18, 31, 53
Long Son (island), 11, 17, 167–171, 177
Long Tan (village), 14, 17, 31, 89–90, 97, 198
Lubke, Pte. R. J., 261

Maizey, Maj. S. J., 20, 31, 177, 210
Mao Tse Tung, 195
May Tao mountains, 9, 11, 180, 181
McAloney, 2/Lt. J., 161–2, 166, 265
McQualter, Maj. M. B., 20, 27, 38, 40, 42–5, 57, 127–8, 232–6, 238, 262
Mealing, S/Sgt. M., 141
Miller, Maj. J. F., 21, 24, 127, 173
Milligan, Capt. R. B., 31, 72, 220, 261
Montagnards, 58
Morris, Lt. E. B., 248
Mulby, Cpl. J., 63

INDEX

Ngai Giao (village), 14, 16, 105, 107, 114–15
Nguyen Nam Hung (*see* Hung, Nguyen Nam)
Nguyen Van Be (*see* Be, Nguyen Van)
Nichols, Cpl. R., 38, 234–5
Nilsen, Pte. E. H., 261
Noack, Pte. E. W., 38–9, 261
Nui Dat, 29–32, 85–6
Nui Nghe (hill), 11, 51, 53–4
Nui Thi Vai (mountain), 119–20, 121, 145, 159, 163–5

O'Dea, 2/Lt. L., 250
O'Hanlon, 2/Lt. T., 42
O'Neill, Capt. R. J., 26, 42–3, 47, 60–4, 73, 77–81, 97–9, 105–6, 108, 124, 172–3, 186–7, 192
Operation
  Beaumaris, 216, 218
  Caloundra, 207–11
  Camden, 211, 212, 213
  Canberra, 120–1, 122–23, 128–30
  Crowsnest, 107, 114–15, 121
  Darlinghurst, 92–7
  Hardihood, 35–54
  Hayman, 171–2, 174–7
  Holsworthy, 73, 75–6, 80–1, 82, 85, 86
  Ingham, 189
  Portsea, 189, 241–4, 245, 247–50
  Queanbeyan, 144–66
  Renmark, 228–37, 238
  Robin, 140, 141–6
  Sydney, 53–5, 56, 60–64, 65
  Toledo, 91, 97, 99–100
  Yass, 171, 174–6
Oxley, Col. P. H. G., 19

Phu My (garrison), 117
Phuoc Tuy (province), 9, 10, 11, 12–14, 110–11, 255
Piper, Maj. A., 127

Poole, Pte. M. D., 261
Pott, 2/Lt. E., 41, 236
Pracy, Pte. N. A., 261
Prescott, Maj. W., 105, 107, 206

RAAF, 90, 186–7
Rainer, 2/Lt. D., 67, 165, 166, 266
Rinkin, 2/Lt. K., 249–50, 262
Royal Australian Engineers, 163

Sandow, Pte. R. W., 261
Seventh Battalion, RAR, 253
Shambrook, Maj. R., 21, 160, 243, 248
Sharp, 2/Lt. G., 89
Sheehan, Lt. T., 131, 215
Sixth Battalion, RAR, composition, 19, 53, 64, 73, 86, 89–90, 99, 118, 147–8, 175, 188, 198, 214, 223–4, 225, 227, 228, 245, 248, 253
Smith, Lt. Col. E., 253
Smith, Maj. H., 85
Song Rai (river), 11, 13–14, 17, 245, 247
Special Air Service, 3 Sqdn., 92, 171, 175
Sullivan, Pte. P. C., 261
Supple, Capt. R., 128, 156
Support Company
  Anti-Tank Platoon, 55, 99, 112, 149–52, 157–9, 229
  Assault Pioneer Platoon, 55, 100, 142, 155, 161–3
  Mortar Platoon, 112, 131
  Reconnaissance Platoon, 229–31, 244
Sweetnam, Pte. J. R., 261
Sydney, HMAS, 24, 47, 253

Tape, Pte., 235
'Tennis' (artillery position), 55, 56
Thomas, L/Cpl. M., 261
Thurman, Col. (US), 32

Townsend, Lt. Col. C. M., 90
Twaites, Pte., 244

United States Army, committed to
    Vietnam, 11; advisers, 15; II Field
    Force, 91–2, 96, 97, 100
  First Infantry Division, 92, 118
  Fourth Infantry Division, 117, 143
  Ninth Infantry Division, 241, 245
  173 Airborne Brigade, 31, 35, 47,
    51, 91–2, 100, 118, 224
  11 Armoured Cavalry Regiment,
    241, 245, 248
  68 Aviation Company, 28, 31
  36 Evacuation Hospital, 236

Viet Cong, emergence of, 9;
    formation of military units,
    9, 193; strategy, 11; growth
    of in Phuoc Tuy, 15–18; and
    national elections, 103–4; North
    Vietnamese and, 193; mentality
    and problems of, 197, 256–7
Viet Cong Army, types of force,
    15–16; situation, May 1967,
    255–6
  Fifth Division, 18, 91, 236–7
  274 Regiment, 17, 18, 48, 51,
    54, 90, 92, 100, 105–7, 118,
    151–2, 157–9, 163–5, 181,
    199–200, 236
  275 Regiment, 18, 25, 90, 199,
    236, 245–6, 247
  C20 Chau Duc District
    Company, 54, 165, 167,
    214–16, 248
  C25 Long Dat District Company,
    216, 218, 224, 225
  D445 Provincial Mobile Battalion,
    16, 17, 90, 181, 186, 216,
    224, 225, 226–8, 245
Viet Minh, 10
Vincent, Maj. Gen. D., 23
Vung Tan, location of, 9; RAR camp,
    24–5, 27–8

Wales, Capt. A., 237
War Zone C, 9, 10
War Zone D, 9, 15, 181
Warburton, Pte. G. F., 112, 113, 261
Warr, Lt. Col. J. A., 19, 20, 27, 35–6,
    40, 47, 58–60, 64, 66, 73, 85, 93,
    105–6, 107, 108, 113, 118, 122,
    127–8, 130–1, 143–5, 149, 152,
    158, 159, 160, 171, 175, 188,
    192, 200, 206, 217–19, 228, 229,
    235, 253, 263
Wass, Sgt., 234
Watson, Pte. B. P., 177, 261
Webster, Pte. J. C., 261
White, Capt. H. A. D., 21, 67, 98,
    99, 113, 135, 139, 152, 157, 188,
    235
Willcox, Capt. D., 21, 75
Williams, Capt. (NZ), 220
Williams, Sgt. E., 57–8
Womal, Cpl. N. J., 152, 157–8, 166,
    261, 269

Xuan, Sgt. Vietnamese interpreter,
    127
Xuan Song, 200
Xuyen Moc (district), 11
Xuyen Moc (village), 13, 14, 17–18,
    179–85, 186, 187–8, 189, 247–8,
    251

www.ingramcontent.com/pod-product-compliance
Lightning Source LLC
Chambersburg PA
CBHW040324300426
44112CB00021B/2864